STORM LANDINGS

STORM
LANDINGS

EPIC AMPHIBIOUS BATTLES IN THE CENTRAL PACIFIC

Joseph H. Alexander

Naval Institute Press • Annapolis, Maryland

ISBN 1-55750-032-0

Printed in the United States of America

Frontispiece: "The Wave Breaks on the Beach" by Kerr Eby (courtesy of U.S. Navy Combat Art Collection).

Epigraph on page vi taken from Saburo Hayashi and Alvin D. Coox, *Kogun: The Japanese Army in the Pacific War* (Marine Corps Association, 1959), page 110.

For Lt. Col. Robert Clark Caldwell,
USMC (Ret.), 1933–1995

The tactics of the Americans called for hurling enormous firepower against the enemy and then making forced landings frontally. So-called "storm landings" were common American practice.

Col. Saburo Hayashi,
Imperial Japanese Army

Contents

Illustrations

Maps

Foreword

Amphibious operations—the movement of armed forces over oceans to be disembarked from ships at sea onto a foreign shore—are as old as the history of warfare itself. However, not until World War II were the military art and science of conducting an assault—the most violent and near-final phase of an attack—perfected from ships at sea against fortified positions. *Storm Landings,* Col. Joe Alexander's second work on amphibious operations in the Pacific during World War II, is the story of that evolution. It is a story worth reading not only because it is told well by a talented writer-historian, or because it is an exciting and instructive look at the past, but more important, it is worth reading because its lessons are a window to the future.

The United States is a maritime nation. Although we have neighbors across our land borders to both the north and south, our most continuous vital interests lie to the east and west—across the great expanses of the Atlantic and Pacific Oceans. Since World War II we have maintained large, standing armies and air forces in foreign lands across these oceans, but that era is drawing to a close. In the decades to come, our national security strategy will change. For a variety of political and economic reasons, far fewer American forces will be permanently stationed in foreign countries. However, our national interests will continue to dictate the need for forward presence, alliance-maintenance, and immediate crisis response through the employment of naval and military forces from ships at sea in places far distant from our shores.

The great majority of these prospective operations will not be the violent, intense storm landings of the past, but some will. Whether they are or not, the perfection of the coordinated assaults from the sea Colonel Alexander has characterized as storm landings in World War II provided the blueprint that has shaped the capabilities of our current and emerging Navy of the twenty-first century and the doctrine by which land forces operate from these modern "sea-bases" now, as they will in the future.

Thus, the true value of Colonel Alexander's insights into the storm landings of the past lies in the relevance of the lessons derived from them to the future. In this, his contributions will be not just novel, they will be enduring.

Carl E. Mundy Jr.
General, U.S. Marine Corps (Ret.)
Commandant of the Marine Corps, 1991–1995

Acknowledgments

This is a tribute to an extreme form of amphibious assault known as "storm landings" developed by American forces in the Central Pacific during the final two years of the war. I have defined storm landings as *risky, long-range, large-scale, self-sustaining assaults executed against strong opposition and within the protective umbrella of fast carrier task forces.* There were seven of these—Tarawa, Saipan, Guam, Tinian, Peleliu, Iwo Jima, and Okinawa—and a potential eighth, Kyūshū.

I concentrate on these specific amphibious epics at the cost of other landings in other theaters. I even omit Operation Flintlock in the Marshalls, a campaign rich in strategic and doctrinal developments but not, by the above definition, a storm landing. I treat these other landings with full respect but not in detail, referring the reader to John A. Lorelli's comprehensive *To Foreign Shores*. As a long-in-the-tooth amphibian myself, I have every admiration for any man of any service who ever landed on a hostile shore. By nature of the beast, there are no amphibious cakewalks. The work is extremely hazardous. Even under the most benign tactical conditions men drown, or get crushed by shifting cargo, or get run over by heavy equipment. Just getting safely ashore in the Pacific War was a minor triumph—storming ashore in the teeth of murderous Japanese fire added a dimension that today defies imagination.

This operational history also examines the desperate Japanese efforts to devise counteramphibious tactics and weaponry. The two antagonists were on a true collision course in southern Kyūshū. Operation Olympic, scheduled for November 1945, would have been—categorically—the bloodiest amphibious campaign of all.

This book is graced by the professional contributions of Mary Craddock Hoffman, who created the maps; Larry E. Klatt (himself a veteran of three storm landings), who sketched the Japanese weapons and defenses; Cindy Wheeler Lee, who illustrated the charts; and Bunichi Ohtsuka, who translated the original Japanese accounts for me.

As always, I benefited from the guidance of Brig. Gen. Edwin H. Simmons, USMC (Ret.), director of Marine Corps History and Museums, and Benis M. Frank, chief historian of the Marine Corps. Other military historians who provided support included Thomas B. Buell, Theodore L. Gatchel, John A. Lorelli, Dr. Allan R. Millett, Dr. Edward J. Drea, Dr. John Ray Skates, Richard B. Frank, Jon T. Hoffman, Dr. George F. Hofmann, Merrill L. Bartlett, Nathan Miller, Thomas J. Cutler, Henry I. Shaw Jr., James R. Davis, Joseph McNamara, and James C. Hitz.

Special thanks to these contributors: Gen. Carl E. Mundy Jr., USMC (Ret.), Lt. Gen. Victor H. Krulak, USMC (Ret.), the Honorable J. T. "Slick" Rutherford, William T. Ketcham, Nick Floros, Don C. Gorham, Douglas J. Colley, Dr. Eugene B. Sledge, Lewis J. Michelony Jr., Brig. Gen. Robert E. Galer, USMC (Ret.), Lt. Gen. James L. Jones Jr., USMC, Norma M. Crotty, Michael F. Keleher, M.D., and Col. Robert J. Putnam, USMC (Ret.).

In four years of researching and writing about the Pacific War, I've been blessed with exceptional editors, including Fred H. Rainbow and John G. Miller of Naval Institute *Proceedings,* Robert Cowley and John Tarkov of *MHQ,* William V. H. White of *Leatherneck,* Fred L. Schultz of *Naval History,* John E. Greenwood of *Marine Corps Gazette,* and Norman C. Stahl, chief creative director, Lou Reda Productions.

I also received invaluable research assistance from the following professionals: Naval Institute Press—Dr. Paul Wilderson, Linda W. O'Doughda, Randy Baldini, Susan Artigiani, Linda Cullen, and Susan Brook; U.S.

Naval Institute—Paul Stillwell, Carol Mason, Mary Beth Straight-Kiss, Charles L. Mussi, Ann Hassinger; Marine Corps Historical Center—Evelyn A. Englander, Frederick J. Graboske, Danny A. Crawford, Robert V. Aquilina, Ann A. Ferrante, Lena M. Kaljot, Richard A. Long, Amy J. Cantin; Naval Historical Center—John Reilly, Kathy Lloyd; Marine Corps University—A. Kerry Strong; National Archives—Dr. Timothy K. Nenninger; Hoover Institution Archives—Linda Wheeler; Admiral Nimitz Museum—Helen McDonald; Pack Memorial Library, Asheville—Charles Cady Jr. I add thanks in particular to my gifted manuscript editor and indexer, Anne R. Gibbons, and to my astute proofreader, Barbara Johnson.

In the realm of close support, my thanks to Richard T. Poore, Stephen W. Woody, Edith H. Livengood, E. Gordon James, Lewis J. Kraus, my brother and fellow historian William T. Alexander, my son and California researcher, Kenneth B. "Keg" Alexander, and my wife, Gale, who patiently allowed storm landings to invade our mountain home and hearth these many months.

STORM LANDINGS

Prologue

Rags to Riches

Enemy task force of twenty ships attacking Tulagi, undergoing severe bombings, landing preparations under way; help
requested.

Commander Japanese Forces,
Tulagi, 0705,
7 August 1942

The sudden appearance of an Allied task force in the Southern
Solomons astonished the Japanese garrison scattered among the
islands. Was it a raid? A feint? Or, heaven forbid, a real invasion?
Excited Japanese officers scanned the threatening armada with
field glasses, noting the presence of fully laden troop transports and
cargo ships. They flinched as U.S. Navy F6F Hellcats and SBD Dauntless
dive-bombers screeched overhead, realizing immediately that the Americans had committed their last remaining carriers to this operation.
When waves of landing craft bearing heavily armed Marines converged
on Tulagi's undefended south coast the local commander knew he was in
deep jeopardy. Radio Tulagi's last message to Rabaul crackled over the
airwaves a few minutes later: "Enemy troop strength is overwhelming.
We will defend to the last man."

Rear Adm. Richmond Kelly Turner's Task Force 62 executed five
separate landings in the Solomons on D-Day. Guadalcanal rightfully
received the main effort, but four other landings occurred among the

Florida Islands, nineteen miles north across a body of water soon to be known as "Iron Bottom Sound."

The distinction of conducting the nation's first offensive amphibious landing in the Pacific War went to Baker Company* of the 1st Battalion, 2d Marines, led by Capt. Edward J. Crane, USMC. Crane's reinforced company of 252 officers and men splashed ashore from eight landing boats from the USS *President Jackson* (AP 37) at 0740 near Haleta on Florida Island. The Baker Company riflemen had the mission of securing the jungled peninsula to protect the left flank of Lt. Col. Merritt A. Edson's 1st Raider Battalion during its assault on nearby Tulagi. This they promptly achieved.

Other American landings occurred in short order. The 1st Raiders charged ashore at 0800. Elements of the 1st Battalion, 2d Marines, seized Halavo Peninsula east of Tulagi half an hour later. To the south, the bulk of the 1st Marine Division landed over Red Beach on Guadalcanal at 0910. So far, so good. The Japanese defenders seemed too stunned to oppose the landings, although the 3d Kure Special Naval Landing Force on Tulagi soon recovered from its initial shock and began delivering a hot fire against the Raiders moving inland.

The Americans lacked sufficient landing craft to execute all five assaults simultaneously. As a consequence, the day's fifth landing, the assault on the tiny islets of Gavutu and Tanambogo east of Tulagi, could not be mounted before 1400. The invaders had forfeited the element of surprise. To complicate matters further, Gavutu's protective reefs permitted a landing approach only from the northeast. The waterborne route from the transport area to the target beach measured fourteen thousand yards—a two-hour transit against an eastern wind. The Americans, in short, telegraphed their punch, and the Japanese machine gunners had plenty of time to orient their killing zones.

Gavutu and Tanambogo were small, hilly islets, joined by the umbilical cord of a three-hundred-yard causeway. The existence of a major Japanese seaplane base made the islets a desirable secondary objective. Close to four hundred members of the Yokohama Air Group and the 3d Kure Special Naval Landing Force defended the two sites, many of them occupying prepared positions in hillside caves overlooking the flat beaches.

The mission of seizing first Gavutu and then Tanambogo went to the 1st Parachute Battalion, commanded by Maj. Robert H. Williams, USMC.

---

* I use the World War II version of the military phonetic alphabet throughout (i.e., Able, Baker, etc., vice the current Alfa, Bravo, etc.).

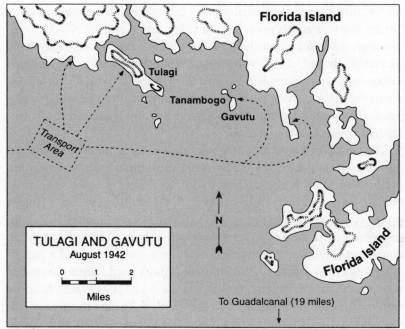

Mary Craddock Hoffman

The Paramarines were well trained, aggressive—and outnumbered. Four minutes of naval shelling and ten minutes of dive-bombing strikes did little to even the odds. The Japanese allowed the first wave to come ashore unmolested in order to mask any residual supporting fires, then cut loose with everything they had. Marines fell along the sandy beaches, in the surf, in their boats. Major Williams went down with a bullet through his lungs; two staff officers died at his side. The Paramarines pressed ahead grimly the rest of the long afternoon, then called for reinforcements.

Captain Crane's Baker Company was available, its outpost duty on Haleta Point done. Crane received urgent orders to reembark and hurry over to Gavutu. Arriving during the abrupt tropical sunset, Crane received further orders to assault nearby Tanambogo by boat that evening. Darkness added to the confusion. Crane could muster only five of his eight boatloads of troops, but these he led toward the neighboring island. As the second boat crunched ashore on Tanambogo, the supporting destroyer proved too helpful, detonating a fuel dump with its prep fires. The conflagration illuminated the entire miniature landing force. Japanese machine gunners scythed down the Marines as they tried to scramble ashore, then ripped their lethal streams the length of the crowded boats, hitting Marines and Navy crewmen alike. Crane and his NCOs somehow restored order out of chaos, set up a base of fire, then evacuated the wounded aboard the shot-up boats. Five hours later, he and his exhausted survivors made it back to the Marine lines on Gavutu. Failure of the night landing brought a sober conclusion to all who participated: the amphibians still had much to learn about assaulting fortified Japanese positions from the sea.

The battle for Gavutu-Tanambogo thus became the first significant opposed landing experienced by American amphibious forces in the Pacific War. Many historians tend to dismiss this early action as an amateurish, backwater skirmish. Indeed, daylight the next day brought rapid tactical success to the invaders. A reinforcing infantry battalion, supported by a destroyer lying barely five hundred yards offshore, landed on Gavutu at midmorning. Two rifle companies and a pair of light tanks then assaulted Tanambogo. A day's hard fighting served to root out the cave defenders on both islands. The 1,300 assault Marines suffered 157 casualties in the two-day battles. Against the greater air-sea-land drama of the nearby Guadalcanal campaign, this action appears inconsequential.

Yet the Gavutu-Tanambogo landings represented a microcosm of the opposed landings to come in the Central Pacific. All the promise and frustration peculiar to forcible seaborne assaults appeared to some degree in this crude little preview—including the excruciatingly difficult task of conducting a ship-to-shore assault against a determined foe.

American armed forces brought two unique and interactive forms of naval warfare to fruition in the later years of the Pacific War: the employment of fast carrier task forces and the execution of long-range, amphibious assaults against fierce opposition. While there were many amphibious landings throughout the Pacific, only a few qualify as storm landings—the Japanese description of America's bold, frontal, daylight assaults into the teeth of prepared defenses.

An amphibious landing per se is an assault launched from the sea by naval and landing forces against a hostile shore. Storm landings in the Pacific War were those amphibious landings distinguished by six additional characteristics. They were all dangerous, long-range, large-scale, self-sustaining assaults executed against defended positions while within the protective umbrella of fast carrier task forces.

For a variety of geostrategic reasons, these storm landings occurred in the Central Pacific from November 1943 to the spring of 1945. The list is short: Tarawa, Saipan, Guam, Tinian, Peleliu, Iwo Jima, Okinawa (where the Japanese 32d Army simply transplaced their beachfront defenses a mile inland), and, by projection, Kyūshū. For the United States, each assault demonstrated a growing mastery of the concentration of overwhelming naval force against a strategic objective and literally kicking down the front door.

Ominously, as American amphibious power became manifest over time, so did the lethality and intensity of the Japanese defenses. These two converging developments were on an exponential collision course in the massive amphibious assaults on southern Kyūshū planned for November 1945. My principal focus therefore covers that twenty-four-month period, roughly from D-Day in the Gilberts to the planned D-Day for Operation Olympic in Kyūshū.

My deliberate focus on this short list of opposed seaborne assaults comes at the expense of hundreds of other landings in the Pacific. I bypass these operations intentionally but with full respect for every web-footed trooper of any service who ever splashed ashore on any godforsaken beach throughout the theater. Each landing had its own story of drama and risk. None were easy. Even Kiska and Morotai cost the landing forces casualties. In part, this universal costliness reflected the tenacity of Japanese defenders, who even when they opted to forgo coverage of a certain beach always seemed to leave behind a die-hard sniper or a series of ingenious booby traps. Many more casualties stemmed from the very nature of amphibious operations—hazardous work with heavy equipment in one of the most unforgiving environments on earth, the surf zone, that jagged seam between land and sea . . . the particular province of the assault amphibians.

The storm landings of the final two years of the Pacific War illustrate both the extreme potential and the great risk of large-scale amphibious assaults. There was nothing of the subtlety of Chinese military theorist Sun Tsu in these landings. The days of combining a tactical defensive with the strategic offensive ended with Guadalcanal and Bougainville. These later operations in the Central Pacific were assaults from start to finish. The landing force never relinquished the offensive. The battles were violent, relatively short, thoroughly decisive, always bloody.

The ability to undertake this most complex and perilous of military operations—the opposed amphibious assault—was the great unknown as the Pacific War opened. The United States fortunately had the rudiments of joint doctrine in place, but many senior officers doubted it would ever work against a well-armed opponent. The doctrine ultimately proved valid, prompting British military historian J.F.C. Fuller to acclaim the development of American amphibious power projection as "the most far-reaching tactical innovation of the war."

But such abstract considerations pale beside the sheer human drama of those precarious, go-for-broke storm landings that cut the heart out of Japanese dreams of preserving an empire in the Pacific Ocean—three-dimensional battles of a magnitude and ferocity that may never again be seen in this world.

The first opposed landings at Gavutu-Tanambogo therefore deserve special mention. In the Florida Islands in 1942 the amphibians forced their way ashore against the equivalent of an enemy battalion. Thirty-two months later, and thirty-five hundred miles to the northwest, Adm. Kelly Turner would order his landing force ashore at Okinawa against a reinforced field army—and prevail. The differences in scale between Baker Company's hasty assault on Tanambogo and the U.S. Tenth Army's complex invasion of Okinawa were enormous, yet the central components hardly varied. The Americans learned from the Gavutu-Tanambogo experience the valuable dichotomy that while amphibious assaults require painstaking planning, the plan serves nothing more than to bring forces in contact with the enemy close to the objective. Thereafter, success or failure devolves quickly under heavy fire and great stress to the improvisational skills of a handful of junior officers and NCOs.

The early amphibious assaults in the Solomons also taught the Americans there would be no easy road to Tokyo. Yet the mere fact that the United States could launch a division-level amphibious offensive in its avowed secondary theater eight months to the day after Pearl Harbor was remarkable in its own right. In the process, and at a cost, the amphibians learned valuable lessons. Maj. Gen. Alexander A. Vandegrift, USMC, commanding the 1st Marine Division in the Guadalcanal campaign, appraised the Gavutu-Tanambogo experience in these terms: "The combat assumed the nature of a storming operation from the outset, a soldier's battle, unremitting and relentless, to be decided only by the extermination of one or the other of the adversaries engaged." These words also proved an apt prediction of the storm landings to follow.

The experiences of Baker Company, 1st Battalion, 2d Marines, at Tanambogo had therefore contributed to the scant body of practical knowledge of waging amphibious war against defended Japanese islands. Night landings would unduly exacerbate the inherent problems of amphibious operations. So would hasty landings executed without decent intelligence or sufficient coordination of supporting arms. Chaos could be expected to rule any opposed beachhead.

Fifteen months later Baker Company would be the first outfit to fight its way across embattled Betio Island in Tarawa Atoll.

Chapter One

Cracking a Tough Nut

To effect such a landing under the sea and shore conditions obtaining and in the face of enemy resistance requires careful training and preparation. . . . It is not enough that the troops be skilled infantry men and jungle men or artillery men of high morale; they must be skilled water men and jungle men who know it can be done—Marines with Marine training.

Maj. Earl H. Ellis, USMC
"Advanced Base Operations in Micronesia,"
1921

Whatever one's opinion of "Pete" Ellis as a self-styled espionage agent, the man was indisputably a prophet of naval warfare in the Pacific in the early interwar years. Ellis was among the first to examine the strategic and operational consequences of a future war with Japan. Ellis saw that America's Pacific naval bases— Pearl Harbor, Guam, Midway, Wake, the Philippines—were few and vulnerable. By contrast, Japan benefited immensely when the League of Nations mandated to them the former German island colonies in the Marianas, Palaus, Carolines, and Marshalls. Ellis clearly envisioned the "island hopping" strategy necessary for American forces to wrest control of these advance naval bases from the Japanese. More significantly, the maverick Marine officer knew each island base would have to be seized forcibly, which to him dictated a clear requirement for specially trained and equipped amphibious forces able to fight their way ashore.

Ellis was little more than a voice crying in the wilderness in those early years. The U.S. military in the 1920s was singularly ill-prepared to conduct an amphibious campaign of the nature and scope envisioned by Ellis. At best, the nation could claim the existence of a series of lightly armed, poorly trained landing parties—mixed, provisional forces of soldiers or Marines and bluejackets in motor whaleboats—good perhaps for expeditionary service in troubled harbors, but hardly a force capable of storming a fortified beachhead. Nor was there much inclination to develop such a capability. Too expensive, too complicated, increasingly too risky.

Yet the art of projecting a landing force ashore against hostile opposition was no twentieth-century newcomer to military science. As early as 55 B.C., British cavalry and spearmen attacked Julius Caesar's VII and X Roman legions as they waded ashore, ten thousand strong, from their transports near present-day Kent. Likewise, French cannoneers and cavalry provided a hot greeting to Gen. Sir Ralph Abercromby's British invaders as they struggled through the surf at Aboukir Bay, Egypt, in 1801. Momentarily at least "the issue was in doubt" for both landing forces, but Caesar and Abercromby eventually prevailed, securing beachheads and penetrating the interior. Military and naval commanders historically viewed disembarking in the face of enemy opposition as a dangerous but achievable mission.

This viewpoint changed sharply as the Industrial Age arrived. In the eyes of nearly every military and political leader of the great powers in the 1920s and 1930s, the successes of Caesar and Abercromby had been eclipsed by the disastrous Allied amphibious campaign against the Turkish Dardanelles in 1915, known simply as "Gallipoli." Here was a campaign in which the Allies violated virtually every known principle of war, yet the persistent image was that of the British landing force being slaughtered in wholesale numbers as they tried to disembark from the experimental "amphibious assault ship," the *River Clyde*. No matter that the *River Clyde* was a converted collier, an unarmored coal-hauler crudely modified to disembark hundreds of troops through open bay doors onto a gangway more or less connected to pontoon causeways alongside—or that in execution the ship made a direct, unsupported approach to the target beach in full daylight, grounded broadside to the Turkish positions, and began spilling her gallant but doomed troops directly into well-aimed rifle and machine-gun fire. The wonder is that the Turks didn't kill the entire force and blow the ship out of the water.

Gallipoli had enormous strategic and political implications within the context of World War I and its aftermath. Military analysts concluded that large-scale, opposed amphibious landings had been rendered ineffective by the fruits of the Industrial Age. If Turkish riflemen and machine gunners could poleax a veteran Allied expeditionary force launched by the Royal Navy in the Dardanelles, what would befall other amphibious forces attempting such landings against opponents equipped with more modern weapons, such as heavy artillery, submarines, and attack aircraft?

The British military analyst Liddell Hart concluded in 1939 that advances in airpower alone had rendered amphibious operations prohibitively costly. "A landing on a foreign coast in face of hostile troops has always been one of the most difficult operations of war," he wrote. "It has now become much more difficult, indeed almost impossible, because of the vulnerable target which a convoy of transports offers to the defender's air force as it approaches the shore. Even more vulnerable to air attack is the process of disembarkation in open boats."

Rear Adm. Kelly Turner had Hart's exact words in hand three years later as he steamed into the Southern Solomons as commander, South Pacific Amphibious Force. In the Solomons, however, Turner's "disembarkation in open boats" went fairly well. But the vulnerability of his irreplaceable amphibious ships received glaring emphasis during the next forty-eight hours. First, Japanese long-range bombers sank the transport *George F. Elliot* (PA 13); next Vice Adm. Frank Jack Fletcher withdrew his carriers; then Japanese Vice Adm. Gunichi Mikawa's striking force of heavy cruisers surprised and thoroughly defeated the Allied cruisers during the night battle of Savo Island, leaving Turner's amphibians at extreme risk. Indeed, only Mikawa's sudden timidity at the height of his tactical victory prevented the Japanese force from annihilating the virtually defenseless transports and cargo ships clustered off the nearby beaches. Turner had little choice but to beat an ignominious retreat, his landing force supplies barely half unloaded, leaving the 1st Marine Division to fend for itself on Guadalcanal and the Florida Islands.

These events occurred in the South Pacific during the second week of August 1942, a period in which the utility of amphibious operations to the U.S. war effort probably reached its lowest ebb. True, America's evolving amphibious capability had enabled this limited offensive in the Pacific, surprising the Japanese and boosting home front morale. But the difficulty experienced in executing the opposed landings at Gavutu-Tanambogo remained troublesome, and the extremely close call of Turner's amphibious task force immediately following the Savo Island battle remained downright harrowing. Maybe Liddell Hart had called it right. Modern technology might have relegated amphibious operations to the diminished role of raids and diversions.

Surprisingly, there existed even in those dark days a reservoir of optimism about the soundness of America's fledgling amphibious doctrine among certain Navy and Marine Corps officers, including Admiral Turner and General Vandegrift, commanding the embattled 1st Marine Division. This optimism in the face of dire setbacks stemmed from years of truly innovative research and analysis performed by a succession of officers from the sea services at the Marine Corps Schools in Quantico, Virginia, during the 1930s. As a matter of ironic fact, the advent of the Amphibious Age had its roots in the flawed Gallipoli campaign. Navy and Marine officers spent several years brainstorming the mistakes and failures of Gallipoli in the effort to determine whether amphibious warfare in fact had any future in the twentieth century.

The process of microexamining the Gallipoli campaign followed the path modern industrialists might describe as "reverse engineering." The analysts painstakingly broke the entire campaign into its most minute components. The Quantico team documented appalling failures in everything from operational security to fundamental leadership, but they also found intriguing possibilities that, properly pursued, might have led to tactical success. The conclusive question remained, Was the Allied amphibious invasion of Gallipoli foredoomed, or did it stand a chance given certain doctrinal changes?

There were no easy answers. Any large-scale amphibious assault against an opposed beach is inherently complex, difficult, and hence vulnerable. The complexity can be daunting, despite Gen. Dwight D. Eisenhower's disclaimer in a 1950 interview that "an amphibious landing is not a particularly difficult thing. . . . You put your men in boats and as long as you get well-trained crews to take the boats in, it is the simplest deployment in the world—the men can go nowhere else except to the beach." Eisenhower was the greatest joint force commander in U.S. history, but these words (spoken seven months before the Inchon landing) reflect too many years as a staff officer and too few as a troop leader. Omaha Beach on D-Day morning at Normandy would have been no place for the Supreme Allied Commander, but had "Ike" been there, or just offshore, he would never have made such a breezy statement.

Eisenhower could have learned from his Normandy invasion that *momentum* is the essence of any successful amphibious assault against a defended shoreline. But everything involved in delivering combat power ashore from the sea degrades momentum. Even under the best conditions the amphibious commander faces a formidable challenge in "stuffing" his landing force into small craft and delivering them to the correct beach with sufficient momentum to attack a fortified enemy. Add hostile fire, barrier reefs, high surf, rip tides, barbed wire, and comm failures, and the "simplest deployment in the world" quickly degenerates into chaos—absolute, unmitigated chaos.

An early and vivid example of the perils inherent in amphibious operations became manifest to U.S. officers during Fleet Operation Number 4, a simulated landing on Culebra Island in February 1924. The single troop transport was so poorly loaded that it took nine days to get medical supplies ashore. Naval boat officers missed their assigned beaches and landed off target and out of sequence. In short, reported Marine brigadier general Eli K. Cole, "chaos reigned." Concluded Rear Adm. Montgomery N. Taylor, commanding the naval attack force: the Navy needed first a doctrine for amphibious assault, then a training program. His advice went largely unheeded for the next ten years.

The Gallipoli analysts at Quantico in the early 1930s tried to examine this latest field evidence in light of their research. Tracing the fault lines of the 1915 campaign was easy enough; determining whether there could be any practical solution required certain leaps of faith. Consider some of the key issues. Would chaos reign along every assault beach— and would that necessarily disqualify the landing? Could naval gunfire adequately support the landing force until field artillery displaced ashore? Could attack aircraft operate within the same "envelope" as naval gunfire without undue risk to the aviators? How much advance naval and aerial bombardment was enough, and who should coordinate it, and by what means? Was there nothing better than motor whaleboats available to deliver combat-equipped assault troops through the surf zone to the beach? How in the world could the landing force ever hope to get tanks and field guns and their prime movers ashore from amphibious ships while under fire? And what of the thorny issue of command relations between the troop commander and the naval commander?

Good fortune brought a nucleus of gifted officers to Quantico during this period who were unafraid to brainstorm such vexing questions. These men reduced their analysis of Gallipoli into a positive breakout of six functional areas applicable to amphibious assault: command relations, naval gunfire support, air support, the ship-to-shore movement, "securing the beachhead," and logistics. By 1934 the Quantico group had not only come to terms with the disasters of Gallipoli but also had defined a working doctrine for successful amphibious assault and published their findings as *Tentative Manual for Landing Operations.* Navy support came swiftly. Following three years of experimentation and refinement, the Chief of Naval Operations issued Fleet Training Publication 167 (FTP 167), *Landing Operations Doctrine U.S. Navy, 1937.* In 1941 the U.S. Army published its own version, albeit nearly a verbatim copy, as War Department Field Manual 31-5, *Landing Operations on Hostile Shores.*

Historians Jeter A. Isely and Philip A. Crowl of Princeton University described the initial *Tentative Manual* as "a remarkable document . . . pioneer work of the most daring and imaginative sort." With it, the Marine Corps made one of its greatest contributions to the nation's military capabilities.

Reading the original editions of the *Tentative Manual* and FTP 167 after six decades of practical application of amphibious warfare gives little sense of the groundbreaking nature of both documents. In certain points they seem almost quaint—describing the Marine landing force as light infantry supplemented with base defense artillery and aviation units, or urging troop commanders to execute the landing "with utmost speed and dash," for example. But in tying together the previously disparate communities of naval gunfire, aviation, logistics, and assault tacticians, the early manuals provided invaluable service. So did insistence on "superiority of force at the point of attack" and "coordination by event not by time." Kelly Turner's attack aviators ignored the latter admonition prior to the assault waves reaching the beach at Tarawa, relying on their wristwatches rather than gauging the extended distance the first waves still had to traverse to the beach. This lapse permitted Japanese gunners time to recover from the pounding and take deadly aim.

This initial concept of a doctrine for amphibious assault suffered from one principal shortcoming. None of the early editions of the doctrinal manuals sufficiently addressed command relations and unity of command. Ground officers generally accepted the fact that the naval "attack force commander" would execute the landing, but at which point, if any, would the troop commander assume full command ashore? And what about "conflict resolution" between the naval and troop commanders, the inevitable clash between strong-willed leaders with sharply different priorities? In the absence of such guidance, Kelly Turner at Guadalcanal acted as if he exercised full tactical command over all units afloat and ashore. Against General Vandegrift's vocal objections, Turner retained control over elements of the 1st Marine Division as force reserves and tried to create new Raider units for separate missions far beyond the force beachheads on Guadalcanal or the Floridas. Fixing this void would take the active intervention of the Commandant of the Marine Corps and the Chief of Naval Operations.

America's new amphibious doctrine had one redeeming grace. Throughout the prewar exercises and the war itself, senior commanders of all services remained amenable to whatever changes seemed necessary to resolve the problem. FTP 167 experienced three major changes between May 1941 and August 1943. Most of these reflected lessons learned in the ship-to-shore movement, naval gunfire support, and shore party operations. The issue of command relations received "off-line" modifications, especially in the Pacific after Guadalcanal, and just prior to Operation Galvanic in the Gilberts.

Other fortuitous developments in the Marine Corps and Navy in the 1930s paralleled and enhanced publication of *Tentative Manual for Landing Operations*. Under the enlightened leadership of Maj. Gen. Commandants Ben H. Fuller and John H. Russell Jr., the Corps finally ended its unbecoming post–World War I attraction to the U.S. Army and returned to its naval roots. Establishment of the Fleet Marine Force (FMF) as a type command of the fleet cemented this relationship. At the same time, the U.S. State Department terminated its long-standing commitment of Marine brigades to occupation duty in Nicaragua and Haiti, making available a substantial body of troops to man the new FMF. Third, the Navy and Marines (and on occasion the Army as well) resumed the annual series of fleet landing exercises that had languished since 1924. These exercises illuminated many of the problems and little of the promise of amphibious warfare, but each one led incrementally toward a better-equipped, somewhat better-trained landing force. Increasingly, the presence of Marine brigadier general Holland M. "Howlin' Mad" Smith began to cast a long shadow at these annual training exercises. Smith became the indisputable apostle of amphibious assault, endearing himself to few senior officers of any service. But by his prickly insistence on amphibious preparedness and realistic training, he did as much as any other serving officer to help prepare the United States for certain key aspects of the forthcoming Pacific War.

Holland Smith's uncompromising efforts, coupled with the visionary productivity of the earlier pioneers at Quantico, gave the U.S. Navy a solid foundation of doctrine and training from which to build amphibious expertise on the eve of World War II. Two major deficiencies remained: the wherewithal (especially transports, landing craft, and tank lighters) to conduct large-scale amphibious assaults, and the necessary trial by fire to validate the new doctrine. These would come in the fullness of time. In the meantime, the initial amphibious advantage in the Pacific would lie with the Japanese.

Japan's amphibious proficiency far exceeded that of the United States at the outbreak of World War II. Japanese strategic planners in the interwar years foresaw the need for seaborne assault landings against such American holdings as Luzon and Guam, as well as against those islands and coastlines in the South Pacific and along the littoral of South Asia currently held by China, France, Great Britain, and the Netherlands. The Japanese could draw on their recent successful amphibious operations in the Pacific against the Germans and Russians in World War I to refine doctrine and tactical concepts. They fielded steel, armored, self-propelled landing craft as early as the mid-1920s. By 1932 the Imperial Army and Navy had forged a rare agreement on a joint doctrine manual, *Outline of Amphibious Operations*. That same year, the Imperial Navy landed twelve thousand troops at Shanghai. It wasn't a pretty operation, but it would take the United States another ten years before it could launch a similar-size landing. Before the 1930s ended, the Imperial Japanese Army had developed, tested, and fielded a family of ramped, shallow-draft, landing craft and several prototypes of multimission amphibious ships. Both programs matured years ahead of any similar efforts undertaken by the Western powers.

Yet interservice rivalry would hamstring the full development of Japanese military proficiency in the war to come, including the application of amphibious expertise. Japan in effect had two amphibious forces—the Army's and the Navy's. The Army had its own transports and landing craft, both operated by organic shipping engineer regiments. As World War II began, Army forces would execute the major landings on the Asian mainland and the larger island groups in the South Pacific. The Imperial Navy featured its own elite naval infantry regiments, the *rikusentai,* or special naval landing forces. At their height, the rikusentai numbered fifty thousand strong, fully an eighth of the Imperial Navy. Typically, they would land as light infantry units from destroyer transports. Their operations were generally smaller and their objectives more limited than the Army landings.

Notwithstanding this costly duplication of effort, the Japanese used their hydra-headed amphibious forces productively in the opening years of the Pacific War. They followed their invasion of Manchuria in 1937 with a double landing near Shanghai. By 1939 Japanese amphibious forces had seized Canton, Wenchow, Foochow, Amoy, Swatow, Pakhoi, Hainan Island, and the Spratly Islands. With forty thousand troops in Canton,

JAPANESE SPECIAL NAVAL LANDING FORCES
Evolutionary Changes, 1941-43

	MAIZURU 2D China/Wake (Nov-Dec 1941)	YOKOSUKA 7TH New Georgia (Feb 1943)	SASEBO 7TH Tarawa (Nov 1943)
Total Strength	1,069	1,820	1,669
Machine Gun, 13mm D.P.	4	10	8*
Flamethrower, Portable	10	n/a	8
AntiTank Gun, 37mm	0	2	2*
Howitzer, 70mm	4	0	2*
Mountain Gun, 75mm	4	0	4
AntiAircraft Gun, 75mm D.P.	0	4	4*
Coastal Defense Gun			
80mm (pedestal)	0	16	0*
120mm	0	8	0*
Light Armored Cars	2	0	0
Light Tanks	0	0	4*

*Augmented by additional weapons by type of 3d Special Base Defense Force, Tarawa [formerly Yokosuka 6th SNLF].

the Japanese were ably poised to go after Hong Kong should a general war erupt. Forcible possession of Hainan helped the Japanese isolate Hong Kong and threaten French Indochina. Seizure of Pakhoi put the vital Haiphong-Kunming railroad within range of Japanese attack aircraft. The stage was set.

The "glory days" for Japanese amphibious forces occurred immediately after Pearl Harbor when they were unleashed for conquest throughout the Pacific. Their successes are familiar: Guam, Hong Kong, the Gilberts, Thailand, Malaya, the Philippines, the Dutch East Indies, northern New Guinea, the Solomons. These amphibious landings followed a peculiar pattern worth noting. Despite their overwhelming air and sea superiority, the Japanese rarely resorted to storm landings of their own. Wherever possible, Japanese commanders preferred night landings by battalion-size units in column against undefended or lightly held stretches of coastline. These operations—tactically bold, strategically conservative—proved well-suited to the highly mobile but logistically stressed campaigns of conquest against a disorganized enemy. One of the Imperial Army's finest moments came with division-level, shore-to-shore night landings across the Straits of Johore to seize the British fortress of Singapore. Accepting the reality that a frontal assault against Singapore from the sea would have proven unacceptably suicidal, Japanese commanders instead executed unopposed amphibious landings to the far north. The expeditionary forces then attacked through the Malayan jungle to seize the fortress from the north, its blind side.

Japanese amphibious forces thus rolled through the self-styled Greater East Asia Co-Prosperity Sphere, but they were not altogether invincible. If we were to rate amphibious landings in the Pacific War on a scale of one to ten in terms of difficulty, with one representing an unopposed frolic and ten reflecting a storm landing against heavy opposition, the Japanese operations in 1941–42 would average about three. There's nothing pejorative about such a rating. The amphibious forces generally succeeded, and they did so at admirably low cost. In relative terms, their missions were not that difficult. These landings rarely tested the mettle of Japanese amphibious assault capabilities. How these units performed against opposition is more revealing.

On four occasions, Japanese landing forces met spirited opposition and prevailed—against British forces at Kota Bharu, Malaya; against U.S. Army and Filipino forces at Baung and Mauban on opposite coasts of Luzon; and against British and Dutch forces defending Koepang, Timor, in

February 1942. Koepang represented one of the few occasions when Imperial Army and Navy forces cooperated to execute an amphibious landing. The Navy rikusentai also employed their own parachute unit to complement their surface ship-to-shore assault. Each operation succeeded against determined resistance, although not truly against prepared fortifications.

In twentieth-century amphibious warfare, however, the trick is not so much getting ashore, but staying ashore. Generally, enough riflemen in the assault waves will survive the gauntlet of defensive fires to reach the beach and establish at least a toehold in the sand. This was the case at Tarawa, for example, where fifteen hundred U.S. Marines stormed ashore essentially intact in their tracked landing vehicles (LVTs), but then had to hang on for dear life for the next thirty hours because the tide and the reef and the Japanese gunners prevented the landing of most follow-on supporting arms and reinforcements. The loss of tactical momentum on such a prodigious scale nearly proved fatal to the 2d Marine Division.

These same circumstances developed during the so-called Battle of the Points in southern Luzon in January–February 1942. The Japanese launched four separate amphibious assaults against points along the western Bataan Peninsula. In each case, assault infantrymen fought their way ashore and secured a tenuous beachhead, but in no case could the Japanese land significant reinforcements, critical supplies, or heavy weapons. General MacArthur's forces eventually threw the survivors back into the sea.

Three months later, a Japanese Army battalion executed a night landing on Corregidor Island, the final American stronghold. This was boldly done, the last straw—the garrison in fact surrendered the next day—but the difficulty must be discounted because of the exhausted state of the defenders.

The most embarrassing amphibious setback experienced by Japan occurred at Wake Island in December 1941 where a spirited little band of U.S. Marines and sailors inflicted heavy losses on the Imperial Navy landing forces, sank several ships, and quashed the entire expedition—for the moment. The isolated garrison could not last indefinitely. The second Japanese attempt, showing greater respect for the Marines' 5-inch coast-defense guns, delivered a substantial landing force ashore at night and soon prevailed.

Both antagonists read the wrong lessons of the battle for Wake Island. The Japanese believed thereafter that coast-defense guns could punish an invasion fleet for a sufficient period of time to allow an effective air-sea-ground counterattack against a beleaguered island. Once they ceded the strategic offensive to the Allies in 1943, their fortification plans for island bastions in the Central Pacific invariably included the emplacement of big, turreted guns from Imperial Navy stocks. Similarly, certain U.S. Navy officers saw in Wake's experience good reason for bombardment ships to lie well offshore, heeding British Adm. Horatio Nelson's axiom "a ship's a fool to fight a fort." Subsequent U.S. successes against major-caliber Japanese coast-defense guns at Tarawa, Saipan, and Iwo Jima proved the fallacy of these arguments. In this case, however, Nelson's ghost died about as hard as the old viscount himself at Trafalgar. Kelly Turner and Holland Smith, it seemed, had to educate every new gunfire support commander in the realities of island bombardment.

Few U.S. strategists caught the real lesson of Wake Island. The small battle provided a revealing preview of Japanese amphibious capabilities that even in December 1941, at the peak of its power, lacked the synergy—the punch—to execute a landing against well-armed opposition. This operational timidity seems uncharacteristic of the Japanese military's well-documented affinity for close, offensive action, the spirit of the samurai. By contrast, even the U.S. Marines' primitive *Tentative Manual for Landing Operations of 1935* stressed utmost warrior qualities in the ship-to-shore assault: "Bayonets are fixed while well off the beach. . . . [The assault troops] charge the immediate beach offensives with the bayonet, and push the attack vigorously to the assigned objective."

In some respects, the issue of Japan's relatively toothless amphibious assault capabilities became academic following the defeats at Midway, Guadalcanal, and New Guinea. What further need would there be for their amphibious forces to fight their way ashore against opposition? In fact, this deficiency had serious implications for Japan's efforts to forestall Allied offensive moves because they could never mount a truly effective counterattack against newly seized enemy beachheads. Japanese counterattacks were typically prompt and furious, consisting sequentially of air strikes, naval surface action, then a counterlanding to wrest the captured ground from the enemy. Japanese aerial counterstrikes remained effective throughout the war—consider the kamikazes at Okinawa in 1945. Japanese naval forces remained a threat, albeit a decreasing one after the Battle of Leyte Gulf. But their amphibious counterlanding operations failed across the board. Counterlandings at Guadalcanal occurred in piecemeal fashion and too far away from the objective, Henderson Field, to succeed. At Bougainville, the counterlanding force stormed

The December 1941 invasion of Guam by Japanese amphibious forces as perceived by a Japanese artist. (*U.S. Naval Institute*)

ashore right where they would be most effective, directly within the Marines' beachhead, but they lacked the staying power to be effective. And at Tarawa, the Ko Detachment never posed a threat—too small, too lightly armed, undertrained, never a factor.

On the other hand, Japanese amphibious forces demonstrated two remarkable proficiencies during 1941–43 that the Americans would have been well advised to replicate: the art of executing night landings and the art of extracting amphibious forces from a desperate situation. Regarding the former, the Japanese seizure of Guam on 10 December 1941 deserves special mention. Put aside for the moment the fact that a tactical assault landing was probably unnecessary (155 U.S. Marines and a few hundred Guamanian Guardsmen defended the entire 228-square-mile island). The Japanese took no chances. They organized a joint landing force of rikusentai and an Army regiment, altogether about 6,000 men, timed their passage over or through the barrier coral reefs at high tide, and came ashore in total darkness at four landing points. For its size, this was one of the most masterfully planned and executed amphibious landings of the war (although whether it would have worked against even moderate opposition is arguable).

The Japanese employed their considerable nocturnal skills to conduct three prodigious missions of amphibious extraction during 1943. They evacuated the entire 5,000-man garrison from Kiska, rescued 9,400 from New Georgia, and pulled out 10,600 starving soldiers from Guadalcanal. While these operations are dwarfed by the Royal Navy's classic evacuation under fire of 360,000 British troops from Dunkirk in 1940, the Japanese achievements reflect masterful planning and execution of one of the most difficult tasks in naval warfare. Of the Solomons extraction, Adm. Chester Nimitz candidly reported, "Only skill in keeping their plans disguised and bold celerity in carrying them out enabled the Japanese to withdraw the remnants of the Guadalcanal garrison. Not until all organized forces had been evacuated on 8 February did we realize the purpose of their air and sea dispositions."

American amphibious developments during the first two years of the war in the Pacific remained hostage to the same limiting factors that existed at the eve of conflict, the lack of specialized wherewithal and a residual lack of confidence in the yet unproven doctrine of amphibious assault against hostile shores. Strategic factors also weighed heavily during these long months. Europe by deliberate choice still received the priority of effort and resources. The Imperial Japanese Navy still wielded sufficient power to threaten U.S. efforts to concentrate "superiority of force at the point of attack" needed to generate a true storm landing.

American forces in the Pacific were learning valuable lessons in this interim period. Among them were these two realities about their Japanese enemies: they were not invincible, but they were tenacious, lethal fighters. Victory seemed achievable, but all hands could sense the great cost in time, treasure, and blood it would require to fight across the breadth of the Pacific Ocean.

In the meantime, local commanders of all three services thought Gen. Alexander A. Vandegrift's assessment of current amphibious capabilities made good sense: "Landings should not be attempted in the face of organized resistance," he wrote in his final Guadalcanal report, "if, by any combination of march or maneuver, it is possible to land unopposed and undetected."

Vandegrift's stricture would prove relevant for most of 1943, but changes in strategy and technology, already in the wind, would soon provide a better road map for victory in the Pacific.

Chapter Two

Pacific Proving Ground

Air raid at 1335—*terrible!* No warning. Right in bull's eye.
Estimate 300 casualties. All HQ hit badly. Gross sights—arms
and legs moving all directions. . . . Nearly crapped out myself.

Lt. Col. David M. Shoup, USMC
Personal journal, Rendova,
2 July 1943

very American landing attempt during 1942–43 in the Pacific ran
the risk of such stinging Japanese counterstrikes as occurred on
D+2 at Rendova. It was a time when neither antagonist could gain
a significant advantage over the other, and the parallel development of U.S. amphibious proficiency and Japanese counterlanding virtuosity remained low key. While the United States lacked the preconditions,
specialized weapons systems, and confidence to launch a true storm landing until late autumn of 1943, the Japanese considered the threat to their
far-flung Pacific conquests as minimal during much of that same period.

With the notable exception of the Gilberts, Japanese base development in the early years consisted principally of building tactical airfields. These they utilized adroitly as interim staging bases, shifting air
units back and forth around the Pacific perimeter, from the Kuriles to
the Celebes, like pieces on a giant chessboard. Otherwise, few Pacific
islands under Japanese control benefited from advanced defensive preparations against potential enemy assaults from the sea in this interim

period. The great defensive citadels of Iwo Jima, Peleliu, and Okinawa did not become fortified until 1944. Most Japanese commanders were so flushed with "victory fever," imbued with the spirit of the offensive, and disdainful of the fighting qualities of their enemies that they gave little serious thought to a sustained Allied counteroffensive in the foreseeable future.

This blinkered mind-set bothered Adm. Isoroku Yamamoto, commander of the Combined Fleet, who had long warned that the Japanese would enjoy only a limited grace period in the Pacific (he figured two years at most) before America's enormous industrial capacity would complete its conversion to a war economy and begin to flood the Pacific with powerful new task forces. But an ULTRA decryption provided Yamamoto's flight schedule to a site within reach of U.S. land-based air units in the Solomons. On 18 April 1943 U.S. Army Air Forces P-38 Lightnings sent the admiral to a watery grave.

There would be other Japanese admirals, some with formidable tactical skills, but the Imperial Navy would never replace Yamamoto. The chronic failure of the Combined Fleet in subsequent years of the war to derail even a single American storm landing would reflect in part the absence of this naval warrior. Had he lived, Yamamoto would not likely have succeeded against America's increasing technological power, but at least he would have failed gloriously, in high seas combat. He surely would not have forfeited the Gilberts, Marshalls, and eastern Carolines without a fight, as his successor would do. Taking Yamamoto off the board improved the odds that America's great naval warfare experiments to follow in the Central Pacific would eventually succeed.

U.S. campaign planners from Pearl Harbor to Brisbane cheered at the muted news of Admiral Yamamoto's aerial ambush, but they still faced other daunting barriers to launching a sustained offensive campaign in the Pacific in 1943.

Vulnerability of the amphibious task force remained the principal concern. Executing conservative, short-range, shore-to-shore amphibious landings against an isolated segment of New Guinea's endless coastline (General MacArthur's preferred approach) was one thing. Cutting loose from the bounds of land-based air support for a distant strike in the Central Pacific would represent quite another—an inconceivable risk to many planners, downright suicidal to others. Limited assets and unproven doctrine reduced strategic options. As a consequence, the prevailing concern about vulnerability would continue to place a premium on surprise, speed, and simplicity in amphibious planning—a limited reach for limited objectives.

American campaign planners also worried about assailability. Japanese defenders on the small atolls of the Central Pacific would be hard to surprise. The vast region also abounded with coral reefs, natural obstacles to even the sturdiest landing boats during most tidal ranges. This was not an unanticipated problem. The intermittent reef surrounding Gavutu-Tanambogo had served to channelize the American assault landing into one open sector, which proved to be well covered by Japanese Nambu machine guns. In the earlier landing on Tulagi, not a single boat in the first wave could negotiate the reef. Troops wading the final one hundred yards ashore in chest-deep water could thank their lucky stars the initial landing was unopposed.

In 1938 Maj. Gerald C. Thomas, soon to become one of the Marine Corps' most influential senior officers, testified before Congress about the protection Guam's fringing reefs would likely provide that island's defenders. Given adequate base defense development funds, Thomas argued, the reefs would help a decent-size defensive force resist up to sixty thousand Japanese invaders. When Congress refused to authorize any base development whatsoever in the Central Pacific, Thomas realized the Marines would face severe problems in the inevitable requirement to recapture Guam by force. Sooner or later the amphibians would have to solve the reef problem.

Certain Pacific Theater commanders and planners shared Thomas's early concern. In fact, a Japanese submarine bombardment of U.S. Navy facilities on tiny Johnston Island on 7 December 1941 was thwarted by the unexpected appearance in those waters of the heavy cruiser *Indianapolis* and a squadron of destroyer minesweepers. Their mission that final day of peace was to test the capability of the Navy's new landing craft, the "Higgins boats," to traverse a coral reef. Higgins boats proved a boon to Allied assault forces in all oceans of the war, but the versatile craft required between three and four feet of water under the keel to clear a coral reef when carrying a full load of troops or equipment.* Marginal water depth over the reef would risk running the craft hard aground and damaging the rudder and prop guard. This operational limitation demanded accurate tidal information in advance. Unfortunately, such precise data were not readily available in many distant reaches of the Pacific.

* The inability of the LCVP (and the larger LCM-3) to negotiate coral reefs takes little away from the fact that these landing craft truly revolutionized amphibious warfare. As designed

For their part, the Japanese had accurate tide information at hand to support their reef-crossing, night landings on Guam in 1941, but that merely reflected the proximity of Japanese bases in the Marianas surrounding the American naval base. Lacking this precise information in 1942, Navy captain Minoru Ota, commanding the 2d Combined Special Naval Landing Force earmarked for the invasion of Midway, planned to transit that island's reefs by rubber boats—once the mighty Combined Fleet crushed the American fleet in the "decisive naval battle" offshore.

The Allies' lack of confidence in their ability to mount a major offensive seaborne campaign in 1942 led to two experiments with large-size amphibious raids. These took place within a week of each other in August of that year at opposite ends of the earth—at Makin in the Gilbert Islands and at Dieppe on the French coast. Neither proved satisfactory. The Dieppe raid turned into a tactical disaster. German defenders recovered from their initial surprise to cut down half the Canadian and British troops along the beaches. Dieppe, however, had redeeming strategic benefits. Adolph Hitler thereafter believed the inevitable cross-channel assault would have to be tied to a port facility, such as Calais or Cherbourg, thereby distracting his attention from the undeveloped Normandy beaches, which would be pierced by the Allied landings sixteen months later.

The Makin raid had considerable potential. Two large transport submarines penetrated the Gilberts undetected, surfaced off Butaritari Island by dark of night to launch Marine lieutenant colonel Evans F. Carlson's 2d Raider Battalion, an elite unit that would shortly earn acclaim for its jungle-fighting exploits on Guadalcanal. Carlson's objective was simply to distract Japanese attention from the landings in the Solomons and spoil their buildup of countervailing forces in the South Pacific. The Raiders surprised and defeated the Japanese garrison, but Carlson's tactical victory was clouded by his hasty withdrawal from the island, in which he inadvertently left nine Marines behind (soon captured and beheaded). Worse, unlike Dieppe, the raid accrued no strategic benefit. Quite the opposite, Carlson stirred up a hornet's nest in what had been a quiet, lightly held backwater of the Japanese perimeter.

---

by Andrew Jackson Higgins, both boats provided the landing force for the first time with reliable, wide-ramped, shallow-draft, high-powered craft with exceptional sea-keeping and surfing capabilities. The advent of the Higgins boats of both configurations quadrupled the landing options available to naval forces. No longer would they be restricted to seizing developed ports for amphibious power projections; any undeveloped beach became a prime access point. Coral reefs, however, remained a vexing obstacle in the Pacific.

Imperial General Headquarters (IGHQ) moved with alacrity to improve the defensive posture of these outer islands. Japanese naval expeditionary forces promptly seized and occupied the Gilberts in force, along with neighboring Nauru and Ocean Islands. The Makin raid sparked the beginning of the Japanese development of tiny Betio Island, Tarawa Atoll, as their easternmost fortified outpost.

Neither Makin nor Dieppe provided encouragement to commanders or strategists regarding the military utility of amphibious operations. The whole business seemed too risky and too complicated to warrant serious consideration in operations against well-organized opposition. Yet there seemed no other operational means of advancing across the Pacific to the Japanese home islands.

By the end of 1942 the United States had launched two large-scale amphibious operations, Operation Torch in North Africa and Operation Watchtower in the Solomons. Torch was a huge undertaking, a triple landing of some 107,000 Allied troops in Morocco and Algeria against brief but sharp opposition by Vichy French forces. The landings reflected more of the inherent chaos of amphibious operations. Many boats landed miles from their assigned beaches, scrambling unit integrity, while rough surf and inexperienced seamanship resulted in the loss of some two hundred landing craft. Although the D-Day beaches portrayed a disaster of classic proportions, the landing force projected sufficient troops and combat support ashore to stay, and the operation continued. An American Army had taken the offensive against the Axis in the European Theater and landed more or less intact in the rear of German general Erwin Rommel's Afrika Korps. There would be hell to pay ahead for the green American troops at Kasserine Pass, but Rommel's desert supremacy would soon wane. Torch worked.

So did Watchtower at Guadalcanal and the Floridas. Smaller, more ragged, and more exposed to major enemy counterattacks than Torch, the Guadalcanal operation literally hung in the balance throughout the three months following the landing. Seizing and holding Guadalcanal, even under such lean and hazardous conditions, produced enormous strategic benefits for the Allies in the Pacific. Perhaps the difficult art of forcible amphibious assault deserved a closer look.

Most strategic planners overlooked the opposed landings at Gavutu-Tanambogo in their review of the state of amphibious virtuosity. This was an unfortunate oversight, because the small-scale but viciously fought landings on those two islands provided a microcosm of the great

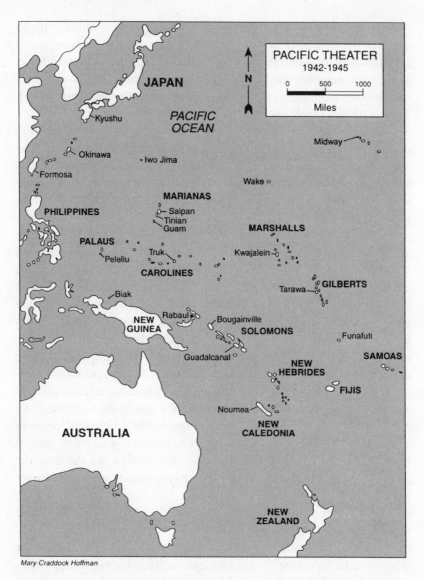

PACIFIC THEATER
1942-1945

0   500   1000

Miles

N

JAPAN

PACIFIC
OCEAN

Kyushu

Okinawa   • Iwo Jima

Midway

Formosa

Wake ○

MARIANAS

PHILIPPINES

Saipan
Tinian
Guam

MARSHALLS

PALAUS

Truk   Kwajalein

Peleliu

CAROLINES

GILBERTS

Tarawa

Biak

New
GUINEA

Rabaul

Bougainville

SOLOMONS

Funafuti

Guadalcanal ○

SAMOAS

NEW
HEBRIDES

FIJIS

Noumea

NEW
CALEDONIA

AUSTRALIA

NEW
ZEALAND

Mary Craddock Hoffman

amphibious campaigns to follow in the Central Pacific. Every flaw in the
Gavutu-Tanambogo operation held a corrective lesson to be learned, had
anyone taken the time for a serious examination.

A good look at Gavutu-Tanambogo would have highlighted the special requirements for amphibious intelligence: the assault force needs
precise information on tides and reefs, obstacles and surf zones, beach

gradient and trafficability—all in addition to reports of the enemy's strength and defensive weaponry. Lacking almost all of this essential information, Captain Crane's rifle company rushed into a buzz-saw in their hasty night landing attempt on Tanambogo.

There would be significant intelligence shortcomings in several of the storm landings to come (Peleliu, Okinawa), but never again would a landing force splash ashore so dangerously blind as did the 1st Marine Division at Guadalcanal and the Floridas. Amphibious intelligence would prove superb at Tarawa (with the notable exception of reliable tidal information). Several factors made such a marked improvement possible in the ensuing fifteen months: the professional growth of the intelligence staffs of the assault divisions (as personified by Lt. Col. Thomas J. "Jack" Colley and his crackerjack D-2 section of the 2d Marine Division); the integration of intelligence efforts with Admiral Nimitz's Joint Intelligence Center, Pacific Ocean Areas (JICPOA); and the onset of reliable aerial photography by the Seventh Air Force and (later) carrier aviation. The missing link remained the absence of on-the-scene reconnaissance of the beach approaches for the storm landings ahead. Tarawa would illuminate the crying need for scout-swimmers. Underwater demolition teams (UDTs) would be available for the Marshalls onward. The amphibians could have used them as early as the Solomons.

The Gavutu-Tanambogo operation should also have indicated the need for greater emphasis on amphibious training. Much of this is unsophisticated familiarization. How to waterproof weapons and equipment. How to use tag lines to lower crew-served weapons into a boat alongside. How to move a unit of troops through the narrow confines of a transport to the designated debarkation station on deck. How to descend via a rope net into the landing craft (never easy— "hands on the vertical, feet on the horizontal, watch that last step!"). When to lock and load. When to fix bayonets. How to roll over the gunwales of the landing craft (until the ramped Higgins boats appeared), hit the water, dash across the beach to the first objective. The simplicity of these tasks is deceiving. Lack of familiarity in any aspect has an accordion effect, which produces the well-documented beachfront chaos. We could have learned this fully from the landings in the Floridas.

Naval gunfire support against Japanese emplacements on Gavutu and Tanambogo proved unsatisfactory, yet we failed to learn this lesson until after Tarawa. Naval officers were slow to accept the fact that rapid, saturation bombardment would not succeed against fortifications or caves, that long-range firing lacked the precision necessary to take out critical targets. The antiaircraft cruiser *San Juan* unleashed 280 rounds from her 6-inch guns in five minutes against Gavutu, but it mainly served to deafen the defenders hunkered in their caves and to announce the approach of the landing force. The destroyer *Monssen*'s 200 rounds of 5-inch fire from 4,000 yards off Tanambogo on D-Day were not nearly as effective as her 92 rounds from 500 yards the following day.

In truth, the quality and quantity of naval gunfire support would continue to be a bone of contention between the landing force and the Navy throughout the war. In the storm landings to come, the landing force would deem naval gunfire support satisfactory only at Guam, Tinian, and Okinawa. The lessons of the Floridas seemed quickly forgotten. Navy commodore Herbert B. Knowles, who would command the transports at Tarawa and many subsequent assault landings, recalled his concern with the deficiencies of preliminary gunfire support against Gavutu when he commanded the transport *Heywood*: "From daylight to noon this little island was subjected to repeated bombing attacks and bombardment by cruisers and destroyers. The results had been most disappointing. Perhaps the reason little was learned from that particular landing was because of the smallness of the island and the few people involved, none of them being of any great rank."

Similarly, close air support at Gavutu and Tanambogo had proven of marginal value. Troops on the ground could not communicate with the aviators overhead. Twice, Navy planes bombed clusters of Marines fighting for Gavutu, the "fratricide" killing and wounding a dozen men and adding further to the frustration of a very long afternoon. Clearly, this critical area needed analysis and improvement. Unfortunately, we squandered the opportunity. D-Day at Tarawa would reflect identical shortcomings. And there was a larger issue of close air support evident in the Floridas. Although we had no alternatives at the time, it was unwise to risk strategic assets like fleet carriers to provide direct air support to the landing force. The U.S. Navy would need two kinds of carriers to prosecute the Pacific War: large, fast carriers to take the war to the enemy on the high seas and small escort carriers to deliver sustained close air support to amphibious operations. Both types were on the way—but not in 1942.

The early, opposed landings in the Floridas also revealed dangerous, momentum-robbing deficiencies in the ship-to-shore movement. The amphibious force supporting the 1st Marine Division contained a mix of six different kinds of landing craft, many of them still without bow ramps. Advent of the thirty-six-foot, ramped Higgins boats, the LCVPs (officially, Landing Craft, Vehicle and Personnel), would simplify and improve this situation, but there remained the problem of crossing coral reefs, and the requirement for larger boats— "lighters"—needed to land artillery and tanks while under enemy fire. The new fifty-foot LCM-3s (medium landing craft, also made by Andrew Higgins) would solve this problem nicely, once the fleet could provide sufficient transports with the boom capacity to handle the heavier craft and their tanks or guns.

The shortage of suitable landing craft limited the Marines' scheme of maneuver for the Floridas. The Paramarines slated to assault Gavutu had to wait several hours until boats used for Tulagi and the neighboring landings could be retrieved and refueled. Nor could the landing force get very many of their organic major weapons ashore in the two-day fight for Gavutu-Tanambogo. The acute shortage of ramped lighters for Watchtower limited the Paramarines and their reinforcements from landing anything more than two light tanks and a battery of 75-mm pack howitzers.

American landing forces would require much greater firepower ashore in the coming assaults. Eventually, the Navy would have sufficient landing craft available to land medium tanks and 155-mm howitzers following the assault waves. In the first years of the war, however, Marine divisions mirrored the lift and assault capabilities of the makeshift amphibious fleet. As one historian commented, the restricted boom capacity of the early amphibious ships limited the choice of Marine tanks and artillery "to the Tinker Toy level." These were the days of the Stuart M-3 light tanks (37-mm gun) and an artillery regiment comprised principally of the pack howitzers.*

Although American amphibious planners overlooked the available lessons of Gavutu-Tanambogo, they began to pay attention to subsequent landings in the Solomons and New Guinea. Two trends began to

---

* These versatile little guns provided yeoman service for the Marines in the Pacific War. Originally developed for mule-borne expeditionary forces, the pack howitzers could be disassembled into several man-portable components. A nightlong effort to manhandle these components ashore from the reef at Tarawa by the 1st Battalion, 10th Marines, made a major difference in the second day of that battle. Many Old Breed Marines, who recalled the stress of trying to unload "French 75" artillery pieces over the gunwales of motor whaleboats in the Potomac River at Quantico in the 1920s, swore by the versatility of the dismountable pack howitzers. So would "New Breed" Marines when they winched the small howitzers up impossible cliffs for point-blank fire against Japanese caves at Peleliu and Okinawa.

develop in the Pacific Theater, a greater appreciation for the role of logistics in amphibious operations and a general disenchantment with large-scale night landings.

The essence of amphibious logistics stems from combat loading, the embarkation of units, supplies, and equipment on assigned shipping to reflect the scheme of maneuver ashore. Combat loading gives little consideration to economic filling of cargo spaces and prime consideration to the principal of "first-needed, last-loaded." The most combat-essential gear must be loaded at the very end and placed in the most accessible spot, such as a hatch square, or preloaded in its assigned boat on board the ship. Sounds simple, but in practice combat loading is one of the most frustrating experiences in military life. Doing the job right assumes several ideal conditions: that there is indeed an approved scheme of maneuver available, with its matching debarkation priority schedule; that sufficient shipping will be assigned to embark the troops, vehicles, and supplies needed to execute the assault; that the "ship's loading characteristics pamphlet" accurately reflects the spaces available for combat cargo on each assigned vessel; and that there will be no last-minute changes. Most of these assumptions are as illusory today as they were in 1942.

A good transport quartermaster (TQM), typically a veteran warrant officer or senior staff NCO, was worth his weight in gold at the onset of each amphibious operation. The best of these not only knew their business but had a lively sense of improvisation. If lucky enough to be paired with an equally flexible ship's first lieutenant or chief boatswains mate, the consummate TQM could somehow survive the vagaries imposed by higher commands. This was the exception. Embarkation of the amphibious ships for Operation Watchtower was a particularly wretched experience, due in part to the degree of urgency and compressed time schedule. The abbreviated offload at Guadalcanal reflected this poor start—too little essential, too much nonessential cargo delivered ashore before the Battle of Savo Island drove the amphibs away.

The impact of logistics on the vital element of acceleration, or momentum, in an opposed amphibious assault cannot be overstated. Assault troops have to dash ashore virtually naked, a storming party of riflemen and light machine gunners who cannot be slowed with logistical burdens. As developed in amphibious doctrine, tactical sustainability gets ashore by increments, first in follow-on scheduled waves, then in designated on-call waves, or "floating dumps," finally by general unloading once the beachhead has been secured to enable unrestricted, administrative flow of boats in and out.

During World War II, there quickly developed an acrimonious difference of opinion between the Navy and the landing forces about the length of time this process should take. The Marines wanted selective unloading following the assault waves to remain the call of the tactical commander ashore—what he needed, when he needed it, delivered systematically to support the battle beyond the beachhead. But Navy commanders had great concerns about the security of the amphibious task force, that group of thin-skinned, lightly armed transports tethered to the beachhead and dangerously lacking the protective mobility available on the high seas. To hell, they said, with the niceties of an orderly offload at the call of the troop commander ashore. The urgent imperative to the Navy was the immediate general offload of all combat cargo in order to release the ships from their vulnerable anchorages.

The Navy's point was valid. The predictable Japanese reaction to each new Allied landing throughout 1942–43 featured major air and surface counterattacks delivered in short order and with great vehemence. The longer the amphibs had to squat and offload supplies, the more critically vulnerable they would become. Kelly Turner's amphibious task force at Guadalcanal had escaped annihilation after Savo Island only by an ill-considered flinch on the part of the victorious Japanese commander. There were other near misses. As a result, Turner and his captains sought to initiate general unloading as soon as the boats returned from landing the first wave. Their measure of effectiveness: how many hours of round-the-clock indiscriminate debarkation would it take before the ships could batten down their cargo hatches, retrieve their boats, and get to sea.

This procedure, fully understandable in the Solomons, became less so in the Gilberts. Hasty unloading of amphibious ships produced enormous problems for the landing force. No one knew which boats held what supplies; urgent requests for plasma, ammo, and water went unfilled; the Southern Attack Force soon ran out of boats—they were all loaded and circling in the lagoon. Some Marines compared the offload process to the Boston Tea Party. The line of departure became absolute chaos.

Chaos also seemed to attend Allied attempts at night landings in the Pacific. The two theaters of war held contrasting views on this subject. In the European Theater, amphibious planners heeded the words of Sir

Roger Keyes about the Gallipoli fiasco, that it was "folly to storm a defended beach in daylight." The Allies conducted successful night landings during the North African, Sicilian, and Italian campaigns.

The Russians had mixed results in night amphibious assaults. The Black Sea Fleet failed spectacularly to execute a night landing at Ozereyka Bay against German and Rumanian forces in February 1943. Yet a nearby diversionary landing by several hundred Soviet Naval Infantry troops that same night led to seizure of Novorossiysk and a seven-month foothold in that strategic sector.

The Pacific was a different story. The Marines, the principal landing force in the early years, recalled the admonitions against night landings of their prophet, Pete Ellis, plus their own adverse experiences in the Caribbean before the war. Captain Crane's abortive night-landing attempt at Tanambogo also left a bad taste. Admiral Turner's experiments with night landings in New Georgia with Army troops the following year left him equally disenchanted. Storm landings, it proved, would by nature require daylight. The final prep fires of ships and aircraft had to be as precise as possible in the morning, and the landing force needed enough residual hours of daylight to get sufficient combat power ashore before dark.

Building sufficient combat power to initiate storm landings would require plenty of specialized amphibious ships and landing craft. These were on the way, but top priority still belonged to the European Theater, which, until the Casablanca Conference of January 1943, still rated an 85 percent share of amphibious assets. The Pacific Theater's share doubled after Casablanca and increased again later in the year with the Allied conclusion that a cross-channel assault into northern France was not possible in 1943. Slowly the trickle of amphibious ships and craft to the Pacific began to increase.

Troop transports were the most immediate need among the amphibious forces. The United States had paid the price for not starting earlier to provide such ships in the prewar years. Only with the "Two-Ocean Navy Act" of 1940 did Congress provide funds for such unglamorous and undersponsored auxiliaries as troop transports. The first transports appeared almost overnight, reflecting the hasty conversion of a dozen passenger–cargo liners from commercial trade. (Captain Knowles's transport *Heywood* was the twenty-year-old former SS *City of Baltimore*.) Most of these steamers were already long in the tooth. Their freshwater, ventilation, and sewer systems could not accommodate a thousand or more "passengers" on any sustained basis. The Navy Department thoughtfully renamed the conversions after legendary Marine Corps general officers—*Doyen, Harris, Zeilin, Heywood, Biddle, Harry Lee*—but the troops developed their own uncomplimentary nicknames, the least offensive of which was "the Listing Harry Lee." Maligned and cussed, these old ships developed a can-do spirit and became valuable workhorses. In fact, much of the early practical body of knowledge of amphibious assaults came to reside in the crews of these journeymen transports simply because they were in demand all over the world. Several rotated between North Africa, the Aleutians, and the South Pacific during the bare-bones years of 1942–43, invaluable amphibious "stormy petrels."

In February 1943 the transports received a morale boost with their redesignation from APs to APAs—still naval auxiliaries, but now "attack transports"—accompanied by a retrofit program that installed multitiered Welin davits to accommodate a range of fifteen to thirty-three Higgins boats.* As 1943 wore on, new APAs joined the Pacific Fleet, built or modified as attack transports from the keel up, such as *Ormsby* and *Sheridan*. These new APAs were bigger, faster, more "spacious" in troop accommodations, and carried better armaments and armor.

Upgrading the transports did little to reduce their overall vulnerability to enemy action. Taking nothing away from their valorous crews, the ships were in no way men-of-war, but rather a fat prize sought by every armed predator on, over, or under the seas. The U.S. Navy lost ten transports (and an additional ten APDs, the smaller, high-speed transports built on modified destroyer hulls) to enemy fire in World War II. These losses included the large, radar-equipped transport *McCawley*, Kelly Turner's flagship at Rendova; four other APAs torpedoed by German U-boats off Fedala, Morocco, following the Torch landings in November 1942; and the *Susan B. Anthony*, sunk by a German mine on D+1 at Normandy. Japanese torpedo bombers sank the APD *McKean* while en route to Bougainville with follow-on forces; 116 men went down. In the North Atlantic in early 1943, a German submarine sank the Allied transport *Dorchester* with the loss of 605 lives, including the inspirational "Four Chaplains." Excepting the *Anthony* and *Dorchester*, our attack transport losses occurred after the main body of troops had already been debarked. Miraculously, in no case did we suffer the catastrophic loss of

* At the same time, amphibious cargo ships, AKs, were modified to carry landing craft and were redesignated attack cargo ships, AKAs. Both APs and AKs also received enhanced antiaircraft armaments in the modification process.

a fully loaded attack transport during any amphibious assault, a reflection of sheer luck and the Japanese Bushido mentality that invariably made them attack U.S. warships instead of the less prestigious auxiliaries.

By contrast, the Japanese lost 97 loaded transports, including 8 in the Battle of the Bismarck Sea in March 1943, in which 3,500 Imperial Army troops drowned.

In the cold-hearted calculus of war, an enemy transport crammed with combat troops on the high seas represents an ideal target. Better to kill these assault troops en masse before they execute a landing and have to be knocked off by twos and threes while swarming over one's beach. The Japanese missed many opportunities to even the odds against the amphibious forces coming to assault their island fortresses. Even at Okinawa the kamikazes usually favored the gunships or carriers over the transports as their final targets. But we now know from declassified ULTRA intercepts that Imperial General Headquarters had finally come to appreciate the logic of preemptive strikes against Allied transports. Japanese plans for the defense of Kyūshū in 1945 featured a heavy concentration of kamikazes and suicide craft against the American transport anchorage at the onset.

What a perfect hell it would have been if one of our transports had been fatally stricken by enemy attack while still laden with embarked troops! In the first place, the transports were invariably overloaded for the assault landings, partly to accommodate unit integrity, partly because there were never enough ships to go around. Imagine fifteen hundred combat-equipped Marines or soldiers on a single transport, in addition to the three-hundred-man crew. Once embarked, the troops had only three places to go: the weather decks, the mess deck, and their "berthing compartments." At General Quarters, all troops by necessity had to be confined to their berthing compartments, the equivalent of a cargo hold filled with floor-to-ceiling bunks, stacked twelve to fifteen high. With no open spaces in which to assemble, the troops had to retire to their bunks, each man further encumbered with rifle, helmet, and pack. These conditions were bleak enough—better than a slave ship, but much worse than the crudest steerage-class passage in turn-of-the-century tramp steamers. But imagine the chaos of a fatal torpedo or bomb strike, and the horror of trying to extricate even a handful of survivors from those jammed compartments to the weather deck in time. We lost hundreds of ships and thousands of seamen under nightmarish conditions in World War II.

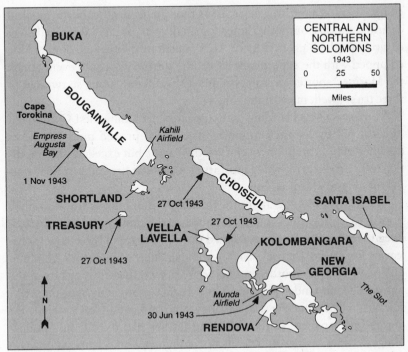

Mary Craddock Hoffman

At least the storm landings were spared from what may have been the ultimate horror on the cruel sea.

As 1943 matured, other new ships of particular value to amphibious assault began to appear in the Pacific Fleet. The first escort carriers, CVEs, participated in the seizure of Attu in the Aleutians in May. The following month Kelly Turner sailed for Operation Toenails, the seizure of New Georgia, with the first contingent of tank landing ships, LSTs.

The ungainly, shallow-draft, flat-bottomed LSTs may have had British origins, but in their down-home utility and versatility these ships had Made in America stamped all over them. They rode rougher than a cob, but they could beach themselves, open bow doors, lower a ramp, and discharge wheeled or tracked vehicles in shallow water or onto a cause-way, conveniently carried on each side. If nothing else, the LST's shallow draft (3'1" forward, 9'6" aft in landing configuration) permitted a much closer approach to any beach, thereby greatly reducing the turnaround time for boats extracting casualties from the fight and receiving more combat cargo to return ashore. LSTs thus made ideal seaborne medical clearing stations, or mother ships for small craft, or relay ships to deliver cargo from the bigger APAs or AKAs much further at sea. Some LSTs, equipped with the experimental "Brodie slingshot," could even launch the Marines' spotter aircraft—or at least succeed in doing so two out of three tries. (Well, most of the time.)

More specialized landing craft appeared, including the LCI (dubbed "Elsie Eye" by lovesick amphibians), which proved marginal in its designed role as an infantry craft in the Pacific but excelled once modified to fire rockets or heavy mortars as a close-in fire support boat during the ship-to-shore assault.

Things were looking up for the threadbare amphibious forces, but the flow of these new ships and craft remained thin for a good half of 1943. Even then, the Pacific Fleet retained the lion's share of these new assets, leaving Rear Adm. Daniel E. Barbey, commanding "MacArthur's Amphibious Navy" in the Southwest Pacific Area with the scrapings from the barrel bottom. Under pressure Kelly Turner grudgingly sent one APA south to Barbey, but the ship had a chronic oil leak, a fatal tattletale for marauding Japanese submarines, and Barbey had to rely on a hodgepodge of other castoffs and derelicts to commence his celebrated drive up the New Guinea coast.

Kelly Turner invaded Rendova in New Georgia with the 43d Infantry Division and the 9th Marine Defense Battalion in late June. In addition to losing his flagship (first to Japanese torpedo bombers, then—a final indignity—to an American PT boat skipper with an itchy trigger finger), Turner experienced several other anxious moments. The Army had trained several companies of elite commandos, Barracudas, who would comprise the assault waves, clear the target beaches, and guide the follow-on waves ashore. Darkness, inexperience, and general "friction" resulted in a late launch of the Barracudas and their landing on the wrong beach. The main body, ignorant of this, sailed shoreward anticipating a covered landing. Turner had to galvanize them with this urgent message: "You are the first to land! You are the first to land! Expect opposition!" All hands experienced anxious moments until the newly designated assault force overcame the few Japanese defending the beach.

The initial landing at Rendova thereby succeeded, but the buildup of combat power ashore suffered from heavy rain, deep mud, and more inexperience. By D+2 supplies and equipment of every description clogged the exposed beach. At that point the joint air defense system failed badly.

A flight of Imperial Navy bombers from Rabaul surprised the landing force and devastated the beach with impunity. Among the many casualties was the senior observer from the 2d Marine Division detailed to Rendova to learn firsthand about amphibious landings. Lt. Col. David M. Shoup barely escaped with his life. Shoup's amphibious odyssey still had a few more twists and turns to follow until his memorable performance as the chief architect and executioner at Betio, but his traumatic experience at Rendova had provided searing lessons. These would prove beneficial at the onset of the great Central Pacific campaign, whose forces were already starting to coil for the first strike.

Chapter Three

Turning Point at Tarawa

But the enemy was also daring. Under our fires they came in
large numbers, one after another, wading the shallows, stepping over their friends' bodies. I in my tank kept shooting until
the gun barrel became red hot. I felt that we were certain to die
because the U.S. fighters came in large numbers.

Petty Officer Tadao Onuki, IJN
Personal memoir, Tarawa,
20 November 1943

The first storm landing of the Pacific War erupted with concentrated violence at dawn on 20 November 1943 against the Japanese
bastion on Betio Island, Tarawa Atoll, in the Gilberts. Imperial
General Headquarters, though shocked by this enemy initiative,
had every confidence that Betio's fortified garrison could withstand any
American landing attempts. Rear Adm. Keiji Shibasaki, highly regarded in
Tokyo, commanded the 3d Special Base Defense Force on Betio, an untested
but well-trained force of forty-six hundred naval infantry and engineers.

Shibasaki realized he was in the presence of a powerful American
naval task force. Each of his strongholds in the Gilberts—Tarawa, Makin,
Apamama, Ocean, and Nauru—had been plastered the preceding week
by carrier aircraft and heavy cruisers, augmented by long-range bombers
from the Ellice Islands. What did it mean? The Japanese high command
believed the American landing at Bougainville in the Solomons earlier
that month represented the principal enemy winter offensive in the
Pacific. Surely this activity in the Gilberts was but a diversion.

The faint gray light of morning nautical twilight on 20 November shattered Shibasaki's reasoned assumptions. The horizon swarmed with scores of enemy warships—battleships, cruisers, the unmistakable silhouettes of troop transports. Already he could see hundreds of tiny dots circling the anchored transports—a landing force. This was no feint! His radio crackled with excited reports from the Makin outpost at Butaritari Island, surrounded by another huge task force. Shibasaki sent an urgent report to the Fourth Fleet commander in the Marshalls and quickly ordered his big coast-defense batteries to open fire.

Shibasaki had drilled his gunners for this precise moment each day of the four months since he had assumed command. The crown jewels of his defensive fire system were four turret-mounted, 8-inch naval cannons, relics of a direct purchase from Great Britain during the 1905 Russo-Japanese War, yet amply suited for interdicting the entrance to Tarawa Atoll or disrupting enemy tactical formations offshore. But the proliferation of live targets seemed to rattle Shibasaki's novice gun crews; they hurried their shots and did little damage. Moreover, their blazing muzzle flashes attracted the immediate attention of a pair of old Pearl Harbor victims with a score to settle. The battleships *Tennessee* and *Maryland*, joined by *Colorado*, leveled their main batteries and methodically demolished three of the Japanese gun positions and their principal magazine in a matter of minutes.* Shibasaki's smaller-caliber coastal guns performed with similar ineptitude. The lagoon entrance, the back door to Betio, now lay uncovered.

Shibasaki could only curse his misfortune. He lacked perhaps two weeks in completing the encirclement of Betio with mines and obstacles. He had placed top priority on the southern and western defenses, figuring the Americans would surely land there, and his laborers had not yet finished work on the northern, lagoon-side beaches. Even now he had three thousand mines sitting uselessly in storage, waiting to be sown throughout the lagoon approaches. Sure enough, Shibasaki's spotters soon reported an enemy task unit of two minesweepers and two destroyers approaching the unobstructed channel.

The Japanese commander ordered every surviving coast-defense gun to engage the new threat from the north. Quickly the green water around the approaching ships erupted in huge geysers. But Shibasaki's luck

---

* The USS *Colorado* (BB 45) had been in overhaul at Bremerton, Washington, on 7 December 1941; she would become extremely popular with the Marines for her willingness to engage shore targets at point-blank range.

Japanese island defenders used these versatile Type 98 (1929) 127-mm dual-purpose gun mounts against American aircraft and landing craft during the Pacific War. *(Larry E. Klatt)*

remained snake-bitten. His most proficient 5.5-inch gun crew nailed the lead destroyer dead center with two quick shots—but both shells were duds. Soon an American smoke screen began to obscure the ships in the lagoon, although not before lookouts reported a long column of landing craft entering the channel five miles northward of Betio.

Admiral Shibasaki did not panic. A veteran himself of amphibious landings along the coast of China, he knew better than most the difficulties the Americans still faced. The heart of the Japanese defenses on Betio lay in their well-sited antiboat and heavy machine guns, enhanced by the natural protection of the coral reef. Shibasaki once taught advanced navigation to other naval officers; he well knew the neap tide that morning favored his defenders. Then, shortly before 0900, the great bombardment by ships and planes suddenly ceased. The enemy assault craft were still two miles away from the beach. Grateful for this opportune blunder, Shibasaki began shifting forces and field guns from the southern defenses to alternate firing positions along the threatened north shore.

As the three ragged waves of enemy assault craft surged into plain view, the Japanese commander realized with surprise that these were not

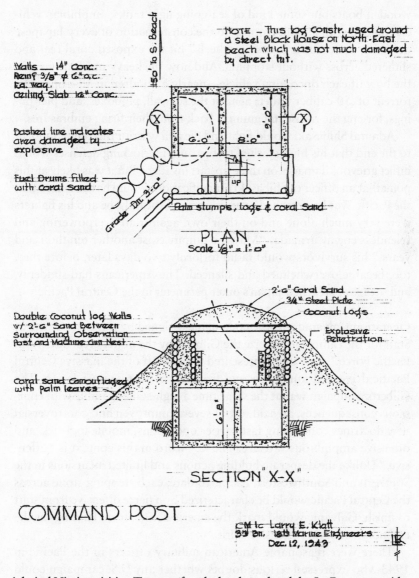

NOTE – This log constr. used around a steel Block House on North-East Beach which was not much damaged by direct hit.

Walls – 14" conc.
Reinf 3/8" ⌀ 6" o.c. ea. way.
ceiling Slab 16" conc.

Dashed line indicates area damaged by explosive

Fuel Drums filled with coral sand

50' to S. Beach

9'-0"
6'-0"   8'-0"

X   X

UP

Grade Dia. 3'-0"

Palm stumps, logs & coral Sand

PLAN
Scale 1/8" = 1'-0"

2'-6" Coral Sand
3/4" Steel Plate
Coconut Logs

Explosive Penetration

Double Coconut log Walls w/ 2'-6" Sand Between Surrounding Observation Post and Machine Gun Nest

Coral sand Camouflaged with palm leaves

6'-8"

SECTION "X-X"

COMMAND POST

CM 1c Larry E. Klatt
3rd Bn. 18th Marine Engineers
Dec. 12, 1943

Admiral Nimitz, visiting Tarawa after the battle, ordered the SeaBees to provide blueprints of the Japanese fortifications for his engineers. Carpenter's Mate 3/c Larry E. Klatt produced this rendering of a sector command post in December 1943. *(Larry E. Klatt)*

wooden boats but some kind of sea-going light tanks, amphibian vehicles loaded with assault troops. To the consternation of every Japanese defender, these "little boats on wheels" hit the exposed coral reef and slithered across without stopping. And now the heavy machine guns in the bow of each oncoming vehicle—nearly a hundred in all—opened a torrent of .50-caliber bullets against the seawall, pillboxes, and pier pilings, forcing the rikusentai gunners back from their firing embrasures.

Admiral Shibasaki would fight and die as a warrior this day, confident to the end that his high-spirited troops and interlocking defenses would inflict grievous damages on these upstart invaders. But it was likely at this point that an officer of Shibasaki's qualifications would have realized that the Pacific War had reached a turning point. Abruptly, he and his fighters were very much alone and on their own against an overpowering and relentless enemy armada. "May the Empire exist another ten thousand years," his survivors would radio forlornly two days later, before they, too, became overwhelmed and silenced. The Americans had suddenly, and savagely, breached Japan's outer perimeter in the Central Pacific.

Operation Galvanic was the code name assigned by the Joint Chiefs of Staff for the campaign to seize the Gilberts by the newly created Central Pacific Force.* Galvanic represented the kickoff of the massive Central Pacific drive, a dramatic second front in the war against Japan. The Gilberts campaign was at the same time a high-stakes gamble with enormous consequences, an acid test of several unproven and controversial new doctrines concerning fast carrier operations, mobile logistics, and offensive amphibious warfare. The key word in this context is "offensive." Unlike the desperate holding actions and limited incursions in the Southern and Southwestern Pacific to date, each stepping stone across the Central Pacific would be characterized by a fierce offensive from start to finish. Galvanic would mark the emergence of storm landings as the embodiment of this offensive spirit.

There were reasonable American military officers in the Pacific in 1943 who expressed serious doubts whether any U.S. campaign could succeed beyond the protective umbrella of land-based tactical aircraft, whether any naval task force could operate at extended ranges beyond fixed repair and replenishment facilities, or whether any fortified island could ever be assaulted by amphibious forces. These men honestly

---

* Soon to be designated the U.S. Fifth Fleet.

believed that the vast ocean expanses and heavily barricaded enemy atolls of the Central Pacific would prove to be the burial ground of any American force foolish enough to "leap off the deep end." It would be wiser and safer, they argued, to concentrate limited resources in General MacArthur's deliberate approach along the Solomons–New Guinea–Philippines axis.

Even the most outspoken proponents of the Central Pacific campaign admitted serious concerns about the risks. Success in this endeavor would provide a shorter road to Tokyo, but it remained an unthinkable strategic option until such time as the United States could deliver the numbers of improved ships and aircraft that would enable the Pacific Fleet to achieve superiority at sea and in the air along the avenue of advance.

Prevailing against the still-powerful Japanese Combined Fleet and the many fortified island outposts in the Central Pacific would require foremost plenty of the new *Essex*-class fleet carriers, with their greater payload (three squadrons), speed, range, and antiaircraft protection. Beyond the fleet carriers the priority list included escort carriers and major-caliber gunfire support ships to enhance amphibious landings; more submarines and destroyers and minesweepers; new, fast replenishment ships and tankers; larger, faster amphibious ships and self-deploying landing ships; improved fighters and dive-bombers; enhanced radar; more reliable torpedoes; variable-time (VT) fuses; medium tanks; more effective flamethrowers. The whole issue of extended range, high mobility, self-sustaining task forces needed validation. Could we really develop the ability to refuel, rearm, and replenish our surface combatants without having to cycle each ship a thousand miles back to rear naval bases? Would we ever have enough ships—transports, cargo ships, merchants—to deliver a combined amphibious assault plus a follow-on base defense force with its heavy antiaircraft guns and air search radars?

The new doctrine of amphibious assault remained unproven in a real trial by fire. Invariably, the principal U.S. objectives in the Central Pacific would be those islands capable of supporting an airfield, and in Micronesia there were only a limited number of islands of sufficient overall length whose long axes conveniently faced the prevailing wind. Most of these already sported Japanese airfields and base defense forces. All were further protected by coral reefs. Prospects for success seemed unlikely.

Operation Galvanic took place twenty-three months after Pearl Harbor, seventeen months after the battle of Midway, and fifteen months following the landings at Guadalcanal and the Floridas. Amphibious planners had devoted much of this time wrestling with the problem of how to get assault forces across a barrier reef while under enemy fire. Some Marines perceived that the means of tactical reef-crossing mobility already existed within their own organizational equipment. Strangely, it was like pulling teeth to bridge the gap between concept and practice.

The humble tracked landing vehicle (LVT—also called "amtrac" and, initially, "amphtrac") provided the solution to the barrier reef. The first model LVT-1s (Alligators), which joined the Fleet Marine Forces in 1941, proved to be true amphibians, capable of being lowered by a ship's boom, swimming shoreward, negotiating a plunging surf, then operating inland through marginal terrain. In the Solomons, however, the Alligators remained simply logistical vehicles, in effect seagoing trucks. Their thin armor, slow speed, fragility, and scary tendency to lose power and watertight integrity in the ocean kept them from tactical mobility applications with embarked troops.

Maj. Gen. Holland M. Smith, rightfully credited as the nation's foremost amphibious pioneer in the early 1940s, became the first senior Marine to propose a tactical role for these primitive LVTs. As commanding general of the Atlantic Fleet Amphibious Force in March 1942, Smith recommended that an amphibian tractor battalion be assigned each division for beach assault. "Swamp areas and coral reefs encountered near the beachline are passable by no other means," he stated. "The use of the amphibian tractor permits a wider selection of landing places and more freedom of maneuver for the attacker."

The Navy listened to Smith's suggestions. Among the new features contained in Change Two to Fleet Training Publication 167, *Landing Operations Doctrine* (August 1942) appeared this modification to the ship-to-shore chapter: "Landing vehicles, track, will be useful and should be available for crossing coral reefs."

In April 1943 Marine colonel David R. Nimmer, a Guadalcanal veteran assigned to the Joint War Plans Committee, evaluated the amphibious feasibility of the proposed Central Pacific campaign. Nimmer asked the Commandant of the Marine Corps whether the current LVT-1 could in fact negotiate a coral reef while being pounded by a plunging surf. The commandant promptly ordered Maj. Gen. Clayton B. Vogel, commanding the I Marine Amphibious Corps (IMAC) in the South Pacific, to conduct a field test. Vogel knew of an officer in his command who had been instrumental in forming and training the first amphibian tractor unit in the Corps, Lt. Col. Victor H. "Brute" Krulak, then commanding the 2d Parachute Battalion.

Brute Krulak conducted a hair-raising series of tests of four Alligators under reef and surf conditions in New Caledonia from 26 April to 3 May. In Krulak's words, "the operation subjected the machines to severe punishment," which created control problems, "shipped considerable water," and made for an uncomfortable ride ("personnel were thrown roughly about"). Surprisingly, the vehicles made the grade. Krulak's conclusion simply stated was, "It is mechanically feasible to employ amphibian tractors as supply and personnel carriers in an amphibious operation executed across coral reefs and involving surf up to ten feet in height."

The IMAC test report sped back to Washington. Colonel Nimmer and the Joint War Plans Committee had it by mid-May. On 10 June the Joint Chiefs released Joint Planning Staff Report No. 205, "Operations against the Marshall Islands." The JCS had come to view the Central Pacific campaign more favorably. Among the many politicostrategic factors leading to this turnaround was one practical operational breakthrough: "Recent tests conducted in the South Pacific indicate that the amphibian tractor can negotiate a fringing reef in all conditions up to a ten-foot surf without too great damage from the pounding or much probability of stranding." The Joint Planning Staff further recommended that amphibious task force commanders use the new tank landing ships (LSTs) to transport assault troops and LVTs to the objective. LSTs could carry seventeen LVTs, launch them ten times faster by bow ramp than transports could by swinging boom, and could approach closer to the shore than the deeper draft transports, thus enabling a faster run to the beach.

The story deserved a happier ending. To this point the Guadalcanal Old Boy Network had worked swiftly to answer a tough question—Nimmer at the JCS to (very likely) Col. Gerald C. Thomas at Marine headquarters to Brute Krulak in New Caledonia and back. But thereafter the details of Krulak's report and the practical suggestions of JPS No. 205 began to fade from sight. Adm. Kelly Turner, for one, would not abide the introduction of LSTs into his attack forces for Galvanic because he believed their slow speed of advance (nine knots on a good day) would jeopardize his formations and forfeit surprise. Worse, while amphibious troop commanders like Vogel and Holland Smith had copies of Krulak's test as early as May and June, respectively, neither thought to share that information with the 2d Marine Division, earmarked to assault the reef-plagued Gilberts for Operation Galvanic in November.*

* Hence, there ensued the stirring but redundant saga of Col. David Shoup and Maj. Henry Drewes, who conducted desperate modifications and tests of the 2d Division LVTs just prior to Tarawa to determine if the vehicles could, in fact, cross a coral reef.

Other knotty problems remained to be resolved before the Central Pacific Force would truly be ready to unleash the first storm landings. The Marines in the Pacific were anxious to receive the M-4 Sherman medium tank, whose 75-mm gun, heavier armor, and enhanced mobility would provide a quantum improvement over the existing M-3 Stuart light tanks. While the Shermans had fared rather poorly in initial encounters against the larger German Tigers and 88-mm antitank weapons in Europe, the Marines figured the new mediums would be ideal in the Pacific against the less lethal Japanese tanks and smaller antitank guns (typically 47-mm).

There were two obstacles to deploying Sherman tanks in an amphibious assault in 1943: the incompatibility of the thirty-four-ton vehicle with existing amphibious shipping, and the delayed arrival in the Pacific of fording kits, the simple exhaust-pipe extensions and engine seals needed to protect the Shermans against flooding during tactical debarkation. In view of the high priority accorded Operation Galvanic, the matter of rushing fording kits to the Pacific should have been readily achievable. The kits nevertheless failed to arrive in time. Five of the fourteen Sherman tanks assigned to the Betio assault drowned in shallow shell craters inside the reef during the ship-to-shore movement on D-Day morning—a critical, nearly fatal, loss.

The larger problem of producing a compatible amphibious ship for the Shermans fared better, albeit in just the nick of time. By mid-1943 the Navy Department had copied a British design and begun producing a revolutionary new amphibious ship of strange proportions whose conventional bow seemed dominated by hunched shoulders and a chopped-off stern. This was the dock landing ship, the LSD, a unique class of amphibious ships still in service in the U.S. fleet. The LSD's enduring utility came from its ability to ballast down at sea, lower a stern gate and flood its well deck to sufficient depth to permit medium landing craft (LCMs), preloaded with, say, Sherman tanks, to float out the stern and proceed directly to the beach—or at least as far as the coral reef.

Here was another ragged edge for the Tarawa assault. The Navy commissioned USS *Ashland* (LSD 1) the first week of August 1943. At the same time, halfway across the world, Vice Adm. Raymond A. Spruance, newly appointed commander of the Central Pacific Force, sat around a map of Tarawa Atoll in a New Zealand hotel room with Maj. Gen. Julian Smith and the senior officers of the 2d Marine Division brainstorming the problem of how to get Sherman tanks ashore. The *Ashland* would play a significant role in Galvanic, delivering the fifty new LVT-2s to Capt. Ray "Hootie" Horner's enterprising amtrackers in Samoa in late October, hastening over to New Caledonia to embark the fourteen Sherman tanks, then catching up with the Southern Attack Force in the New Hebrides only two weeks before D-Day. The *Ashland* succeeded in delivering the goods in the lagoon at Tarawa, but so close had been the schedule that the first time the 2d Marine Division ever laid eyes on the new Sherman tanks was that very chaotic morning.

Some staff admirals in Pearl Harbor derided Raymond Spruance for trying to build his new Central Pacific Force into an overwhelming armada. "Spruance," said one, "wants to use a sledgehammer to drive a tack." The new force commander shrugged off the criticism. Although inexperienced in amphibious warfare, he could sense its inherent risks. Years later, after commanding the great amphibious victories in the Gilberts, Marshalls, Marianas, Iwo Jima, and Okinawa, Spruance would declare that the principal lesson he learned at Tarawa was the need to use "violent, overwhelming force, swiftly applied." Even in 1943 he knew how big a task lay ahead.

The Marines likewise knew in advance that Tarawa would be a tough nut to crack. Lt. Col. Jack Colley's enterprising intelligence section provided Julian Smith and his commanders a wealth of tactical information about the Japanese garrison, their weapons, numbers, and dispositions. Smith was particularly uneasy about the artificial restrictions imposed on his division.

The Gilberts would be merely the first step, a modest-size operation to shake down new forces, test new doctrine, and seize advance air bases— all in preparation for the pending assault on the larger, more strategically valuable Marshalls, five hundred miles west of the Gilberts. So be it. But Smith perceived the Marshalls "clock" to be driving every Gilberts decision. Galvanic, in effect, had to be executed in time to preserve the Marshalls schedule, whose D-Day was a mere six weeks away. That inflexible mandate, coupled with the Navy's natural concern with a major engagement with the Combined Fleet, put a premium on speed of execution for Galvanic.

"Get the hell in and get the hell out," said Nimitz to Spruance. Nimitz and Spruance therefore scotched Julian Smith's proposals for advance seizure of neighboring Bairiki Island for an artillery fire support base, an amphibious feint against Betio's north shore, and several days of naval bombardment. The Southern Attack Force would instead have three hours at first light on D-Day to pummel Betio with everything in the book. What the hell, many officers reasoned, the island was a small spit of sand and coral. Three hours' concentrated fire by the force of battleships, cruisers, and destroyers—augmented by attack aircraft—would constitute the biggest preliminary naval bombardment of the war to date. The admiral commanding the fire support ships even promised Smith he would "obliterate" the island.

The initial counterbattery fire delivered by the battleships against Admiral Shibasaki's 8-inch guns at the onset of the battle seemed to underscore this boast. From that point, however, the preliminary bombardment went downhill sharply. All hands—commanders, gunners, directors, spotters—simply had too much to learn about this specialized mission. The bombardment proved spectacular to watch, but it was all sound and fury, with scant little damage to Betio's five hundred pillboxes and gun positions. These deficiencies became exacerbated when Adm. Harry Hill ordered cease fire twenty minutes before the first assault waves reached the beaches.

The biggest surprise encountered by the 2d Marine Division in their assault on Betio was not low water over the coral reef—most had been advised to expect this—but the unsettling realization that the Japanese garrison had somehow survived the "war's largest bombardment" with their tactical integrity, crew-served weapons, and fighting spirit intact. That's when the "issue in doubt" reports began to emerge from the bloody fighting.

The next thirty hours were excruciating for the commanders offshore and further distant—Harry Hill and Julian Smith on the battleship *Maryland,* Ray Spruance nearby on the heavy cruiser *Indianapolis,* Kelly Turner and Holland Smith on the battleship *Pennsylvania* near Makin (observing the 27th Army Division's assault, but glued to radio reports from Tarawa), Chester Nimitz at his headquarters at Makalapa Heights, Oahu. "Issue in doubt" at Tarawa meant the whole Central Pacific campaign was now at risk. This first storm landing had to succeed.

The twin American offensives in the Solomons and the Gilberts whipsawed and confounded the Imperial General Headquarters and caused Admiral Koga to fritter away his Combined Fleet in misdirected countermeasures. But there was a world of difference between Operation Galvanic and Operation Dipper, the Bougainville campaign.

Unlike Galvanic, which envisioned an unremitting offensive surge from start to finish, Dipper resembled the Guadalcanal initiative months earlier, in which the Allies combined a strategic offensive with a tactical defensive. The mission of the 3d Marine Division was not to conquer Bougainville, but rather to seize an unoccupied sector of jungle near Cape Torokina on the island's southern coast, then hang on for dear life while the SeaBees built from scratch two airfields to be used against Rabaul. Like Galvanic, campaign planning for Dipper emphasized surprise and speed of execution.

A diversionary landing by Brute Krulak's 2d Parachute Battalion on Choiseul Island distracted Japanese attention long enough for the amphibious task force to venture into Empress Augusta Bay. Here there was no brash admiral to proclaim his intention of "obliterating" Bougainville. Four destroyers opened up on the target beachhead without great effect. The 3d Marines and the 2d Raiders, leading the assault, were soon on their own.

By all definitions, this was not a storm landing. Bougainville would soon become a deadly and prolonged campaign fought under brutish jungle conditions. But the decision to attack an unimproved stretch of the long coastline paid dividends on D-Day morning because fewer than three hundred Japanese rikusentai constituted the immediate defensive force. A single Japanese 75-mm gun, unscathed by the naval gunfire, had a field day delivering enfilade fire against the Higgins boats approaching the beach. Knocking it out took exceptional personal courage by Marine sergeant Robert A. Owens, whose family later received the posthumous Medal of Honor on his behalf. Five squadrons of Marine and Navy torpedo bombers and dive-bombers swept in low to hammer the beach shortly before touchdown.* Meanwhile, a vicious surf disrupted the landing more than enemy fire, swamping scores of boats and scattering the assault waves. In all, the 3d Marine Division sustained about two hundred casualties getting ashore. The troops dug in quickly. The small assembly of amphibious ships offloaded limited supplies in great haste, as agreed, then retreated, in dire jeopardy.

* Effective as this close air support was by their brothers in arms, Bougainville would represent the last time USMC tactical air provided direct support to a Marine landing force until the attack on Ngesebus Island at Peleliu ten months later. The striking distances in the Central Pacific exceeded the "legs" of Marine land-based fighters, and it would take nearly a year before USMC squadrons assigned to CVs and CVEs would coincide with a major amphibious assault. These occurred effectively at Iwo Jima and Okinawa.

Within hours, more than a hundred Japanese bombers and fighters began screeching over the beachhead. Rear Adm. Aaron S. Merrill prevailed against a major surface counterattack in the Battle of Empress Augusta Bay. Admiral Koga then deployed two entire air groups—120 planes and crews—from his carriers remaining at Truk. He also detached a force of heavy cruisers to Rabaul. Adm. William F. Halsey's thin resources were stretched to the breaking point.

Bull Halsey reacted to these threats by launching a high-risk preemptive strike. On 5 November he deployed his only two carriers, the old *Saratoga* and the smaller *Princeton,* in a daylight foray into the Northern Solomons. The carrier pilots caught the Japanese task force by surprise in Rabaul's Simpson Harbor, damaging eight cruisers and shooting down scores of Koga's transplaced naval aviators.

Halsey's initiative earned tremendous strategic dividends for Americans throughout the Pacific. These preemptive raids saved the Bougainville beachhead, for one thing, and by annihilating the equivalent of two entire carrier air groups, the strikes rendered Admiral Koga essentially toothless throughout the ensuing U.S. campaigns in the Gilberts and Marshalls. Koga would not dare deploy the Combined Fleet without carrier air cover. His decision to reinforce Rabaul thereby proved disastrous. Moreover, his surviving aviators returned with wildly exaggerated claims of having sunk a dozen U.S. carriers and battleships. Blindly accepting their claims, Koga concluded that he had at least derailed any possible American incursion into the Central Pacific by a matter of months. He had no clue that an enormous new enemy force was already steaming toward the Gilberts.

The Central Pacific Force thus achieved strategic surprise, assembling its disparate components in the Gilberts from half a dozen distant ports before finally being detected by Japanese maritime patrol aircraft two days before D-Day. Both Koga at Truk and Shibasaki at Tarawa refused at first to believe the reports. Surely this was a diversionary raid. . . .

The Marines struggling to seize Betio Island would need every possible advantage to gain the edge. The twin gambles of attacking through the lagoon and using jury-rigged LVTs as assault craft had succeeded handsomely—but then the wheels came off. The vaunted obliteration of Betio by preliminary bombardment had proven so ineffective that a battery of four Japanese dual-purpose (antiaircraft-antiboat) 75-mm guns in open revetments along the reentrant of Red Beach One remained untouched.

These guns, firing horizontally at point-blank range, exacted a fearsome toll among the LVTs trying to shuttle reinforcements from those units in boats stalled by the exposed reef. The battery maintained this deadly fire for a full hour after touchdown until an improvised storming party of Marines snuffed them out one by one with grenades and bayonets.

The Japanese fought like banshees. The naval infantrymen in their pillboxes or fighting holes displayed none of the "buck fever" of the coast-defense gunners in the opening rounds of the battle. Shibasaki had identified every yard of the island with a firing grid. Howitzer crews plotted their targets using pre-positioned aiming stakes; machine gunners maintained assigned fields of fire along the barbed wire and tetrahedrons; riflemen kept their cover and concealment. The attacking Marines fought with their own ferocity, but any man who lifted his head above the seawall attracted bullets from a dozen sources, most of them dangerously close at hand. Hoarse cries arose along the ragged beachhead: "Corpsman!" "Demolitions!" "Flamethrowers!" These vital resources would remain scarce throughout the day.

Here was the classic vulnerability of an opposed amphibious assault. The initial assault force, ashore but hard hit, held on virtually by its fingernails. Behind them, stalled by the reef and receiving heavy fire, hovered the critically needed reinforcements for momentum, acceleration, and support. The tide was inexplicably weird. Even a neap tide should have risen enough by now to permit boat passage over the reef—but low water prevailed for nearly thirty hours.[*] The Marines' alternate plan to use empty LVTs to shuttle fresh troops in from the reef came a cropper as Japanese gunners found the weak spots on the thinly armored vehicles. Machine guns drilled them full of holes; howitzers and knee mortars dropped high explosives squarely on their open hatches; high-velocity, dual-purpose guns blew them apart and set them ablaze.[†]

Julian Smith's attempts during the next twenty-four hours to land three sequential infantry battalions by wading from the jumbled reef provided a shooting gallery for Japanese gunners, cost hundreds of casualties, and scattered the survivors—disorganized and often weaponless—along a mile and a half of ghastly beach.

---

[*] It would be forty-four years before physicist Donald W. Olson would discover that D-Day at Tarawa occurred during one of only two days in 1943 when the moon's apogee coincided with a neap tide, resulting in a tidal range of only a few inches rather than several feet.

[†] The 2d Amphibian Tractor Battalion would lose its intrepid commander, Maj. Henry C. Drewes, half its men, and 72 percent of its LVTs in this battle.

As the battle hung in the balance that first afternoon, the outcome would be shaped by the powerful personalities of the opposing commanders on the ground, Adm. Keiji Shibasaki and Col. David Shoup. Both were hard-nosed, competent military professionals. Both had emerged from relative obscurity to sudden prominence in this fierce battle.

Julian Smith had gambled twice on Shoup before the battle began. Shoup had little to commend his continued services as division operations officer when Smith assumed command. He had only slight experience in command or combat and had never planned a division-level amphibious assault. But Smith recognized a fighting heart within Shoup's barrel chest and stuck with him. Then, after Shoup had prepared the intricate landing plan, Smith promoted him to colonel and gave him command of the 2d Marines, the regimental combat team destined to lead the assault on Tarawa. By these two decisions, Julian Smith did more to win the forthcoming battle than he would do throughout D-Day.

Shoup proved worthy of Smith's confidence. Seared and embarrassed by his experience at Rendova, Shoup set his face to the horrors and chaos he knew to expect. His personal landing on Betio on D-Day was a five-hour odyssey. He straggled ashore at noon, wounded and waterlogged, but immediately took charge. Ignoring the crippling effects of the laggard tide and his awful communications, Shoup rallied his surviving battalion commanders, maintained relentless offensive pressure, and exhibited rocklike faith that his Marines would prevail.

Shibasaki's principal contributions came before the Marines landed. He had trained and motivated his troops superbly. Though surprised by the Americans' assault waves penetrating the lagoon and reef, he had reacted coolly in shifting forces from primary to alternate positions. He also demonstrated a humanitarian side to his character. We now know from recent translations of Japanese accounts of the battle that Shibasaki died that first afternoon—not the third day as recorded in our histories. He gave up his concrete blockhouse to be used as a hospital for his hundreds of casualties, assembled his staff in the open, and began to move to a secondary command post several hundred yards away. In one of the ironic flukes of battle, a Marine with perhaps the only working field radio on the island spotted the cluster of officers in the open and quickly called in naval gunfire. The two destroyers in the lagoon, *Ringgold* and *Dashiell*, cut loose with salvos of 5"/38 rounds fused as air bursts. Steel shards rained over the exposed Japanese, killing Shibasaki and his entire staff. By these few salvos, the Navy fire support task group made up for all its shortcomings of the day.

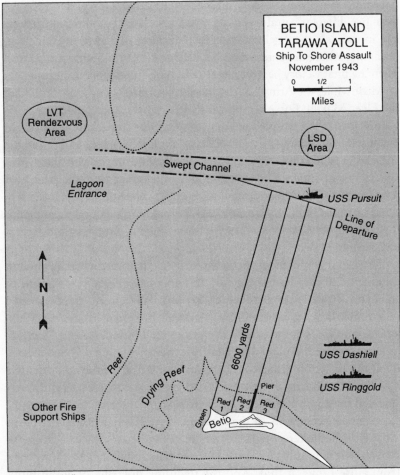

BETIO ISLAND
TARAWA ATOLL
Ship To Shore Assault
November 1943

0   1/2   1

Miles

LVT
Rendezvous
Area

LSD
Area

Swept Channel

Lagoon
Entrance

USS Pursuit

Line of
Departure

N

6600 yards

USS Dashiell

USS Ringgold

Reef

Drying Reef

Pier

Red
1

Red
2

Red
3

Green

Betio

Other Fire
Support Ships

Mary Craddock Hoffman

That's why the Japanese were unable to launch their expected counterattack the first night. They did so two nights later, a ferocious and
well-coordinated affair, which by then was doomed. The greatest opportunity for the Japanese to throw the invaders back into the sea existed
that first night, with scarcely more than three thousand Marines ashore,
clinging to irregular pockets of narrow beachhead. Here the issue was
indeed "in doubt." Shibasaki, had he lived, would have thrown everything into the attack.

With the dawn of the second day, however, the crisis for the Americans passed. While getting ashore over Red Beach never got any easier,

the enterprising Maj. Mike Ryan patched together a force of "orphans" from five different battalions to seize the western end of the island. There, late in the day, the 1st Battalion, 6th Marines, landed by rubber boat, streaming ashore uncontested with full unit integrity and supporting arms. Then the final victory became a matter of time—no longer conjecture.

Meanwhile, the Army's 27th Division prevailed on Makin Atoll, and the Fleet Marine Force Amphibious Reconnaissance Company stole ashore from the transport submarine *Nautilus* to capture lightly held Apamama. Suddenly, Galvanic ended. Admiral Spruance had seized the Gilberts in exactly two weeks. The time schedule for the Marshalls invasion remained intact. The redoubtable SeaBees had "laid the table" for the next invasion. Already, medium bombers were taking off from captured or newly built airstrips in the Gilberts to begin pounding and photographing the Marshalls—now within range of bombers and fighter escorts alike.

The senior commanders in Galvanic then conducted a brutally honest critique of all they had learned in the campaign. There was no time to spare, no sensitivity for bruised reputations. This agreement generated a remarkable outpouring of frank assessments by men of all services. Problems abounded, but the basic doctrines seemed sound. Despite Tarawa's frightful costs (a thousand dead Marines; twenty-four hundred wounded), the commanders concluded that the inaugural trials of the new offensive naval warfare doctrines had succeeded. The fast carriers had effectively shielded the amphibious task force from surface sorties from either the Combined Fleet at Truk or the Fourth Fleet at Kwajalein. Carrier-borne air patrols had intercepted most of the Japanese air attacks against the beachheads. Gunships had proven they could in fact "fight a fort," and from close range at that. And the fledgling doctrine of amphibious assault against a fortified objective had finally been validated, albeit at high cost. Most senior commanders recognized that if the new doctrine could work at Tarawa under the worst imaginable hydrographic and tactical conditions, it could likely work anywhere in the world—given better coordination of naval gunfire and aerial bombardment, improved communications, more LVTs, and stealthy, lion-hearted swimmers to scout the reefs and enemy offshore obstacles in advance. Each of these critical deficiencies were significantly improved for the Marshalls campaign, an impressive, joint effort in precious little time.

Moreover, the thorny issue of command relations in amphibious operations seemed to be resolved. At Tarawa, the attack force commander,

Admiral Hill, retained overall command of the operation until his counterpart landing force commander, Gen. Julian Smith, had established full control ashore at 1458 on D+3. Here was a significant improvement, not only over the Gallipoli debacle but also over Guadalcanal the year before Galvanic.

Tarawa was thus a vital proving ground for the storm landings to come. Yet it had also been riskier and costlier than expected because so many elements of the complex assault had been undertaken for the first time. Each of the major commanders made mistakes. As Kelly Turner admitted, the experience proved invaluable but "it was a goddamned painful lesson." Turner erred twice. He failed to ensure that Admiral Hill knew the submarine *Nautilus* would be operating near Betio in the path of the Southern Attack Force's final approach. (Hill's "friendly fire" damaged the sub and nearly wiped out the Apamama invasion force.) Turner also failed to notify Hill that he had earlier agreed to a half-hour delay in the first air attacks on Betio on D-Day morning. (Hill, unaware, stopped firing, waiting on the planes, giving Shibasaki his first grace period to recover.)

Hill's decision to cease all firing during the most vulnerable final approach of the ship-to-shore assault provided a second, more critical respite for the Japanese defenders. His insistence on pell-mell unloading of landing force supplies and equipment—while understandable in light of the expectation of Japanese counterattacks—became a grievous burden to the embattled troops ashore. At one point on the third day, everything came to a halt. All boats were filled and awaiting the impossibly long sequence of unloading at the pierhead. Julian Smith could not transfer Lt. Col. Ray Murray's fresh troops from Bairiki into the lines on Betio—the amphibious force had lost its tactical mobility.

Julian Smith's main error stemmed from having to marry two of his first three assault waves with their assigned amphibian tractors on the high seas in total darkness. His intricately choreographed landing plan proved dangerously complicated. Troops disembarked into boats in the dark, which then set off searching for the new LVT-2s (from LSTs that might or might not arrive in time), executed a time-consuming and dangerous gunwale-to-gunwale transfer at sea, then endured a ten-mile run to a fortified beach against a punishing headwind. The friction of war provides a high coefficient in opposed landing operations. Smith and Hill had to delay H-Hour twice, and even then the first waves landed twenty to twenty-five minutes late.

The price in men and machines to assault Betio Island, Tarawa Atoll—the first storm landing. *(U.S. Naval Institute)*

The performance of Holland M. Smith as commanding general of V Amphibious Corps (VAC) in Galvanic needs a critical review. On one hand, the senior Smith deserves credit for bucking Turner and getting the LSTs laden with fifty additional LVTs for the 2d Marine Division in time for Tarawa (at one point fulminating: "No LVTs, no operation!"). But "Howlin' Mad" Smith missed many other opportunities to enhance the 2d Marine Division's preparations for the forcible seizure of Tarawa. Specifically, the corps commander seemed ineffective in these areas:

• **Distributing "Lessons Learned."** Holland Smith was commanding general, Amphibious Corps, Pacific Fleet before assuming command of the new V Amphibious Corps for Galvanic. In either capacity he should have been the principal collector and disseminator of amphibious lessons learned in the Pacific. But the 2d Marine Division never received Brute Krulak's "LVT Crash Test" report, even though the commandant sent Smith a copy five months before

Tarawa. Nor is there evidence that Smith made any efforts to standardize the successful use by amphibious forces in the South Pacific of LCIs converted to fire 40-mm guns and heavy mortars in support of the assault waves. Moreover, Marines in the Solomons had reported improved tank-infantry communications by jury-rigging EE-8 field phones to the back of their tanks. This report would have been a great benefit to the Sherman tanks assigned to the 2d Marine Division. At Tarawa, tankers and riflemen could find no common frequency for their radios; no one knew to experiment with "bustle-mounted field phones"; and an undue number of tank commanders became casualties when they had to dismount to talk face-to-face with their supporting infantry.

• **Unequal Distribution of Critical Items.** The 27th Division, slated to assault lightly defended Makin, received half the new LVT-2s, half the borrowed Sherman tanks, plenty of new bazookas, barrage rockets, and flamethrowers—even sufficient lumber to build sleds and toboggan pallets for their supplies. The 2d Marine Division had to scrounge flamethrowers from Army units in the South Pacific and received no bazookas, rockets, or lumber. And their long-sought fording kits for the Sherman tanks never arrived.

• **The Missing "Daisy-Cutters."** The 2d Marine Division requested in October that the Seventh Air Force drop two-thousand-pound daisy-cutter bombs (so-named because they would detonate above-ground and annihilate troops and weapons lacking strong overhead cover) on Betio on D-Day before the landing. Delivered with any degree of accuracy at the time requested, these munitions would have made mincemeat out of the garrison's exposed dual-purpose gun crews, the beachfront installations with the greatest potential for devastating the landing force. The Seventh Air Force never got the request. Nor is there evidence that Holland Smith made any supervisory effort to ensure that this critical, interdepartmental appeal would in fact be honored. Likely, some starch-khakied staff officer pigeonholed the request, fearing such heavy munitions might damage the airstrip. This bureaucratic ineptitude should have received the full blistering heat of Smith's unholy wrath. The issue was saving Marine lives, not preserving a level runway. "For God's sake," Smith should have thundered, "that's why we have two battalions of veteran SeaBees attached to the assault force! Get Julian Smith his damned daisy-cutters!"

Smith's failure to follow through on this fundamental request from his most endangered division represented an inexcusable lapse. Survivors of the assault waves have recounted a half century later how they kept looking skyward all the way to the beach, still expecting to see the B-24 Liberators arrive overhead with their payloads of daisy-cutters.

Holland Smith, to be fair, had his hands full with many matters, and so did Marine Corps Headquarters, frantically trying to help four separate divisions get ready for major assaults within three months (Bougainville, Tarawa, Cape Gloucester, the Marshalls). But Smith clearly knew in advance which of these would be the most critical. He also had a superb chief of staff in Brig. Gen. Graves B. Erskine. Even amid all the competing, gargantuan tasks, it still should have been easy for Smith and Erskine to ensure that the forces bound for Tarawa would be as well-armed and fully supported as humanly possible. The 2d Marine Division had the right to expect nothing less from their senior headquarters. Afterward, Julian Smith and (particularly) David Shoup believed they had been forced to rely on their own devices in far-distant New Zealand on too many operational and logistical matters beyond their jurisdiction. Shoup would go to his grave still bitter about the failure of the division's request for daisy-cutters on D-Day to reach the Seventh Air Force. After Galvanic the V Amphibious Corps (and the IIIAC, as well) would greatly improve in stewardship to component commands. At Tarawa the gap was unseemly and critical.

In retrospect, perhaps it was helpful that the Tarawa landing proved less than perfect. True, the new doctrine of amphibious assault against fortified opposition had been validated in a consummate trial by fire. But commanders and strategic planners needed to accept and appreciate the two enduring realities that would characterize the storm landings to come: each would feature a high degree of vulnerability; each would slip at least temporarily into unmitigated chaos.

For all their strategic benefits, storm landings would always exact a high price. Sensible tasking, solid intelligence, competent staff work, first-class training, and disciplined leadership could reduce the costs significantly, but—as a Cold War amphibian would later say— "it is not the nature of amphibious warfare to be bloodless." The Navy would face greater threats during landing operations in the Marianas, Philippines, and Okinawa. Newer-model Marine Corps LVTs would be sturdier, faster, more seaworthy—yet still protected by nothing heavier than a quarter-inch of armor. Accepting this fact, the VAC standard operating procedure for LVTs in 1944 simply directed each crew to "carry a supply of wooden plugs to plug bullet holes caused by enemy fire."

Regarding the chaos factor, Lt. Col. Evans F. Carlson, an observer at Tarawa from the newly formed 4th Marine Division, contributed this comment after the battle: "Leaders must be trained to adapt themselves quickly to unexpected and unfamiliar situations when units have become disorganized. . . . This might be called training in SNAFU leadership." A fellow observer from the 4th Division was Lt. Col. Walter I. Jordan, who assumed command of the shot-up remnants of the 2d Battalion, 2d Marines, with the death of the battalion commander on D-Day. Jordan recommended: "Landing teams should practice landings wherein all units are mixed up while in small boats. Then permit only a certain percentage of each company to land. Furthermore, have those units land on the wrong beaches without their officers and NCOs and little or no communications equipment."

The Japanese also endeavored to learn lessons from the shocking loss of their Betio fortress in such short order. Island commanders in the Marshalls received urgent messages from Imperial General Headquarters to beware of the Americans' amphibious tanks and their propensity to attack through the lagoon against an island's weakest defenses. The Japanese tried frantically to send fortification materials and automatic cannons to their garrisons in the Marshalls, but conditions were changing in the Pacific. The Imperial Navy had enjoyed fifteen months of relatively unimpeded access with which to build up the defenses of Betio. Now American submarines had drastically tightened their ring. And time was running out.

Admiral Spruance's Central Pacific Force, bolstered immeasurably by success in the Gilberts, hit the Marshalls with twice the size force. Using his fast carriers as an effective shield, Spruance bypassed the eastern Marshalls to strike at Kwajalein and Roi-Namur, then Eniwetok. Sharp fighting ensued locally, and a thousand Americans died in a dozen landings, but nowhere did conditions approach the level of desperation and savagery as at Tarawa. Galvanic had paved the way. In less than three months the new American offensive had chewed a thousand-mile bite out of the Japanese perimeter.

Chapter Four

The Marianas

Storming the "Absolute National Defense Sphere"

> The enemy met the assault operations with pointless bravery, inhuman tenacity, cave fighting, and the will to lose hard.
>
> *Adm. Chester W. Nimitz, USN*
> Commander in Chief, Pacific,
> July 1944

Saipan looked enormous to the Marines in the assault LVTs crossing the line of departure just before H-Hour. These men of the 2d and 4th Marine Divisions were veterans of the Gilberts and Marshalls—landings executed against small coral atolls. Now, a thousand miles further west than the last U.S. outpost, the Marines were approaching an island so large that all of Tarawa, Roi-Namur, and Eniwetok would have fit into a single stretch of scalloped headland looming dead ahead. The Marines knew their enemy. They could sense Japanese officers watching their approach through binoculars from concealed gun emplacements along the entire west coast—hands cradling lanyards or firing keys. Now came the coral reef.

PFC. J. T. "Slick" Rutherford, a Tarawa veteran, manned a .30-caliber machine gun on the port side of his LVT-2 Water Buffalo on the right flank of the first wave. Tarawa's lagoon-side reef had at least been free of surf, but here at Saipan the long Pacific rollers broke viciously on the shallow coral ledge. Rutherford watched in horror as a plunging wave caught the stern of the adjacent LVT and flipped it "ass-over-teakettle," trapping the Marines underneath. Rutherford's crew could not stop to help. The Japanese storm of fire and steel had erupted all around them. Now came the gauntlet—the final heart-pounding surge to the beach.

A hail of small-arms fire greeted Rutherford's LVT as it lumbered ashore onto Saipan's dirty sand. Japanese marksmen shot the driver in the head. A rifle bullet glanced sharply off the side of Rutherford's helmet. As he lurched to the right, a mortar round exploded just off the port side, which flattened him and killed the troop commander. The LVT crew's mission had been to proceed inland several hundred yards. Now all they could do was limp back to sea. Half the crew and troops were dead or wounded. The bloodied survivors stared at each other. "Welcome to Saipan!"

In the heights above the beaches, a Japanese defender wrote in his journal, "On this day the enemy has landed, and the time has come at last."

American victory in the Marianas would not come easily. Operation Forager, the forcible seizure of Saipan, Guam, and Tinian, would require two months of unremitting close combat and cost twenty-seven thousand casualties, an unprecedented expense, but the United States had stormed into Japan's Absolute National Defense Sphere in great force, and the Pacific War would never be the same.

History, justifiably, tends to overlook the Marianas campaign. Operation Overlord, the dramatic Allied invasion of Normandy, constituted the "main event" of June 1944, and it eclipsed all concurrent operations. Additionally, Forager's three storm landings, plus the epic carrier battle in the Philippine Sea, overlap and compete with one another for historical recognition. Some of Saipan's vignettes—the suicides of Japanese and native civilians off the cliffs at Marpi Point, the Smith vs. Smith controversy—distract from the flesh and bones of the complex air-sea-land campaign. Forager deserves better recognition. The campaign manifested the revolution in naval warfare then underway in the Central Pacific. It also manifested the true nature of storm landings—the audacious concentration of overwhelming force at the point of attack.

None of the major commanders on either side in the Pacific in mid-1944 seemed to appreciate the unexpected acceleration of combat power represented by the U.S. Fifth Fleet and its integral amphibious components. This was as true of Adm. Soemu Toyoda, now commanding the Combined Fleet, and Lt. Gen. Hideyoshi Obata, commanding the Central Pacific's 31st Army, as it was of General MacArthur. Even Admiral

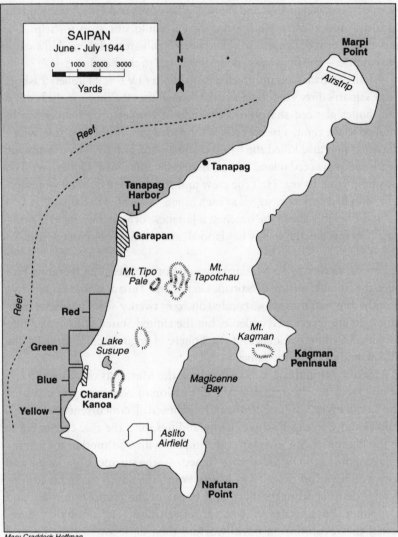

SAIPAN
June - July 1944

0   1000   2000   3000
Yards

N

Marpi
Point

Airstrip

Reef

Tanapag

Tanapag
Harbor

Garapan

Reef

Mt. Tipo
Pale

Mt.
Tapotchau

Red

Mt.
Kagman

Green

Lake
Susupe

Kagman
Peninsula

Blue

Magicenne
Bay

Yellow

Charan
Kanoa

Aslito
Airfield

Nafutan
Point

Mary Craddock Hoffman

Nimitz, the theater commander responsible for unleashing the Fifth Fleet, suffered second thoughts about its chances for success against the distant and formidable Marianas.

Consider this latter fact in context. Nimitz's misgivings occurred during a Pacific strategy conference at Pearl Harbor during 27–28 January 1944. This occurred after Tarawa, before the Marshalls. Nimitz was still receiving hate mail from anguished parents of Marines slain at Betio, still being excoriated in the press. He had gambled in the Gilberts; he was about to gamble again in the Marshalls, striking deep at Kwajalein instead of nibbling at the defended islands along the outer ring. Barely ten weeks earlier he had sweated blood while Halsey risked his only two carriers in the preemptive strike against Rabaul.

Meanwhile, General MacArthur stridently called for a return to his single-axis campaign through the Southwest Pacific; indeed, his chief of staff and other senior officers came to the Pearl Harbor meeting to argue for consensus on that strategy. Meanwhile, MacArthur had just forwarded an appeal to Secretary of War Henry L. Stimson, in which he argued: "Give me central direction of the war in the Pacific, and I will be in the Philippines in ten months. . . . Don't let the Navy's pride of position and ignorance continue this great tragedy to our country."

Chester Nimitz was the man in the middle. He knew Adm. Ernest King, his direct commander in Washington, advocated seizing the Marianas after the Marshalls. But he also listened to MacArthur's representatives. When his own staff argued that the Marianas were too far, too big, and of marginal strategic value, Nimitz concurred that MacArthur's single-axis strategy should prevail after the Marshalls campaign. The Marianas would have to wait, perhaps indefinitely.

Two things happened to change CINCPAC's mind. First came a blistering message from King, who expressed "indignant dismay" at Nimitz's waffling on the Marianas. The second, more important catalyst came with the news of the overwhelming success of the Marshalls campaign. Vice Adm. Marc Mitscher, newly appointed commander of the fast carriers of Task Force 58, provided an early glimpse of how abruptly the Pacific War had changed. Throughout the first twenty-seven months of the war Nimitz had safeguarded his few carriers as if they were the nation's crown jewels. Suddenly the floodgates had opened. Carrier task forces and the Central Pacific were made for each other. Mitscher's Task Force 58 bore no semblance to the bare-bones U.S. deployments during Coral Sea and Midway. Mitscher stormed into the Marianas as the vanguard of the Fifth Fleet with an awesome force of fifteen carriers, seven fast battleships, twenty-one cruisers, and sixty-nine destroyers.

The Central Pacific drive accelerated the pace of operations as well as the lethality of American combat power. With the capture of Eniwetok in late February 1944, the Fifth Fleet had conquered the Gilberts and Marshalls in less than one hundred days, an achievement undreamed of in 1942. Admiral King, more strategically oriented than Nimitz, saw immediately that the war could be shortened by continuing the momentum westward, cutting off the flow of war materials from the Dutch East Indies to the Japanese home islands, providing a base for the heralded new B-29 long-range bombers, and provoking a decisive battle with the Combined Fleet. Nimitz, whose earlier audacity had sent Spruance striding across the Marshalls in seven-league boots, turned conservative again, fixated with seizing Truk in the Central Carolines. The CINCPAC staff dutifully prepared campaign plans. Although not at all the Gibraltar of the Pacific described in the western press, Truk would have been both a man-eater and a time-eater. Nimitz planned to send three Marine divisions (the 1st, 3d, and 4th), with two Army divisions in reserve (the 7th and 77th) against Truk.

Once again King "nudged" Nimitz along the path to the Marianas. Taking Truk no longer made strategic sense, he argued. Mitscher had already forced the Combined Fleet to evacuate Truk's anchorage and seek shelter a thousand miles to the southwest, near Tawi Tawi in the Sulu Sea. American bombers flying from newly captured fields in the Gilberts and Marshalls could suppress Truk's residual air power. Seizing the Marianas would close the door on Truk altogether. Nimitz, virtually unflappable, said "aye, aye, sir" and put his planning staff to work on the Marianas. The time was mid-March. King, speaking for the Joint Chiefs, had already assigned a D-Day of 15 June.

Rear Adm. Forrest Sherman—razor sharp, acerbic, driven—became chief war planner for Nimitz after the Marshalls and would serve as the mastermind behind the great campaigns of the remainder of the war. The Marianas presented a daunting first challenge. He and his staff stared at the huge chart of the Central Pacific in the CINCPAC headquarters on Makalapa Heights, Oahu, and shook their heads with concern. The Marianas lay 3,300 miles from the fleet base at Pearl Harbor, 1,300 miles past Kwajalein, and 1,100 miles beyond Eniwetok, "the last frontier." Moreover, the target islands of Saipan, Guam, and Tinian were large, mountainous, populous, and heavily defended—as befitting their location well within Japan's proclaimed Absolute National Defense Sphere.

Sherman and Nimitz fully expected the Combined Fleet to sortie from the Sulu Sea to seek a "decisive battle" against the invading Fifth Fleet, the same kind of climactic sea fight waged by the legendary Admiral Togo against the Russian Baltic Fleet in the Battle of Tsushima in 1905. The Japanese would have two advantages in such an engagement. Their carrier aircraft, unencumbered by such safety features as armor-shielded gas tanks, could outrange their American counterparts by a distinct margin. The second advantage reflected the "unsinkable" Japanese carriers—their airfields in the Marianas. The Imperial Navy's carrier planes could strike Mitscher's task force, swing by Guam (among many other islands) to refuel and rearm, then strike again on their homeward leg.

Forrest Sherman thus specified multiple objectives for the Fifth Fleet: establish air and sea superiority in the Marianas; pulverize the local airfields; forcibly seize Saipan, Guam, and Tinian (the principal task); deliver and protect a major construction force to build strategic bombing bases; be prepared to engage and destroy the Combined Fleet. Raymond Spruance would need an enormous force, the largest assembled in the Pacific War to date.

In that respect, Operation Forager's timing was terrible. The Normandy landings rated top priority on amphibious transports, cargo ships, and self-deploying landing craft. In any earlier period this would have killed the Pacific operation. Not this time. American shipyards had attained unprecedented heights of productivity. There would be plenty of LSTs, for example, to support both massive landings. Moreover, the Allied Fleet, operating in the narrow seas of the English Channel, had a minimal requirement for carriers, and General Eisenhower's landing force opted not to adopt LVTs to enhance their ship-to-shore assault. And there was another fortuitous coincidence. Forager took place just as William Halsey's South Pacific Command ran out of missions. MacArthur and Nimitz divided Halsey's warfighting assets. MacArthur got an abundance of land-based bombers. Nimitz got enough amphibious troops and craft to make Forager executable. Halsey himself would rotate future fleet command with Spruance.

Spruance, Kelly Turner, and Holland Smith again teamed up to lead the joint naval expedition to the Marianas. Turner would be ably supported by two up-and-coming amphibious admirals, Harry W. Hill, veteran of Tarawa and the Marshalls, and Richard L. Conolly, who had served coolly in command of the Kwajalein and Roi-Namur landings. General Smith would coordinate two corps—rarified atmosphere for a Marine officer—the new III Amphibious Corps (IIIAC), commanded by a can-do aviator, Maj. Gen. Roy S. Geiger, and Smith's own V Amphibious Corps (VAC), commanded by himself at Saipan and by the rock-steady Maj. Gen. Harry Schmidt at Tinian. Altogether, Spruance would lead 535 ships and 166,000 troops into the Marianas.

The Marines who had survived Tarawa marveled at the improvements in hardware available for Forager. While each target island would be surrounded by a coral reef, this time there would be plenty of LVTs for the landing force, including newer versions configured for the assault mission—LVT-4s with stern ramps and overhead hatch covers as well as LVT-As, new armored amtracs equipped with turret-mounted cannon. The Marines assaulted Tarawa with 125 field-modified LVTs. Seven months later they would land with 732 LVTs at Saipan, 456 at Guam, 519 at Tinian. And LCI-G gunboats had finally joined the Central Pacific Force. These would precede the H-Hour assaults, delivering concentrations of final preparatory fires from point-blank range with 4.5-inch rocket launchers and 40-mm and 20-mm gun mounts.

Certain tactical improvements for Forager brought grim smiles to Tarawa veterans like Merritt Edson and David Shoup. Now the Navy would devote much more time to preliminary air and naval gunfire bombardment. The Navy also agreed to utilize deception landings— amphibious feints—at Saipan and Tinian, as well as advanced force operations with UDT teams and minesweepers at all three islands. A compromise of sorts evolved between the Navy's Gun Club—the diehard battleship advocates—and the Airdales, the fast carrier advocates. Since the prewar battleships lacked the speed to keep up with the carriers, they would find a permanent home in the amphibious forces, where their 14-inch and 16-inch main batteries would be most welcome additions to shore bombardment. The new, fast battleships would accompany the carrier task forces.

These improvements in amphibious doctrine notwithstanding, the work-up for Forager developed ragged edges. The landing forces lacked sufficient cargo ships to fully embark their organic vehicles. This had not been a factor on the small islands. But fighting ashore in the Marianas would require a major logistic effort to keep frontline troops armed and equipped. Shortage of prime movers in Guam, for example, would significantly slow the forward displacement of artillery units. Extended combat ashore also dictated a much greater need for ammunition. Truckloads of ammo kept appearing dockside during embarkation— well after the ship's captain and the landing force had agreed on the extent, stowage, and off-load priority of the loading plan.

Haphazard loading of ammunition and gasoline on eight LSTs in the West Loch section of Pearl Harbor led to a tragic disaster that marred the beginning of Forager. The ships, nested together and overloaded with dangerous and incompatible cargo, constituted an accident waiting to happen. A spark ignited on 21 May, and all of West Loch seemed to explode at once. The conflagration killed 163 men, injured 396 more—irreplaceable veterans. Six precious LSTs were totaled.*

A disaster of this proportion would have scuttled any previous expeditionary mount-out. Only three LSTs, for example, participated in the assault landings at Tarawa. Losing six of these increasingly useful ships, with all their combat cargo, seemed staggering. Yet Kelly Turner replaced the ships in a fortnight; Holland Smith found substitute vehicles and ammo; and the huge task force sailed on schedule. Yet the troops would not readily forget the West Loch nightmare. Five hundred good men gone. . . .

The West Loch disaster reflected the critical shortage of ammunition ships in the Pacific Fleet. Indirectly, the incident may also have stemmed from the overriding sense of urgency that characterized the mount-out for Forager. Several units in fact complained that the whole schedule seemed too frenetic for adequate planning, training, and combat loading, but Admiral Spruance persisted in his belief that strategic momentum would prove to be the great equalizer. Events in the Central Pacific never proved him wrong. The Fifth Fleet's dash for the Marianas caught the Japanese flat-footed. Admiral Toyoda, preoccupied with MacArthur's landing on Biak in the Schouten Islands off New Guinea's north coast, had deployed his main forces southward. General Obata chose the week of 8–15 June to leave his Saipan headquarters and tour the outer islands of his command. News that American carrier aircraft were suddenly savaging the Marianas on 11 June in advance of the invasion fleet came as a great shock to both commanders. The Marianas were not yet ready to withstand an American invasion—and would not be until autumn.

Japanese troops in the Marianas would defend all three islands fanatically, but they would go to their deaths cursing their fate at not receiving sufficient soldiers, major weapons, or fortifications material to prepare adequate defenses. Maj. Kiyoshi Yoshida, intelligence officer of the 43d Division on Saipan (one of the few field grade officers of the Imperial Japanese Army ever captured alive), admitted to his interrogators that the completion date for the island's defensive construction program had slipped until November.

---

* Admiral Nimitz narrowly missed becoming a casualty himself at West Loch. Seeing the explosions, he ordered his driver to approach the bluff overlooking the disaster, then told him to drive down a dirt road to the water's edge. Eighteen-year-old Marine corporal Loren F. "Sonny" Paulus, the admiral's bodyguard, overruled the commander in chief. "Shrapnel was already landing near us on top of the bluff; if we'd gone down that trail we would've been hit for sure. I ignored the admiral and ordered the driver the hell out of there."

Major Yoshida's statement begs the question of why IGHQ would allow a full year to lapse after the fall of Tarawa before completing the urgent upgrade of defenses in the Marianas. This inordinate delay reflected neither bureaucratic bumbling nor interservice rivalry—but rather the emergence of a terrible new menace to Japanese prosecution of the war. Ship after ship left Japan for the Marianas loaded with troops, weapons, and material. But the Western Pacific was no longer a Japanese lake. American submarines, their faulty torpedo fuses finally fixed, now prowled the underseas with a vengeance. Aided by ULTRA intercepts of routine reports of ship schedules between Japanese port captains, the subs began to eat the heart out of Japanese maritime power. Time and again these subs positioned themselves to torpedo Japanese cargo ships laden with tanks, heavy guns, cement, and steel bound for Saipan. The "silent service" likewise helped even the odds for the Marines ashore by sinking—in one celebrated case—five of seven transports conveying the veteran 43d Division from Pusan, Korea, to Saipan. Those troops who survived the sinking of their ships arrived in the Marianas waterlogged, disoriented, and often weaponless—barely two weeks before the U.S. storm landings began.

Lt. Gen. Yoshitsuga Saito took command of the twenty thousand Japanese soldiers and sailors on Saipan in General Obata's absence. Although Saipan's rugged terrain made it ideal for a disciplined defense in depth, Obata had adhered to the prevailing philosophy of "defend-at-the-water's edge," and Saito had no time to make major adjustments. Saito figured the Americans would land on the east coast, over Magicienne Bay's broad beaches, and he arrayed much of his firepower in that quadrant. But his artillery officers were professionals. All points on the coastline—including the western beaches chosen for assault by the Americans—would be covered by howitzers, heavy mortars, and dismounted naval guns.

Holland Smith, ever the realist, warned his landing force commanders of the tough job ahead. "We are through with the flat atolls now," said Smith. "Now we are up against mountains and caves where the Japs can really dig in. A week from now there will be a lot of dead Marines." Smith might have added another caveat: in the Saipan town of Garapan the Marines would face house-to-house fighting for the first time since Vera Cruz in 1914.

Neither Holland Smith nor Kelly Turner wanted to repeat the complicated choreography of Tarawa. The amphibious task force therefore stopped at Eniwetok Atoll to "shoe-horn" assault troops into LSTs, already loaded with amtracs. The rough-riding ships steamed directly for Saipan's southwest coast. Arriving in darkness early on D-Day, 15 June, the LSTs dropped anchor on line fifty-five hundred yards offshore, opened their bow doors, and launched their loaded LVTs toward the beach. The line of departure lay directly ahead.

As dawn broke, Navy and Marine control officers in offshore small craft were startled to see small red flags along the reef. They had not been there yesterday. The Japanese, tipped off by the preliminary UDT survey, had placed range markers offshore for their artillery spotters.

The Japanese maintained good fire discipline, waiting until the LVTs struck the reef line before opening fire. Naval observers, recoiling at the sudden curtain of explosions that erupted all along the line, thought the reef had been mined. What they were seeing was a well-orchestrated "time-on-target" artillery and mortar barrage performed by Japanese gunners firing from a hundred reverse-slope emplacements. Although never as grim as Tarawa had been—or Peleliu would soon be—the ship-to-shore assault at Saipan nevertheless had its own moments of sheer horror. One large-caliber round made a direct hit on an LVT carrying the assault elements of Company C, 1st Battalion, 6th Marines. The force of the explosion blew several men to bits. Lt. Paul M. Dodd was grievously wounded by bones blasted from the Marines next to him. The vehicle foundered in the surf, then drifted out to sea, a gruesome, smoking relic.

But Turner and Smith's insistence on direct delivery of preloaded LVTs just seaward of the line of departure served to maximize surprise and minimize exposure to the Japanese killing zones. Somehow the Marines lost only twenty LVTs to the combination of high surf and enemy fire in the initial assault. A formidable force of twenty thousand men had stormed ashore by nightfall, but they sustained nearly two thousand casualties, mainly from unrelenting artillery and mortar fire delivered along the crowded beaches, the most skillful the Marines had yet faced. Both divisions landed their artillery units early to help equal the odds, but the Japanese that first day were looking right down the Marines' throats.

Night counterattacks characterized the fighting on Saipan throughout the weeks of the battle. One of these, shortly after the landing, included the first armored counterattack the Marines had experienced, some forty Japanese medium tanks roaring through the darkness toward the beach. But the Marines were ashore to stay. This time they had plenty of bazookas and Sherman tanks at hand. There was never a question of "issue in doubt" as at Tarawa.

The only real threat to the capture of Saipan came when Admiral Toyoda dispatched his principal task force, the Mobile Fleet, into the Philippine Sea with orders to sink the American carriers, then destroy the amphibious task force off Saipan. Spruance did not overreact. He directed Turner and Smith to offload the 27th Infantry Division immediately and prepare for curtailed support from the fleet. The amphibs would still dart in to unload critical supplies; the gunships could still return for called fire missions. Spruance then uncoiled Mitscher's Task Force 58. The resulting Battle of the Philippine Sea, which included "the Great Marianas Turkey Shoot," became a convincing naval victory for the United States. While the carrier admirals (and even genial Chester Nimitz) expressed keen disappointment when Spruance allowed the major components of the Mobile Fleet to escape destruction, the landing force appreciated his caution. Spruance took the heat calmly. His primary mission, he reminded his critics, was to capture Saipan by amphibious assault. "We were at the start of a very large amphibious operation, and we could not afford to gamble and place it in jeopardy." These words did little to placate his critics, but some strategists would take another look at Spruance's practical conservatism later that fall after Halsey abandoned the Leyte beachheads to chase what he believed to be the Japanese fleet.

Nor did Spruance's distraction with the Mobile Fleet result in another Guadalcanal for the landing force. Amphibious ships unloaded 11,500 tons of combat cargo across the beach at the height of the naval battle. General Saito then knew his cause was lost. There would be no rescue by the Japanese fleet, no reinforcements for his beleaguered garrison.

Late in the battle, surviving Japanese troops staged a massive banzai attack, some four thousand troops screaming out of the night with swords and grenades. Finding a wide gap in the American lines, the human waves penetrated several thousand yards to overlap the artillerymen of the 14th Marines. The cannoneers died by their guns in desperate, close-range fighting. Daylight brought reinforcements and succor, but the slaughter had been great on both sides.

Another horror followed. As Marines and soldiers converged on the final enemy positions near Marpi Point in the north, hundreds of Japanese and native civilians, convinced by the garrison that Americans would torture them, began jumping off the cliffs onto the rocks below—entire families, including infants. In a war increasingly marked by cruelty and devastation, these scenes proved awful to behold by even the most battle-hardened Americans. Admiral Nimitz, visiting the site several days later,

"Chaos Reigned." D-Day on Saipan. Hell on earth. *(U.S. Naval Institute)*

became visibly moved at the sight of the bodies strewn along the rocks far below. The experience convinced Nimitz that an invasion of the Japanese homeland would result in the virtual extermination of the civilian population.

Holland Smith declared Saipan "secured" on 9 July, putting an official ending to twenty-four days of close combat. American casualties reached sixteen thousand. Virtually all of the twenty-thousand-man Japanese garrison perished. Now Spruance directed his commanders to the other two objectives in the Marianas: first, Guam, then Tinian, separate and nearly simultaneous operations.

Spruance had to postpone the Guam landing by a month once he committed his force reserve, the 27th Division, to the Saipan flail. The 77th Division, in theater reserve on Oahu, had to hustle aboard ships and join General Geiger's IIIAC at sea. The long delay rode heavily on the Guam landing force. At Admiral Conolly's suggestion, Spruance returned the amphibious task force to Eniwetok for a little R&R, a dubious interlude, little more than a few hours of exercise on a forlorn sand spit, followed by two cans of warm beer per man. Conolly's subsequent announcement of reembarkation for a new "W-Day" of 21 July inspired cheers from the bored troops.*

The Marines liked Conolly, had already nicknamed him "Close-In" Conolly for his willingness to steam close ashore in the Marshalls to deliver naval gunfire virtually at "bayonet point." Command relations between Conolly and his counterpart Roy Geiger exemplified the best characteristics of both men—open, honest, cooperative. No other force in Forager conducted such a systematic work-up for amphibious assault, capped by a detailed rehearsal landing and critique. And at Guam, the landing force would enjoy one of the longest sustained preliminary naval bombardments of the Pacific War—thirteen days, during which "Close-In Conolly" again lived up to his name.

Geiger's landing force proved to be a diverse but highly competent body of fighters. Maj. Gen. Allen Turnage's jungle-savvy 3d Marine Division had established the Bougainville beachhead. Brig. Gen. Lemuel C. Shepherd's 1st Provisional Marine Brigade (soon to become the nucleus of the 6th Marine Division) was new and untested as an entity, but the combination of former Raiders in the 4th Marines plus the Marshalls veterans among the 22d Marines would fight with the equivalent ferocity of a full division. Guam would be the 77th Division's first fight, but Maj. Gen. Andrew D. Bruce's soldiers had received superb amphibious and jungle training. Initially slated for reserve duty, the 77th would begin entering the battle for Guam as early as W-Day. The soldiers would acquit themselves well, and after a series of hard-fought subsequent landings in the Philippines and Okinawa would end the war as one of the most adept amphibious divisions in the Pacific.

The Americans had an emotional stake in recapturing Guam, their Pacific possession since 1899. Many "Old Corps" Marines had been stationed there and had developed a special relationship with the native Chamorros. A generation of Marine officers had studied "the Guam Problem" in tactics courses at the Marine Corps Schools in Quantico during the interwar years. Most knew that Guam stood to be more difficult to seize than Saipan. Guam had three times the size, more mountains, more jungle growth, fewer suitable beaches.

The Japanese defended Guam with thirteen thousand army and fifty-five hundred naval troops. General Obata, unable to return to Saipan,

---

* The amphibians used alternate letters to designate landing dates when campaign planning overlapped. Hence, in the Marianas, it was D-Day at Saipan, W-Day at Guam, and J-Day at Tinian.

had slipped ashore on Guam to reestablish his 31st Army headquarters, but Obata would yield tactical direction of the coming battle to Lt. Gen. Takeshi Takashina, a veteran of action along the Manchurian frontier against the Soviet Union. Takashina believed the Americans would attempt to land at Tumon Bay, the site of the principal Japanese landing in 1941, and developed his main defenses there.

As at Tarawa and Saipan, the Japanese guessed wrong about American landing intentions. Geiger and Conolly decided to forgo Tumon Bay and hit two smaller beaches, five miles apart, the 3d Marine Division in the north, the 1st Provisional Brigade in the south. This was hazardous. Rough terrain just inland from the beaches would slow the link-up of the two forces, leaving both vulnerable to a concentrated counterattack.

Geiger worried needlessly. Thirteen days of preliminary shelling served to disrupt and innervate the Japanese hierarchy. UDT teams performed sparkling work in clearing mines and obstacles from the boat lanes (even having the cheek to leave a sign pointing seaward saying Welcome Marines). Naval aircraft from both the escort carriers and Mitscher's fast carrier veterans executed a spectacular eighty-plane strike just before H-Hour, strafing and bombing the beaches and the high ground inland. The supporting armada assembled around Guam's northwest coast included 274 ships, conveying the fifty-four-thousand-man landing force and their weapons and equipment. Here was truly a storm landing in process.

And yet, Japanese defenders, dazed and deafened, somehow emerged from that awful pounding to man their guns and resist the landing. One officer of the 9th Marines reported: "I was particularly impressed to see Japanese soldiers still alive right on the landing beaches after almost . . . incessant bombardment by naval gunfire." To the south at Gaan Point, a solitary 75-mm gun crew, protected throughout by a camouflaged, concrete blockhouse, opened a disciplined fire against oncoming LVTs at a range of one hundred yards, knocking out nearly two dozen in a row, spilling their troops into the shallows, before Marines from adjacent landing points could overwhelm the position from the rear.

Like Saipan, Guam's coral reef would prevent all boats from landing on the beach, so LVTs would have to maintain the assault momentum by conducting transfer line operations with the boats along the beach. Loss of so many LVTs in the assault put a premium on their use to land ammunition and other critical supplies. That situation precluded the use of LVTs to land the reserve force, the 77th Division, whose introduction to amphibious combat in the Pacific War thus consisted of having to wade ashore from the reef under intermittent enemy fire.

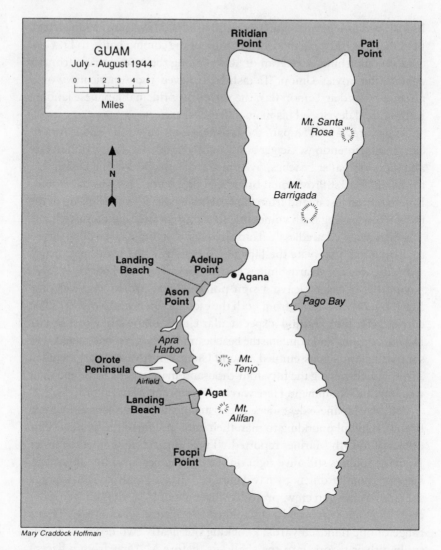

GUAM
July - August 1944

0   1   2   3   4   5
Miles

N

Ritidian
Point

Pati
Point

Mt. Santa
Rosa

Mt.
Barrigada

Landing
Beach

Adelup
Point

Agana

Ason
Point

Pago Bay

Apra
Harbor

Orote
Peninsula

Mt.
Tenjo

Airfield

Agat

Landing
Beach

Mt.
Alifan

Focpi
Point

Mary Craddock Hoffman

    A paradox developed in the nature of the Japanese defense. Takashina and his lieutenants fought with a singular lack of imagination, squandering their sizable forces in suicidal counterattacks. On their own, however, the Japanese junior officers and NCOs fought with great elan and daring, prolonging the inland battle, and selling themselves dearly. Some of the roughest fighting the Marines would experience in the Pacific occurred well after W-Day on Guam, including the protracted battle for Bundschu

Ridge by the 3d Marine Division and the "minicampaign" to seize Orote Peninsula by the 1st Provisional Brigade.*

The spirited if uncoordinated resistance by the Japanese garrison combined with Guam's rugged terrain to slow the efforts of the two landing forces to merge and drive northward. The reef proved to be the weak point in the massive logistic effort needed to sustain the campaign ashore. General Shepherd found this to be the case as early as W-Day when he came ashore to establish his brigade command post. "Supplies not coming ashore with sufficient rapidity," he signaled the control ship offshore. "Believe delay at transfer line at edge of reef. Expedite move-ment with preference to all types ammunition." Hours later he reported the situation unchanged: "Our casualties about 350. . . . Critical short-ages fuel and ammunition."

Navy beachmasters and shore party Marines provided a dozen or so floating cranes along the reef to speed the exchange of cargo between boats and LVTs, but this produced only marginal improvements. Logis-tics problems intensified as frontline units deployed further from the beachheads. The paucity of tracked and wheeled prime movers slowed artillery displacements, medical evacuation, and critical resupply efforts throughout the campaign. Guam, in fact, proved to be one of the most labor-intensive logistic efforts of the Central Pacific drive. At one point, nearly ten thousand troops from all three divisions—virtually one-fifth of IIIAC—could be found wrestling with combat cargo in ships' holds, along the reef, or among inland supply dumps.

On 29 July, W-Day+8, the 22d Marines raised the American flag above the ruins of the former Marine barracks on Orote Peninsula. The next day, tactical aircraft of all three services began using the two-thousand-foot airstrip on the captured peninsula. On 4 August Marine Air Group 21 began flight operations from Orote Field, soon providing twelve squadrons of attack and fighter aircraft in support of the campaign.

Guam "fell" on 10 August, the official end of organized resistance. Nearly 11,000 Japanese died in the defense, including both Obata and Takashina. Incredibly, as many as 10,000 more Japanese troops simply vanished—went to ground in Guam's subtropical jungles. American forces would continue to flush them out for the duration of the war (and for decades thereafter). If the fighting spirit of the Japanese troops on

---

* General Shepherd's masterful coordination of naval gunfire, field artillery, and close air support of his Orote operation would place him in good stead for assaulting two more peninsulas the following year: Motobu and Oroku on Okinawa.

A Marine wounded in the battle for Guam is carried aboard a waiting landing craft for the run out to a hospital ship. *(U.S. Naval Institute)*

Guam had been matched with the same kind of resourceful leadership exhibited by Imperial commanders at Tarawa, Peleliu, Iwo Jima, or Okinawa, the campaign might well have followed a more dramatic and extended course. As it was, Guam proved costly enough. General Geiger's IIIAC suffered 8,000 casualties (Marines and soldiers) in the twenty-day fighting, including 1,796 killed.

Where Saipan had been clouded by interservice acrimony, Guam served as a model of how smoothly a joint-service campaign could function. The harmonious relations between Admiral Conolly and General Geiger extended downward and outward. The salty Marines, innately suspicious of the unproven soldiers of the 77th Division, soon marveled at that unit's courage and proficiency. Indeed the Guam Leathernecks would ever after refer to their Army teammates as the "77th Marine Division." General Bruce recognized the compliment. Naval historian Samuel Eliot Morison was equally complimentary of those who won victory by storming Guam. Citing Julian Corbett's axiom that amphibious landings are only successful when both naval officers and troops "are schooled for it, hand in hand, by constant and well-ordered practice," Morison concluded that "Dick Conolly's and Roy Geiger's units were superbly schooled."

At dawn on 24 July 1944, while the battle of Guam raged at full intensity, two U.S. amphibious task forces approached the west coast of Tinian. One seemed vast and powerful—battleships and heavy cruisers surrounding attack transports. The second force, an unimpressive scattering of LSTs and smaller craft, loitered behind, near Tinian's northwest tip, as if merely a follow-on echelon.

The larger task force steamed directly for Tinian Town, site of the island's best beaches and consequently the heart of the Japanese defenses. Gunships commenced a fierce bombardment. Transports lowered landing craft, formed them into waves, dispatched them shoreward in formation. Japanese naval gunners opened fire from camouflaged coast-defense batteries. The boat waves hesitated four hundred yards from the beach, then retired at full speed to the transports. The exultant Japanese commander wired Tokyo: "We have repelled an American landing with one hundred barges!"

But something strange was happening with that sleepy group of LSTs up north, an area where no real landing beaches existed. To the shock of the Japanese garrison, hundreds of troop-laden LVTs appeared in the water, streaming in parallel columns toward two narrow patches of rock and sand. The demonstration against Tinian Town had been an artful ruse. Here was the main assault. Seasoned troops of the 4th Marine Division swarmed quickly ashore. Similar to the Allied invasion of Normandy, the American seizure of Tinian would depend heavily on tactical deception, favorable weather—and audacity.

No island seized by the Fifth Fleet in the Central Pacific produced greater strategic dividends at less cost. Tinian, in fact, was a model of amphibious ingenuity. Where each previous storm landing had been characterized by a costly loss of momentum at the beachhead, Tinian was just the opposite—a waterborne blitzkrieg; indeed, an early forerunner of "maneuver warfare from the sea."

Tinian would reflect the emergence of a new breed of amphibians. Gen. Holland Smith's long span of influence in the Pacific War waned sharply after Saipan. Although Spruance and Turner would recall him from the sidelines to help with Iwo Jima, Smith would never again exercise direct tactical command of troops in an amphibious assault. Chester Nimitz, striving mightily to preserve a spirit of interservice harmony among his often fractious command, would never forgive Holland Smith, a Marine, for his heavy-handed relief of Gen. Ralph Smith, an Army commander, for ineptitude. Nimitz ordered Holland Smith back to Pearl Harbor to assume command of the newly established Fleet Marine Force, Pacific, an important but administrative—and backwater—billet. Maj. Gen. Harry Schmidt assumed command of VAC. Maj. Gen. Clifford B. Cates relieved Schmidt in command of the 4th Marine Division.* The two younger generals would work well together at Tinian and again half a year later at Iwo Jima—and in both cases in harmony with the amphibious force commander, Adm. "Handsome Harry" Hill, who replaced Turner.

Compared to Saipan's mountains and Guam's jungled ridges, Tinian was relatively flat, its northern two-thirds covered by a checkerboard of open canefields and small farms. Operation Forager sought air bases for the new B-29 Super-fortresses, and Tinian's canefields offered a bonanza. Three decent airfields already existed. Engineers figured they could enlarge these, then build three more from scratch, eventually giving the U.S. Army Air Forces six bomber strips with the necessary eighty-five-hundred-foot runways.

Nearly nine thousand Japanese troops—half Army, half Navy—stood ready to defend Tinian against the inevitable American invasion. Col. Keishi Ogata held nominal command over all forces on the island, including his own 50th Infantry Regiment, veterans of the Kwantung Army. Like his counterparts on Saipan and Guam, Ogata proved brave but uninspired.

Tinian's shortage of suitable landing beaches presented the biggest challenge to Marine planners. Forcing a landing at Tinian Town would be foolhardy ("another Tarawa" warned Holland Smith, sourly, before he departed). The island did offer two tiny beaches on the northwest coast, near Ushi Airfield, but they were rocky and narrow, more like trails leading onto the plateau. The more the planners studied the aerial photographs, however, the more they liked the idea of deviating radically from established doctrine by landing two entire divisions over these improbable entry points. Tactically, it made sense: a surprise strike with plenty of mobility; early seizure of the best airfields; maneuver room for

---

* Cates was one of six future Commandants of the Marine Corps who fought in the Marianas. David M. Shoup and Wallace M. Greene Jr. served at Saipan and Tinian; Lemuel C. Shepherd, Robert E. Cushman Jr., and Louis H. Wilson Jr. served at Guam.

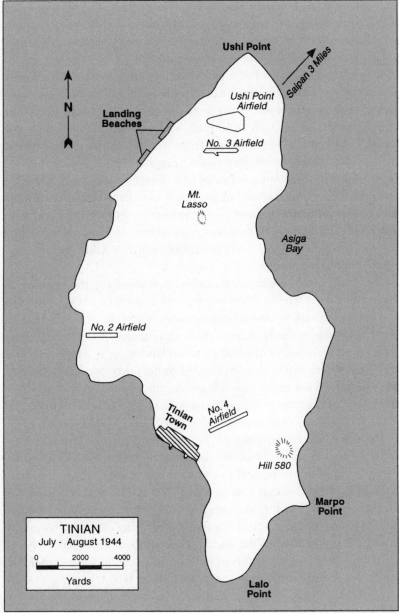

N

Ushi Point

Saipan 3 Miles

Ushi Point
Airfield

Landing
Beaches

No. 3 Airfield

Mt.
Lasso

Asiga
Bay

No. 2 Airfield

Tinian
Town

No. 4
Airfield

Hill 580

Marpo
Point

TINIAN
July - August 1944

0   2000   4000

Yards

Lalo
Point

Mary Craddock Hoffman

both divisions to shoulder into line and swing south. The big risk came in the arena of logistic support. Could Hill and Schmidt really support two divisions through those tiny bottlenecks in the escarpment? Weather became a concern. The monsoon season loomed.

Schmidt and Hill launched an exceptional preliminary bombardment of Tinian. For once, the Americans in the Central Pacific were close enough to their next objective to pound it with their own field guns from a fire support base. As early as 20 June, while the fighting for Saipan still boiled, U.S. Army 155-mm "Long Toms" began bombarding northern Tinian. The number of artillery pieces firing on Tinian grew as the battle of Saipan waned. Soon Schmidt had thirteen batteries of the XIV Corps artillery firing day and night, using a greater number of cannon than Union general Meade employed in defense of Cemetery Ridge at Gettysburg. Hill's veteran gunships worked over the rest of the island, while carrier air and Army P-47s flying from Saipan's Aslito Airfield contributed to the pounding.

This integrated bombardment reached a crescendo on the morning of J-Day. Hill's decoy landing effectively froze the main body of Ogata's forces in place in the south for several critical hours. Members of the 2d Marine Division, watching the feint from the relative safety of their transports, quickly saw the wisdom of avoiding a real landing at Tinian Town. The popular old battleship *Colorado* closed to within thirty-one hundred yards off shore when a battery of Japanese 6-inch guns opened up from a hidden cave above the harbor. In fifteen minutes these guns scored twenty-eight hits on the battleship and her escort destroyer, inflicting 285 casualties.

The 4th Marine Division took full advantage of this distraction to hustle its assault elements ashore, using more than 500 LVTs and 130 DUKWs (amphibious trucks) to cross the reef and penetrate Japanese defenses at White Beach.* Enemy mines and machine guns slowed the advance initially, but the Marines soon had the mass and mobility in place to roll inland. Cates well knew that everything depended on maintaining the momentum of the assault. Conventional shore party operations would not do the job. There must be no stopping on the beach for any reason. Everything coming ashore—bullets, beans, bandages—had to travel on tracks or wheels, prepared to move directly to supply points well past the escarpment.

---

* DUKW is not an acronym but rather an arcane construction code: D = 1942, U = utility, K = all-wheel drive, W = twin rear wheel axles. Troops for forty years called the vehicles "Ducks."

Assault troops of the 4th Marine Division race toward Tinian's northwestern beaches during the decoy landing farther south. *(U.S. Naval Institute)*

An enterprising SeaBee officer devised a portable vehicle ramp that could be emplaced by LVTs, thus offering more beach exits. Before long the Navy warped two floating pontoons into place, invaluable facilities captured from the Japanese at Saipan. The tempo of offloading never slowed. Before nightfall, Cates had 15,000 Marines ashore. The cost had been astonishingly light: 15 killed, 225 wounded.

Cates had fought the Japanese at Guadalcanal and knew what the night would bring. He brought his tanks, half-tracks, and light artillery ashore well before dark. Cates also landed enough barbed wire to secure the extended perimeter, and he coordinated night defensive fires with the cruisers and destroyers assigned in support.

As expected, Colonel Ogata, chagrined at misjudging the main thrust of the American landing, sought to reverse the situation that night by marshaling several thousand of his troops and half a dozen tanks around the American perimeter. Ogata's veterans, adept at night fighting, launched a well-coordinated tank-infantry attack on the heels of a stinging artillery barrage. In essence, this close, violent combat between two experienced forces became THE Battle of Tinian. Here General Cates's forethought paid dividends. Star shells fired from offshore destroyers helped backlight the attackers. Marine tanks, half-tracks, and machine guns took a heavy toll of Japanese infantry caught up in barbed wire. The Marines' versatile M3A1 37-mm antitank guns proved particularly well-suited for this kind of close-range fighting, firing canister rounds like some super-caliber, semiautomatic shotgun. The whole affair was as vicious a little battle as would be seen in the Pacific War. And one of the most one-sided. The Marines held. At daybreak they counted fifteen hundred dead Japanese in and around their perimeter. "We've broken their backs," said Cates grimly.

With the dawn also came the 2d Marine Division, landing in trace over White Beach, maintaining the high mobility of the previous day. The two divisions moved out together, reached the east coast, then wheeled southward. Scattered Japanese units fought bitterly, but most of Ogata's surviving forces melted away toward the south. The terrain opened up, becoming ideal tank country. For several days after the landing, the Marines enjoyed the rarest of combat experiences in the island warfare of the Pacific, riding on tanks and half-tracks pell-mell down farm roads in pursuit of a retreating enemy. The troops soon outran the range of the artillery support on Saipan and began relying more heavily on Army aircraft, Navy gun ships, and their own 105-mm artillery battalions, now ashore.

Tinian was a magnificent fight for Marine artillerymen. As one captured Japanese soldier admitted, "You couldn't drop a stick without bringing down artillery." Maj. Frederick J. Karch, operations officer for the 14th Marines, recalled an incident where an airburst artillery round cut down an entire Japanese machine-gun crew. "Each man fell in position, carrying his assigned component of the gun, just like a picture out of a training manual."

General Schmidt declared the island secured on the afternoon of 1 August. The V Amphibious Corps had seized Tinian in nine days at the cost of 2,355 casualties. Most of the remaining Japanese garrison died defending the southern palisades or in hopelessly outgunned banzai attacks.

Tinian epitomized the fusion of innovative planning and violent execution, the hallmark of an effective amphibious assault. For its size, there is no finer example of amphibious virtuosity in the Pacific War.

Tinian became the largest B-29 base in the world and within a year would launch the B-29 *Enola Gay* with its single atomic bomb destined for Hiroshima. Yet the shock waves of Japan's sudden loss of the Marianas—forcibly ripped from within their presumably impregnable Absolute National Defense Sphere—produced more immediate results. The Tojo government resigned in disgrace. A senior Japanese official in the emperor's retinue exclaimed, "Hell is upon us." Civil defense officials in Japanese cities received orders to begin preparing for American air raids. Garrisons on Peleliu, Iwo Jima, the Philippines, and Okinawa began a frantic race to enhance fortifications.

Adm. Kishisaburo Nomura admitted to his postwar interrogators that, from Tarawa onward, "everywhere you attacked before the defense was ready. You came more quickly than we expected." Nomura's assessment was right on the mark regarding the Gilberts, Marshalls, and Marianas. Beyond that point, however, the Japanese learned to anticipate their enemy more realistically. They would prove fully ready for the storm landings to come. Especially at Peleliu. . . .

Chapter Five

Sharpening the Amphibious Ax

The invasion generates into what is purely and simply assault.
By assault we mean the last stages of an attack. The operation
becomes assault from beginning to end.

Lt. Gen. Alexander A. Vandegrift, USMC
Commandant of the Marine Corps,
August 1944

The Japanese high command faced an intolerable dilemma in
August 1944. Painful to admit, difficult to believe, but the Americans had thoroughly whipped their forces in the Marianas. The
U.S. invasion force had crippled the Mobile Fleet and practically
annihilated an entire field army. From all reports, the Americans had outfoxed, outfought, and literally steamrollered each Japanese garrison into
oblivion. The enemy now held airfields within thirteen hundred miles of
Tokyo. And there was no telling where the next storm landing would
occur. Both Iwo Jima and Okinawa were now very much at risk.

With hindsight, and from a purely political viewpoint, this would have
been a smart time for Japan to have sued for peace. The savings in lives
and property would have been incalculable (although the postwar implications are murky to perceive). But capitulation was not a strategic option
to the senior military officers who dominated the Japanese government.
Instead, IGHQ reacted to the loss of the Marianas with shame, fury, and
controlled desperation. Imperial forces would fight on—and fight smarter.

Both sides therefore devoted the late summer of 1944 to appraising the new U.S. practice of storm landings. The Americans saw little need for improvement. The Tinian operation in particular generated great pride— a planning and logistical masterpiece, executed with such ferocity by the veteran landing force that the island fell in nine days at a casualty rate of less than 5 percent. In contrast, the Japanese examined their performance in the Marianas and found discouraging evidence of uninspired leadership, interservice squabbling, wasteful banzai charges, and inadequate heavy weapons and fortification material. IGHQ saw clearly that the legendary spiritual supremacy of the individual Japanese warrior could not prevail in the face of overwhelming firepower and mobility that characterized the recent American landings across the Central Pacific. Obviously, their traditional counterlanding doctrine—defend at the water's edge, counterattack any penetration immediately with all forces—needed urgent, radical revision.

Japanese leaders believed until the end of the war that the American public would not tolerate a protracted war with high casualties in the Pacific. After the Marianas, IGHQ generally agreed that the best defensive doctrine would be one that bogged down an American campaign indefinitely and inflicted maximum casualties. This was attrition warfare, anathema to the samurai tradition, but the tactics would capitalize on two great strengths of the Japanese troops—their ability to dig and their ability to endure the most god-awful shelling.

The Japanese received an unexpected grace period in which to refine this new doctrine when the Americans turned away, momentarily, from Iwo Jima and Okinawa to concentrate on the Palaus and the Philippines. IGHQ was elated with the reprieve for its northern outposts. Two extremely gifted lieutenant generals, each bearing the approval of Emperor Hirohito, had just left Japan to begin the defensive enhancements of their respective island citadels: Tadamichi Kuribayashi at Iwo Jima and Mitsuru Ushijima at Okinawa. Within six months both generals would be poised and waiting among some of the most daunting defenses the Americans would face in the war. As they prepared for the coming firestorms, both commanders studied reports of the ways their enemy executed forcible seaborne assaults.

American amphibious proficiency developed unevenly as the war progressed. Major differences existed between the conduct of amphibious operations in the European and Pacific theaters. Landings in the

Mediterranean and in France tended to be larger than those in the Pacific. They usually involved combined operations with Allied forces and often integrated airborne and glider units into the assault plan. Most took place under the protective umbrella of land-based air, and all required a high degree of logistical ingenuity to succeed. Landing forces in Europe rarely encountered reefs and thus remained satisfied with landing boats rather than assault amphibian vehicles. With the major exception of Normandy, most Allied commanders favored night landings, in which the duration and importance of preliminary naval gunfire became secondary to achieving tactical surprise. Allied landings in Italy and France invariably provoked a strong counterattack by German panzer forces. The extended beachhead lines at Anzio and Normandy remained major battlefields for weeks. Some landings were easier. Yet the "amphibious hazard axiom" remained constant: no one in any theater ever landed on a foreign shore without risk—if the enemy didn't hurt you, the high surf would.

Night landings were not common in the Pacific. The prevalence of coral reefs dictated precision (daylight) navigation, as well as more attention to the timing of rising tides rather than conditions of light or darkness. Control of the ship-to-shore movement, complex enough in daylight, became dangerously complicated after sunset. Any landing plan that involved preliminary naval bombardment—an inevitable requirement in the Central Pacific (and Normandy, as well)—demanded several hours of daylight for satisfactory observation and execution.

The celebrated storm landings at Tarawa and Iwo Jima were conducted by Marines; those in the Marianas, Peleliu, and Okinawa by joint landing forces of Army and Marine divisions. Both services also conducted dozens of other landings with only slightly less intensity than those featured in this book. The Army rarely gets sufficient credit for its considerable amphibious role in the Pacific War. As a matter of fact, historian Allan R. Millett has calculated that eighteen Army divisions executed twenty-six amphibious landings in the Pacific, while the six Marine divisions executed fifteen.

Nowhere did the Army gain amphibious proficiency more rapidly than in "MacArthur's Amphibious Navy"—the Seventh Amphibious Force commanded by the enterprising Rear Adm. Daniel E. Barbey. MacArthur and Barbey executed an unbeatable record of fifty-six amphibious landings in two years, delivering a cumulative total of 1 million men over enemy-held shores. That most of these landings were conducted against light opposition simply reflects MacArthur's tactical genius and the advantage of attacking along the immense coastlines of New Guinea, Leyte, or Luzon.

Barbey achieved these series of hopscotching operations with an amphibious fleet literally gathered from the boneyard—castoffs after the Atlantic and Pacific Fleets got first pick. Where amphibious force commanders in other theaters went to sea in battleships, cruisers, or special command ships, Barbey for years flew his flag in an "Able Peter little Charlie," an APc, a wooden-hulled coastal transport the size of a small tugboat. Barbey modified his "flag-configured 'apple cart'" to accommodate a few extra bunks, a typewriter, and a mimeograph machine. From his tiny "flag bridge," Barbey coordinated the movement of his flotilla of flat-bottomed LSTs, LCIs, and LCTs along the dark coasts. Here, speed of execution dominated all other tactical considerations. The beachheads may have been lightly defended, but MacArthur and Barbey knew to expect a major Japanese air strike within the first hours. The soldiers learned to load their ships so adroitly that an acceptable level of critical supplies could be rushed ashore by H-Hour+4—the witching hour—at which the ships would hightail it for safer waters. Barbey therefore preferred to land by the first blush of dawn, sacrificing preliminary naval gunfire (such as was available) to enhance surprise and permit a running start on the offload.

"Uncle Dan" Barbey conducted all of his New Guinea landings without the luxury of carrier support—with one major exception. In April 1944 an unusually congenial agreement between Nimitz and MacArthur led to the temporary augmentation of Barbey's ragtag amphibious force by a wealth of carriers, battleships, and transports loaned from the Pacific Fleet for Operation Reckless. This was MacArthur's bold end run of several hundred miles to strike at the Japanese command and supply center near Hollandia, New Guinea.* Since such a movement would exceed the operating range of land-based tactical aircraft, MacArthur borrowed Marc Mitscher's Task Force 58 and several escort carriers from Nimitz. Barbey suddenly commanded 217 ships—an embarrassment of riches. He even upgraded his flagship to a destroyer for the occasion.

Operation Reckless succeeded handsomely. Barbey's forces landed eighty thousand Army troops in simultaneous assaults at Humboldt Bay,

---

* Although smaller in scope and less significant strategically, MacArthur's end-run amphibious strike at Hollandia would approximate his subsequent brilliant strike at Inchon during the Korean War six years later.

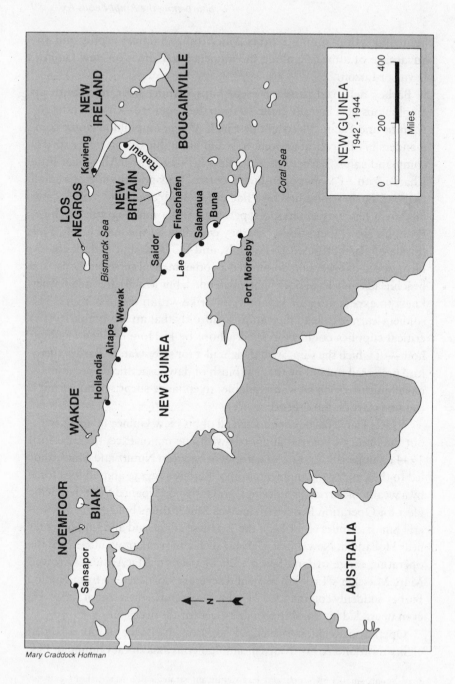

NEW GUINEA
1942 - 1944

Miles

0   200   400

NEW IRELAND

Kavieng

Rabaul

NEW BRITAIN

BOUGAINVILLE

LOS NEGROS

Bismarck Sea

Saidor

Finschafen

Salamaua

Buna

Coral Sea

Lae

Wewak

Aitape

Hollandia

WAKDE

NEW GUINEA

Port Moresby

NOEMFOOR

BIAK

Sansapor

N

AUSTRALIA

Mary Craddock Hoffman

Aitape, and Tanahmerah Bay. Japanese forces in the area, confounded by the sudden landing, fled into the jungles. Thousands of more resolute Imperial troops had been effectively bypassed and neutralized. Army Chief of Staff George C. Marshall complimented MacArthur, calling the operation "a model of strategic and tactical maneuver."

Hollandia indeed represented one of the most economical uses of amphibious power in the Pacific War. But here again, heavy congestion of supplies along the exposed beaches continued to represent the Achilles' heel of amphibious operations. A lone Japanese bomber penetrated the screen at Humboldt Bay during the second night, dropped one stick of bombs amid the crowded stacks of ammunition and fuel along the narrow beachhead, and set fires that exploded and burned for four days—destroying the equivalent of twelve LST loads of critical supplies. The 125 casualties from this incident exceeded the total lost to enemy fire in securing the beachheads on D-Day.

Amphibious troops and the "Gator Navy" had been wrestling with the problems of delivering combat cargo over the shore for a decade. Tinian's signal success—the rare beachhead that never became a bottleneck—was more a reflection of an uncommon abundance of LVTs and DUKWs, plus northern Tinian's open country inland, than any doctrinal breakthrough. As the amphibious war progressed, however, there developed a knowledgeable cadre of Navy beachmasters and landing force shore party professionals who took perverse pride in creating order out of chaos—the essence of amphibious logistics. Iwo Jima would provide their supreme test, but the body of knowledge was now steadily increasing.

Ironically, the Marines saw their own original mission change significantly as the war progressed. After forty years of developing the capability of seizing advance fleet bases in support of a naval campaign, the Marines increasingly found themselves storming ashore to establish airfields in support of the strategic bombing campaign against Imperial Japan. The Marianas and Iwo Jima exemplified this new thrust. Gen. Henry H. "Hap" Arnold, chief of the Army Air Forces, thus became keenly interested in Marine amphibious expertise in the Pacific. By late November the first B-29s of the Twentieth Air Force would take off for Japan from the new airfields in the Marianas.

The distinguishing characteristic of amphibious operations executed in the Central Pacific would remain the convergence of strategic and tactical offensives—General Vandegrift's aptly described "assault from start to finish." Such an emphasis on unrelenting assault meant heavy demands on shipping, intricate organizations, concentrated detailed planning, and complex tactical execution.

These demands revealed a fundamental split between the tactics of the Army and the Marines once they crossed the high-water mark on the beaches. Army divisions, in general, made maximum use of supporting arms, preferring to pulverize Japanese strongholds with integrated fire-power before ordering an infantry attack. Army commanders also proved methodical in sweeping their entire frontage as they advanced, leaving no pockets of resistance in their rear. The Marines, less endowed with organic supporting arms and more attuned to the spirit of momentum by their amphibious nature, preferred to charge ahead, accepting casualties and bypassing pockets, hustling for the far shore. The Army approach undeniably saved casualties. The Marine way saved time.

The Navy favored any tactics that would expedite the assault, hasten the general unloading of landing force supplies, and permit an early departure from constricted waters of the task force. The Navy's sense of desperate vulnerability during an amphibious assault—the apt metaphor of "one foot ashore, the other still in the water"—did not diminish throughout the course of the Pacific War. Indeed the Navy's heaviest losses and closest encounters with disasters after Pearl Harbor occurred in and around amphibious beachheads: Savo Island in 1942; loss of the escort carrier *Liscome Bay* in 1943; Leyte in 1944; the kamikazes off Okinawa in 1945.

The Japanese fleet submarine *I-175* torpedoed the merchant-hulled escort carrier *Liscome Bay* off Makin Atoll during Operation Galvanic. The torpedoes caught the ship at sunrise, just as her aircraft began to spool-up for launch, all fully armed and fueled. The resulting explosions were terrific—Admiral Hill saw the smoke plume from Tarawa, ninety-five miles away—and the ship sank like a stone, taking 644 of her 959 officers and men to their deaths.

Kelly Turner and Holland Smith held Maj. Gen. Ralph Smith and his 27th Division partly responsible for this disaster. The Army National Guard outfit, engaged in their first combat, had taken nearly four days to subjugate the small Japanese garrison on Butaritari Island, thereby extending the requirement for the *Liscome Bay* and the other support ships to loiter in harm's way. This resentment clearly influenced the Smith vs. Smith controversy at Saipan months later, but the criticism is a bit unfair. Losses to Japanese submarines in the Gilberts could well have been greater and in fact could have occurred days earlier. Admiral Koga dispatched nine long-range submarines to the Gilberts from the Carolines on 18 November, two days before D-Day at Tarawa and Makin. Every ship in Spruance's fleet had been in jeopardy throughout the landings. In the eyes of the Navy, however, the loss of the *Liscome Bay* illustrated the imperative for unrelenting, aggressive tactics by the landing force—the Marine way, not the Army way. Nor did these adjectives always follow service lines; the Navy admired the rambunctious spirit displayed by the Army's 77th Division at Guam, Leyte, and the offshore islands at Okinawa.

For its part, the Navy now demonstrated an increased willingness to support amphibious assaults from dangerously close range. This had not been the case in the narrow waters of the Solomons. When Admiral Nimitz visited Guadalcanal at the height of the campaign in late September 1942, General Vandegrift complained about the tactical conservatism of the warships intended to support his Marines ashore: "Out here too many commanders have been far too leery about risking their ships." Nimitz, who had survived the blemish of a court-martial as an ensign for running his destroyer aground in the Philippines, agreed that the preservation of a fleet-in-being would be meaningless if the United States lacked the naval power to win the protracted battle for Guadalcanal. He then placed "Bull" Halsey in command of the South Pacific Theater, and Vandegrift quickly had the support of a warrior who would risk every ship in his arsenal to support the troops ashore.

Kelly Turner proved equally fearless in commanding his task forces against enemy-held islands. "Close the range or cease firing," he chided one cruiser at Makin. His battleship commanders needed little encouragement. When Turner queried the *Mississippi* why her number 2 turret was no longer firing at Butaritari, the skipper reported a turret explosion had killed forty-three officers and men, but his other main batteries had assumed the fire missions of the stricken turret until the carnage could be cleared.

Similarly, Admiral Hill did not hesitate to risk dispatching two destroyers and two minesweepers into Tarawa's lagoon on D-Day to blaze the way for the assault craft despite the gauntlet of fire that greeted them. He even chided Spruance's flagship, the cruiser *Indianapolis*, for opening fire on Betio at twenty-two thousand yards—"an extreme range." The valor of the battleship *Colorado*, closing to thirty-one hundred yards at Tinian, drew a punishing fire from shore batteries but helped make the decoy landing all the more convincing. Adm. "Close-In" Conolly's personal bravery in this regard at Guam and the Marshalls also illustrates the

Close fire support: the older battleships, now too slow to accompany the fleet carriers, found a welcome home with the amphibious forces. Here the battleship *Pennsylvania* delivers fire from her 14-inch batteries in support of the III Amphibious Corps assaulting Guam. *(U.S. Naval Institute)*

point. So does the case of the destroyer that approached "within rock-throwing range" to knock out the Japanese mountain gun at Guam's Adelup Point on W-Day. "This was a beautiful bit of seamanship [that] saved the lives of lots of Marines," said Maj. Louis Metzger, who had lost several of his LVT-As to this troublesome gun crew.

The daring of battleships and cruisers steaming in harm's way to pound the amphibious objective provided one measure of the Navy's intent to add ferocity and momentum to the assault, but these large ships at least had armor protection. Gen. Julian Smith had rather forcibly reminded the shore bombardment admiral before Tarawa that his Marines would be "crossing that beach with no more armored protection than a goddamned khaki shirt." The same could be said of the "small boys" of the amphibious task force—the minesweepers, LCI-G gunboats, and UDT boats. The "Elsie Gee" gunboats would attract increasingly deadly counterbattery fire in the storm landings to come.

Few naval craft would ever be so vulnerable to major-caliber enemy fire at such short ranges.

The increasing employment of minesweepers, UDT teams, and close-in fire support craft reflected the Navy's increasing confidence in maintaining command of the sea and air around their amphibious objective in the Central Pacific. Spruance and Turner had overruled Julian Smith's request for "advance force operations" at Tarawa on the basis of their concern with major surface and air counterattacks. The advent of the fast carrier task forces changed that equation drastically. Once the fleet and amphibious force commanders accepted that reality, they stopped placing such a premium on strategic surprise and tactical speed and began to develop a full menu of preliminary amphibious measures.

These initiatives included a more sensible use of the Fleet Marine Force Reconnaissance Company, commanded throughout the war by Capt. (later Maj.) James L. Jones. The unit had distinguished itself in the Gilberts by teaming with the troop submarine *Nautilus* to capture vital Apamama Atoll, but their most valuable contributions came later, especially at Tinian, where their stealth swimmers executed a rock-by-rock, mine-by-mine, nighttime reconn of alternate landing beaches. The force reconn Marines' surreptitious work complemented the more brazen deployment of the underwater demolition teams. After the Marshalls, Turner learned to use his UDT frogmen in daylight, which they needed for the ticklish work of rigging explosives to offshore obstacles and mines. This required a regular armada of ships to provide smothering protective fire while the men did their work close to the beaches. Such noisy and obvious daylight operations could not help but alert the Japanese as to the exact beaches chosen for assault.* But by then (typically D-Day-minus-1) it was too late to execute major troop redeployments during the concurrent naval shelling and aerial strafing.

Preliminary naval gunfire ran the gamut of effectiveness during the seven storm landings: inadequate at Tarawa and Peleliu, marginal at Saipan and Iwo Jima, superb at Guam, Tinian, and Okinawa. Tarawa's failures stemmed from inexperience. Iwo Jima's shortcomings had more to do with logistic limitations and a preoccupation by the fleet commander with suppressing enemy air counterattacks by striking the Japanese homeland. Sometimes the difference lay in the nature of the amphibious

---

* This was the case at Saipan, Peleliu, and Okinawa, but multiple UDT operations at Guam further confused the Japanese, and the frogmen at Iwo Jima conducted identical sweeps on both coasts.

force commander. "Close-In" Conolly, brilliant at Guam, did not participate in the Peleliu campaign. Sometimes the difference reflected differing
service priorities. With the exception of Guam and Okinawa, the landing
force always wanted more preliminary naval gunfire support than the
Navy was prepared to give. Holland Smith and Harry Schmidt fought for
ten days of preliminary naval shelling of Iwo Jima. They got three.

If preliminary naval bombardment varied widely in duration and effectiveness in these major landings, the record of subsequent naval gunfire
support to troops ashore proved consistently outstanding. As at Tarawa,
once shore fire control parties made it safely ashore with working radios—
one of the battle's turning points—naval gunfire improved dramatically.
Even in the leanest of amphibious operations in the Central Pacific, a division could count on the full-time support of a designated battleship; a regiment got a cruiser; each infantry battalion on the line rated a destroyer.
Nor did this support end at sunset. Other designated ships would take station prepared to fire star shells over the approaches to the main line of
resistance; other ships awaited the inevitable call for high-explosive shells
once the parachute flares illuminated a Japanese raiding party. In addition
to star shells, destroyers often bathed the contested ground at night with
their searchlights—as at Iwo Jima when they surprised Japanese troops
swarming from caves on Suribachi for a counterattack.

While beachhead logistics problems represented the biggest operational
hurdle to increasing the velocity of amphibious assault in late 1944, close
air support remained the biggest disappointment. The efficiency of air support of amphibious assaults seemed to function in the reverse of naval gunfire: good in the preliminary pounding, ragged after troops stormed
ashore. Much of this had to do with the failure of the landing force to
incorporate a workable, survivable system of command, control, and communications for tactical air support. Another factor was the absence of
opportunities to train with air control systems under realistic conditions. A
third detriment concerned the uneven proficiency of the Navy squadrons
assigned to support the landing force from their escort carriers. Most
squadrons lacked the experience of precision bombing and strafing in the
proximity of friendly troops. Typically, their missions within the amphibious task force extended to combat air patrols, antisubmarine patrols,
search and rescue—even delivering pesticides like DDT over troop concentrations in battle. Frequently pilots flying close support missions for
troops ashore were restricted to maximum bomb loads (often only five
hundred pounds) and minimum elevation (say, fifteen hundred feet).

Ground troops became much concerned with minimum elevation restrictions on support pilots after Tinian, where napalm bombs were first introduced. In that battle, Army pilots dropped 150 jettisonable wing tanks filled with gasoline and napalm jelly. U.S. forces originally intended the napalm strikes as a defoliant, but veteran infantrymen quickly saw the tactical benefits of the new weapon. The bombs were inaccurate and not altogether reliable, but when they worked they were awesome. But no Marine on the ground felt comfortable with a tank-full of napalm tumbling down in his vicinity from fifteen hundred feet. Fifty feet was more like it!

In truth, the Marines still hankered for an operational reunion with their own aviation units. The desire was understandable. Marine pilots were trained first as infantry officers—many served subsequent exchange tours with ground units—and developed a natural inclination to provide more responsive close air support to their counterparts on the ground. Marine Corps aviation units filled several vital operational needs in the Pacific War, and their numbers grew exponentially—from a scant prewar configuration of 2 air groups and 11 squadrons in mid-1940 to a peak of 5 air wings, 32 groups, and 145 squadrons in the fall of 1944. But the leap-frog strategy of the Central Pacific campaign removed the assault troops beyond supporting range of all their land-based fighters and dive-bombers. Holland Smith's long struggle to get the Navy to dedicate escort carriers to Marine fighter and attack squadrons for amphibious support did not bear fruit until Okinawa in 1945.

Actually the Marines fighting ashore on Tinian and Iwo Jima received exceptional close air support from Army P-47 squadrons, an uncommon role for the long-range fighters, but one performed with great elan. The Navy squadrons, however, would continue to deliver the bulk of the calls for air support ashore. As air command and control systems evolved during Iwo Jima and Okinawa, so would the proficiency, responsiveness, and safety of those on-call missions.

In the other critical dimension of amphibious assault, the surf zone, the landing forces benefited not only from the advent of newer, more reliable LVTs and upgunned LVT-As, but also from an ugly-looking hybrid vehicle developed by the Army and soon used in all theaters of the war, the DUKW amphibian truck. The DUKW was in effect a 2.5-ton, six-wheel truck configured to a boat-shaped flotation hull. Waterborne, the vehicle used a propeller driven by a power take-off from the transmission and steered by a standard rudder. Wheels and propeller operated together as

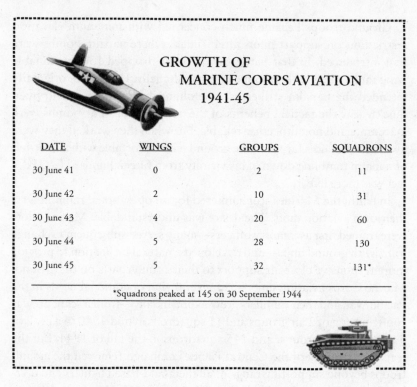

GROWTH OF
MARINE CORPS AVIATION
1941-45

DATE	WINGS	GROUPS	SQUADRONS
30 June 41	0	2	11
30 June 42	2	10	31
30 June 43	4	20	60
30 June 44	5	28	130
30 June 45	5	32	131*

*Squadrons peaked at 145 on 30 September 1944

the vehicle emerged from the surf zone. At thirty-one feet long and eight feet wide, each DUKW could carry twenty-five men, but the best way to use a DUKW was to stuff it with five thousand pounds of critical supplies (freeboard permitting) for the ship-to-shore movement, then load a dozen wounded men in litters and evacuate them back through the surf to a hospital ship. Then repeat the process—around the clock.

DUKWs and LVTs complemented each other rather than competed for missions. With their slightly more generous armor plate and more machine guns, LVTs retained their tactical role as assault vehicles. DUKWs, with much greater cargo capacity, filled and surpassed the logistic role formerly held by LVTs, and typically landed in waves just after the assault LVTs. Both vehicles were displacement hulls in the water, meaning neither could generate much speed or creature comfort in rough seas. LVTs had slightly better seakeeping and surfing capabilities than DUKWs and proved superior in some inland swamps. But DUKWs had much greater reliability and maintainability, operated with exceptional agility over most marginal terrain ashore, and provided a capability no LVT could ever do—transport a 105-mm howitzer (a shoe-horn fit). For Army and

Marine divisions alike, the ability to land 105-mm battalions early in an assault represented a most welcome tactical enhancement. Moreover, DUKWs proved worth their weight in gold in delivering a steady stream of artillery ammo directly from ship to firing batteries ashore.

Storm landings and armored amphibian vehicles—the LVT-As—were made for each other in the Pacific War. Barrier reefs and shallow water kept the LCI-G gunboats (even with their admirable five-foot drafts) and Navy wave guide boats at arm's length; the Marines were on their own for the final thousand yards. As Adm. Harry Hill instructed his boat control officers at Saipan: "The reef marks the limit of Navy responsibility for leading in the assault. . . . Your job is to get them to the correct part of the reef." Thereafter the first wave would consist of LVT-As, firing on the move from turret-mounted 37-mm guns (LVT-A1s) or 75-mm howitzers (LVT-A4s). Subsequent employment of the LVT-As ashore went through several variations. Planners learned to reject the temptation to use the armored amphibians as light tanks. The top-of-the-line LVT-A4 weighed nineteen tons and featured half-inch frontal and turret armor— enough to deflect small-arms fire, but the vehicle proved vulnerable to every larger Japanese weapon. If hydrographic conditions permitted, the LVT-As were better employed by diverting them to the flanks just before reaching the beach—where, still enjoying the relative protection of their low freeboards in the water, they could maintain direct or indirect fire to assault troops until the field artillery could land. The vehicles proved at their best in such operations close to the shore. At Guam, Maj. Louis Metzger's 1st Armored Amphibian Tractor Battalion led the initial ship-to-shore assaults, helped anchor Navy landing craft to the reef for the offload of Sherman tanks, led subsequent assaults on Cabras Island and Orote Peninsula, and conducted long-range water patrols along the northern coastline.

The most significant developments in weapons organic to the Marine division during this period related to the tactical use of flame. Tarawa had demonstrated the urgent need for both portable and vehicle-mounted flamethrowers. There the 2d Marine Division had faced the task of overcoming nearly five hundred Japanese pillboxes with only twenty-four back-pack flamethrowers. Short-range systems mounted on M-3 Stuart light tanks appeared in time for the Marshalls. Another system appeared as a replacement for the Sherman bow machine gun. Both proved unsatisfactory in the Central Pacific. Assault troops needed a turret-mounted flame launcher with greater range, enhanced safety, and more endurance. An ad hoc team of Army Chemical Corps officers, Marine

Corps tankers, and an enterprising SeaBee officer then developed a prototype turret-launcher and mounted three of them on LVTs for Peleliu. These proved invaluable except for the traditional limitation of all amphibian vehicles—too thin-skinned for adequate protection in close combat ashore. Adapting an official version of the prototype Sherman turret took longer than it should have, but at least eight were ready in time for Iwo Jima, where they were without a doubt the weapons of choice. Factory-built versions of the Sherman flame tank appeared in quantities in Army tank battalions in time for Okinawa.

Another munition that saw wide use in the Pacific War was white phosphorous (then and now: "Willy Peter"), packaged in every size from hand grenades to heavy artillery rounds. Maj. Kiyoshi Yoshida, the 43d Division staff officer captured by the Americans on Saipan, admitted during interrogation that Japanese troops "feared the phosphorous shells much more than high explosives."

The Marine Corps in May 1944 revised its division-level organization and equipment for the third time in the war. The "F Series Division" reflected the latest lessons of the Pacific War. Increased lethality and embarkability factors dominated. At 17,465 men, the division now became the smallest of any of its wartime configurations—more than 2,000 fewer men and 80 fewer trucks than the Guadalcanal-era division, for example. Sherman medium tanks replaced the last of the light tanks. The number of 75-mm pack howitzer battalions decreased, reflecting the trend toward larger caliber artillery pieces now that the ship-to-shore problems had been solved. The number of portable flamethrowers increased tenfold. The widely unpopular Reising submachine guns had been fully replaced by a combination of 12-gauge shotguns and Thompson submachine guns.

Browning Automatic Rifles (BARs) increased from 558 to 853 in the new division, a reflection of the fundamental restructuring of the rifle squad, subdivided for the first time into three four-man fire teams, each built around a BAR man. The Marines thus continued their thirty-year love affair with the BAR. ("Oh, the BAR," exclaimed Gen. Lemuel C. Shepherd after the war, "now there was a weapon—the finest we had!") Marines in the Pacific did not cotton to the M1918A2 version of the BAR, with its fancy bipods and hinged butt-plate. Troops quickly "lost" the 2.4-pound bipods in the boondocks, preferring the "lean" World War I versions. The popularity of this reliable automatic rifle can be measured by photographs of combat action in Okinawa, the final battle of the war, in which every other Marine, it seems, had acquired a BAR of his own.

U.S. MARINE CORPS DIVISION
EVOLUTIONARY CHANGES, 1942-44

	SERIES D (July 42)	SERIES E (April 43)	SERIES F (May 44)
Total Strength	19,514	19,965	17,465
Flame thrower			
Portable	0	24	243
Submachine Gun			
Reising .45	4,208	0	0
Thompson .45	0	78	49
Shotgun			
Riot, 12-gauge	0	306	306
Browning Automatic Rifle			
(BAR)	513	558	853
Mortar			
60mm	63	81	117
Howitzer			
75mm Pack	36	36	24*
105mm	12	24	24*
Jeep			
4x4, one -quarter ton	427	509	408
Truck			
6x6, Cargo, 2.5 ton	229	198	150
Tank			
M3 Light (37mm)	72	54	0
M4 Med. (75mm)	0	0	46

*By mid-1945: 75mm pack = 0, 105mm = 36, 155mm = 12

The 1944 F Series Division achieved some of its economies in personnel by reassigning the organic Naval Construction Battalion to force troops. This made sense—the SeaBees were in constant demand for both combat and postcombat missions—but it broke up an excellent team. The Marines valued the SeaBees' infectious "can do" spirit. The most prized weapon system at Tarawa on the second and third days of the battle, for example, was often a SeaBee bulldozer. SeaBees had served as shore party cargo handlers as well as construction troops and adjunct riflemen. Others volunteered to serve with the initial UDT teams, helped devise the turret-mounted flamethrower, and designed mobile ramps to help reduce the congestion at Tinian's White Beach. The SeaBees would still be very much in the thick of the action, but from henceforth the Marine divisions would not have their very own "battalion of sergeants," the abundance of skilled petty officers in the construction trades.

Even without the SeaBees, each Marine division still included more than a thousand Navy personnel under the new T/O. These were the surgeons, dentists, chaplains, and hospital corpsmen who served as an integral part of every Marine tactical unit. A special bond already existed between the infantrymen and their assigned corpsmen, resourceful "country doctors" who shared every hazard with their Leathernecks. Indeed, all seven men of the Navy Hospital Corps who received the Medal of Honor in World War II were corpsmen with the Fleet Marine Forces, Pacific. And always, Navy medical personnel ashore paid a high price for their calling. A total of 414 surgeons and corpsmen were killed or wounded at Saipan, eight times the number for Tarawa. The figure would double again for Iwo Jima.

The accelerated pace and violent execution of the storm landings in the Central Pacific were exacting a high toll among the landing forces, and by the fall of 1944 the strain was beginning to show. As combat correspondent Robert Sherrod noted at war's end: "Only eleven divisions of troops (six Marine, five Army) were involved in the [Central Pacific] battles from Tarawa to Okinawa, though often those divisions carried as heavy a responsibility as ever was placed on the men with infantry weapons." Sherrod took particular note of the 4th Marine Division, which fought four complete battles (the Marshalls, Saipan, Tinian, Iwo Jima) in barely one year, suffered nearly 75 percent casualties—"yet it was in action only 61 days throughout the war."

Many proven combat leaders found little respite before being tested again on yet another hellacious beach. Five infantry battalion commanders who survived Tarawa went down in the Marianas—Lt. Col. Kenneth McLeod and Maj. John F. Schoettel killed; Lt. Col. Henry P. Crowe, Lt. Col. Lawrence C. Hays, Lt. Col. Raymond L. Murray wounded. A Japanese sniper shot Lt. Col. Evans F. Carlson on Saipan, in effect knocking the controversial former Raider out of the war. Another sniper on Guam killed Lt. Col. Samuel D. Puller, executive officer of the 4th Marines and brother of the legendary Col. Lewis B. "Chesty" Puller.

These losses were matched by proportional, if less heralded, losses among the key NCO ranks. Survival odds for infantrymen, engineers, and amtrackers were never good; spread over several battles along the seemingly endless road to Japan they seemed prohibitive. A sign post on Tarawa in mid-1944 seemed to reflect this cynicism. One arrow read "To Tokyo, 3130 miles"; another: "To Frisco—what the hell do YOU care? You're not going there"; and another predicted: "The Golden Gate in '48; the Bread Line in '49."

American troops invading the final bastions of the Central Pacific would face larger, more experienced, and more heavily armed Japanese garrisons, each offering an elaborate defense in depth among convoluted terrain. Japanese commanders from this point forward would prove very adept at training and motivating the assortment of veterans and rookies, soldiers and sailors in their ranks. Imperial Army artillery units, absent from the Gilberts and Marshalls, had shown their worth under disorganized conditions at Saipan. Now, increasingly, they would dominate the fighting to come at Peleliu, Iwo Jima, and Okinawa. The Japanese 70-mm howitzers fired by rikusentai troops at Tarawa had proven deadly enough; ahead lay 155-mm field guns, 8-inch naval rockets, 320-mm spigot mortars.

Also ahead, waiting for the U.S. amphibious forces, would be mines—more numbers and a greater variety than ever used in the Pacific. Among the most common would be the Type 98 hemispherical antiboat mines—"the steel basketball with horns"—which were packed with forty-six pounds of trinitroanisol boosted by picric acid. More lethal improvisation lay ahead: converted depth charges and thousand-pound bombs buried vertically under the sands with contact detonators.

The Japanese in the coming fights would continue to demonstrate their mastery of the night. "They've taken Indian warfare and applied it to the 20th century," said Merritt A. "Red Mike" Edson, the highly decorated veteran of Tulagi, Guadalcanal, Tarawa, and Saipan. But now there would be far fewer of the wasteful banzai charges and much greater emphasis on small-unit infiltration— "prowling wolves," General Kuribayashi would call them.

And still to come would be the greatest threat yet to the seemingly unstoppable American amphibious juggernaut—the special attack units, Japan's last, forlorn, deadly hope—the young kamikaze pilots, suicide boat crews, and "human bullet" antitank squads.

Chapter Six

Bloody Peleliu

Don't kid yourself that the end is in sight out here; we're still
nibbling at the edges, and the predominant Japanese Army has
not yet really been hurt.

Vice Adm. Theodore S. Wilkinson, USN
Commander, III Amphibious Force,
Summer 1944

B y September 1944 Adm. Chester Nimitz commanded more men
and machines of war than all the fabled conquerors of antiquity
combined. His joint staff had expanded tenfold since 1941 and
now operated at an intensity level best described as "controlled
frenzy"—peaking with the mount-out of each new campaign. Such had
particularly been the case in getting Operation Stalemate II underway,
the prophetically named, frequently altered campaign to seize the Palau
Islands in the western Carolines. Stalemate II had seemed snake-bit from
the start—delayed and short-changed by the extended Guam campaign,
shackled by late-arriving combat equipment and too few ships, marred
by costly collisions and other accidents during the training phase. But the
diverse components of the task force had sailed on schedule and now,
12 September (Pearl Harbor time), had converged off Peleliu. Indeed,
Vice Adm. Theodore S. Wilkinson's III Amphibious Force had already
commenced advanced operations against that small island.

Nimitz, who had learned the ways of the sea from his mariner grand-father, knew he had done his best to prepare his lieutenants for the assault. Now came the hard part: waiting for the battle reports. Few commanders handled this nail-biting pressure better than Nimitz. Those who knew him best, however, discerned a pattern to his activities during these periods of tense anticipation. When he was upbeat and confident, Nimitz passed the time by pitching horseshoes. When he was concerned, the admiral sought to steady his nerves by firing his target pistol on the small range adjacent to his Pearl Harbor headquarters. Nimitz fired thousands of rounds while waiting for news of the storm landing at Peleliu.*

Nimitz had promised Douglas MacArthur in the presence of President Roosevelt the previous summer that he would support his adjoining theater commander's long-anticipated return to the Philippines. MacArthur worried about the threat to his right flank in advancing from New Guinea to Mindanao posed by Japanese airfields on Peleliu in the Palaus and on Morotai in the Moluccas. The two commanders agreed to attack both islands on 15 September, MacArthur against Morotai, Nimitz against Peleliu.

Nimitz knew he had gotten the short end of the stick. Less than two hundred Japanese defended Morotai. He already knew from documents captured on Saipan that more than ten thousand veterans from the Kwantung Army defended Peleliu and neighboring Angaur. He also knew the Japanese had expected his forces to strike the Palaus immediately after the Marshalls. He had outfoxed them by attacking the Marianas instead, but now came the payback—the Peleliu defenders would surely have taken every advantage of the three-month grace period to enhance their fortifications. Both "Bull" Halsey and "Howlin' Mad" Smith had dourly predicted in advance that Peleliu could be "another Tarawa." While neither Nimitz nor his staff shared that pessimism, no one expected a cakewalk. Nimitz also realized he did not have his "first team"—Spruance, Turner, Hill, Smith—assigned to this campaign, but that fact didn't bother him. Nimitz's great strength lay in his ability to appraise and select commanders. He had plenty of confidence in the newly formed Third Fleet team of Halsey, Wilkinson, Rear Adm. George H. Fort, and Marine major general Roy S. Geiger. Still, Nimitz fired his target pistol, magazine after magazine, waiting.

Abruptly, at this eleventh hour, came a thunderbolt from Halsey. In a flash precedence, top secret message to Nimitz, intended for the Joint

* The author is indebted to H. Arthur "Hal" Lamar, flag lieutenant to Nimitz, and Loren F. "Sonny" Paulus, the admiral's bodyguard, for these personal insights.

Chiefs, Halsey recommended major revisions to the conduct of the Pacific War. While rampaging through the Philippines with his fast carrier task forces, Halsey had found surprisingly light opposition. In his view, the door to the central Philippines lay open ("this was the vulnerable underbelly of the Imperial Dragon"). His message suggested mind-boggling changes: cancel the invasion of Mindanao altogether; strike instead at Leyte, and do so two months early; cancel the entire Palaus operation; redeploy the Army's XXIV Corps (scheduled to seize Yap and Ulithi) to MacArthur for Leyte.

Nimitz never kept a diary nor wrote a "tell-all" book after the war. We can only surmise that Halsey's breathless message caused him great irritation. For one thing, there was very little time to decide. Operation Stalemate II had already begun; D-Day at Peleliu was less than three days off. Second, the timing couldn't be worse. These decisions would affect the entire Pacific War, but MacArthur was under way with the Morotai assault force under radio silence and Adm. Ernie King out of town at the Combined Chiefs' "Octagon" Conference in Quebec. There was probably another, more subtle factor at work. While Nimitz and his staff admired the tactical bravery of "Bull" Halsey, they had less regard for his strategical acumen. Then, too, the CINCPAC staff had worked hard to get the Stalemate II forces under way; reversing that momentum would be costly to do and bad on morale.

Against this background, Nimitz and his valued planner Forrest Sherman reviewed the bidding. Nothing Halsey said really changed the obligation of CINCPAC to protect MacArthur's return to the Philippines by forcibly eliminating the Japanese threat at Peleliu. Yes, they could forgo Yap and loan MacArthur the temporary use of the XXIV Corps. Bypassing Mindanao, advancing Leyte? MacArthur's call. But Peleliu would go as planned.

That was the substance of the CINCPAC endorsement on Halsey's message. King and the other Joint Chiefs, with subsequent input from MacArthur's staff, bought the recommendations as modified by Nimitz. Peleliu's storm landing would stand.

Nimitz made decisions every day of the war that sealed the fate of men under his command. This decision had terribly fateful consequences. Yet it is difficult to fault the man based on what he thought he knew at the time. Peleliu's unsavory aftertaste would be more a product of unexpected tactics by the Japanese garrison and unimaginative division-level leadership on the part of the landing force than the strategic rationale for the campaign. More than anything else, Peleliu would represent the dynamic relationship between American's growing amphibious virtuosity vis-à-vis the Japanese search for effective countermeasures the final year of the war.

Maj. Gen. Roy S. Geiger, the gregarious Marine aviator commanding III Amphibious Corps at Peleliu, became the first senior American officer to sense the changes in Japanese "antiamphibious doctrine." Eight weeks earlier he had commanded IIIAC against stiff but predictable Japanese defenses at Guam. But this D-Day—15 September 1944—seemed different. Status reports reaching Geiger on the flagship *Mount McKinley* from assault elements ashore were garbled and incomplete. He could neither grasp the situation nor understand why the assault momentum seemed so badly stalled.

His staff knew Geiger to be a commander who liked to see things firsthand. In earlier campaigns (and again at Okinawa) the Old Man was prone to disappear from headquarters, "borrow" an aircraft, and fly over the battlefield to assess the situation directly. On D-Day at Peleliu, frustrated by conflicting reports, Geiger simply walked down the ship's accommodation ladder, hailed a passing landing craft with all the nonchalance of a man flagging a taxi, and took off for the beach.

As he approached the reef, Geiger immediately recognized two facts. First, the truncated naval gunfire bombardment had failed to take out several cleverly hidden antiboat guns on both flanks of the beaches. At least twenty-four LVTs and countless DUKWs now burned in the shallows from direct hits at short range. Second, judging from the recurring booms of heavy artillery firing from a forbidding ridgeline dominating the island—and where the hell did that *ridge* come from?—the Japanese had adopted a defense-in-depth for Peleliu. Gaining the beach with considerable difficulty, Geiger worked his way forward and stuck his head up over the berm to appraise the airfield. At that instant, a major-caliber Japanese round nearly tore his head off. The Corps commander slithered quickly down to cover, visibly shaken. Guam had been rough. But Peleliu looked absolutely lethal. Now they were facing a pro team.

The forcible seaborne assault of Peleliu and its subsequent battle ashore would prove Geiger right. This was a strange, transitional, costly campaign. The landing was bad enough. There followed a desperate, prolonged battle under unimaginable conditions of hellish heat and twisted terrain—vicious, point-blank fighting that would last ten weeks and cost nearly ten thousand American casualties. "Everything about Peleliu left a bad taste in your mouth," said one survivor. Indeed, the battle became one of the most controversial—and obscure—conflicts in the entire war. Yet for all its waste and sacrifice, the fighting on Peleliu yielded useful operational benefits. While no one knew it at the time, it would be Peleliu—not Saipan or Guam—that would reflect the future of storm landings to come at Iwo Jima and Okinawa and, potentially, Kyūshū. Whatever could be learned here, at whatever cost, would help prepare for the even bigger bloodbaths ahead.

The Palaus anchor the western edge of the Carolines, the most extensive island chain in the world, spanning thirty-three degrees of longitude just north of the equator. The Palaus themselves are an unremarkable string of islands ranging about one hundred miles from Ulithi in the north to Peleliu and Angaur in the south. Babelthuap, by far the largest, almost as large as Guam, lies just south of center. Adjacent to Babelthuap, the Japanese maintained an administrative center in Koror, the long-time capital of their mandated possessions in the Pacific. The strategic value of the Palaus stems from pure geography: they lie nearly equidistant from New Guinea, the Marianas, and Mindanao. The Japanese called the Palaus "the spigot of the oil barrel," the gateway to their petroleum resources in the East Indies.

Admiral Koga's precipitous abandonment of Truk with his Combined Fleet during the Marshalls campaign left all of the Carolines vulnerable to American amphibious assault, including the lightly fortified Palaus. The degree to which IGHQ took this vulnerability seriously can be measured by their decision to withdraw the 14th Division from the Kwantung Army for deployment to the Palaus as early as April 1944. The 14th Division had a proud combat record dating back to the Sino-Japanese War of the last century. Many of the current troops had fought the Russians or the Chinese. This was a well-trained, cohesive, heavily armed unit, proud to be "Manchukuoan" veterans and boastful of their new motto, Breakwater of the Pacific.

Maj. Gen. Sadae Inoue deployed most of his division—some twenty-five thousand troops—on Babelthuap, expecting the main American attack there. He also assigned a large garrison to defend Yap. To Peleliu he dispatched a reinforced regiment; to Angaur a reinforced battalion. While Babelthuap had a military airfield, the one on Peleliu was better, a two-strip, hard-surfaced facility for medium bombers and fighters. Japanese engineers also had an auxiliary strip under construction on the small island of Ngesebus, joined to Peleliu by a causeway.

Col. Kunio Nakagawa commanded the 2d Infantry Regiment (with two battalions of the 15th) on Peleliu. Altogether, Army and Navy combined, the Japanese force on the island would number well over ten thousand. When early Army-Navy squabbling threatened to interfere with defensive preparations, Inoue sent down his trusted assistant Maj. Gen. Kenjiro Murai, who served unobtrusively as Nakagawa's "tactical assistant" and kept the Navy admiral in line.

Peleliu's unique and remarkable defenses may have had several architects. Inoue and his talented chief of staff, Col. Tokechi Tada, certainly contributed; Murai and Nakagawa contributed the most; the faceless IGHQ provided top-level doctrinal impetus.

IGHQ took exceptional measures following the fall of the Marianas to devise more practical countermeasures against American storm landings. Indeed the Imperial Army, increasingly taking on the lion's share of defense responsibilities within the Absolute National Defense Sphere, formed antiamphibious research teams to analyze lessons learned from each battle. Among the lessons learned from Saipan, for example, emerged these blunt recommendations:

- "Prepare for the worst on the assumption of defending without control of either the air or the sea."

- "Enemy preparation fires for a beach assault are beyond imagination, which is ten to twenty thousand tons. The enemy will continue to increase preparatory bombardment in order to minimize his casualties."

- "The enemy is expected to choose landing sites where he can land at relative ease, disembark rapidly, and have easy access to airfields."

Japanese forces on Guam had little time to inculcate lessons learned at Saipan into their own defense plans, but they did experiment successfully with employing a few major weapons forward along the beach in heavily fortified and camouflaged positions. The final reports from the Guam garrison, like those at Saipan, suggested the futility of trying to defend the shoreline. "Although there is a need for beach positions to disrupt the enemy landing," said one staff officer, "it is dangerous to depend on them too much. There is need for preparation of strongpoints from which to launch counterattacks, and for deep resistance zones adjacent to waterfront positions."

Imperial General Headquarters in August 1944 published "Defense Guidance on Islands," which reflected the bitter lessons of the Marianas, recommended defense in depth, and advised against "reflex, rash counterattacks." Army field commanders noted the transition from seeking the elusive "decisive engagement"—ludicrous in the absence of air or naval superiority—to a much more realistic policy of "endurance engagement." Policy statements began to include the phrase "*Fukkaku* positions," defined as underground, honeycombed defensive positions.

The Americans had first encountered primitive Fukkaku positions as early as Gavutu-Tanambogo in 1942. By May 1944, when the 41st Division landed on Biak in the Schouten Islands as part of MacArthur's New Guinea campaign, the Japanese had developed Fukkaku positions to a disturbingly systematic level. MacArthur had promised Nimitz he would provide shore-based, long-range bomber and reconnaissance support from captured Japanese airfields on Biak in time for the Saipan invasion. Two weeks, planners figured, should be enough time to overcome the forty-four-hundred-man garrison and get the fields operational. When the 41st Division's vigorous landings on Z-Day met only sporadic resistance, it seemed the planners had been right.

Unfortunately, the American invasion of Biak coincided with an inspection visit by Lt. Gen. Takazo Numata, chief of staff of the 2d Area Army. Numata assumed command of the garrison, deployed them in natural caves and hastily enlarged extensions along the high ground dominating the airfields, and settled in for an "endurance engagement." The battle for Biak's caves took two months and cost three thousand U.S. casualties, plus the relief of the division commander. MacArthur was doubly embarrassed. His promised support to Nimitz failed to materialize, and his press communiqué announcing victory on Biak was several weeks premature. But Biak had been a hell of a fight. Had the Marines and soldiers of the III Amphibious Force studied that battle in the adjoining theater in advance they might not have been as surprised at Peleliu.

The driving force for Peleliu's innovative defenses seems to have emanated from the personality of Colonel Nakagawa. We may never know the extent to which he may have benefited from General Numata's experiences defending Biak or from all the antiamphibious wisdom being collected and disseminated by IGHQ, but Nakagawa had plenty of combat experience in his own right. He had a keen eye for the lay of the land and a respect for the firepower the Americans would bring against his reinforced regiment. He knew their objective would be the airfield. He knew the field lay too close to the obvious landing beaches for him to defend for long. Then he examined the high ground, the ungodly ridges and hills that dominated the island along the northern length. Here he would make his stand.

Peleliu is barely six miles long by two miles wide and shaped like a lobster claw. The airfields—the main complex in the south and the fighter strip under construction on Ngesebus in the north—lay fully exposed in flat ground. But along the northern edge lay the badlands—a jumble of upthrust coral and limestone ridges, box canyons, natural caves, and sheer cliffs. The natives called this forbidding terrain the Umurbrogal; the Japanese named it Momoji. The Americans would call it Bloody Nose Ridge. But here was a critical intelligence failure. Dense scrub vegetation covered and disguised the Umurbrogal before the bombardment began. Overhead aerial photographs failed to reveal this critical topography to U.S. analysts. That's why General Geiger was so astonished on D-Day to see such dominant terrain overlooking the airfield and beaches.

At Nakagawa's request, General Inoue prevailed on IGHQ to send mining and tunnel engineers to Peleliu to help build the defenses. Within months the forbidding hills and cliffs were honeycombed with more than five hundred caves. Some were five or six stories deep. Some had sliding steel doors to protect heavy weapons. All had alternate exits. All were mutually supporting by observed fire. Here was a classic Fukkaku position defense.

Roy Geiger's IIIAC consisted of two divisions, one Army, one Marine. Maj. Gen. Paul Mueller commanded the 81st Division, nicknamed "the Wildcats." The Wildcats had yet to face combat, but they were enthusiastic, well-trained, ready to fight. Geiger would hold the Wildcats in reserve initially, then unleash them against Angaur and Ulithi. They would also be on call to help out the Marines on Peleliu, if needed. The honor of assaulting Peleliu itself went to the 1st Marine Division, the "Old Breed," veterans of the earliest pitched battles in the Pacific, Guadalcanal and Cape Gloucester. Many of the rank and file of the Old Breed had been deployed in the Pacific for more than twenty months. Said one salty noncom to a greenhorn replacement: "Sonny, I've worn out more seabags than you've worn out socks!"

Maj. Gen. William Rupertus commanded the Old Breed. He had seen plenty of fighting in the Solomons and New Britain, but he was impatient, stubborn, and dour. Some contemporaries said he never recovered from the trauma of losing his wife and two children to a scarlet fever epidemic in China a few years earlier. Unlike Geiger, Rupertus held a low opinion of Army forces and viewed Mueller's Wildcats with suspicion. Rupertus figured his three infantry regimental commanders—Cols. "Chesty" Puller, "Bucky" Harris, and Herman Hanneken—had more combat experience between them than all the officers combined in the Army division.

The 1st Marine Division had fully earned its spurs and its Presidential Unit Citation at Guadalcanal. By 1944 their veterans were likely the best jungle fighters in the world. But the division also had some shortcomings. While their collective fighting spirit would forever sustain them in combat, the Old Breed would need more than jungle fighting skills to prevail in the cave and mountain warfare waiting them at Peleliu. Also, this would be the division's first major storm landing. For all the subsequent savagery of the fighting for Guadalcanal and Cape Gloucester, the Old Breed had never executed a landing against major opposition in prepared defenses, the Florida Islands notwithstanding. Rupertus did little to close the gap. While the rest of Fleet Marine Forces, Pacific leapt at the opportunity after Tarawa to convert their LVTs into tactical assault vehicles, Rupertus demurred. He preferred their original employment as logistic support vehicles. Nor did Rupertus put much stock in naval gunfire planning. Geiger was shocked to discover that the division went into combat at Peleliu without a designated naval gunfire officer on its general staff. Nor was Geiger impressed with the division's proposed landing plan: three regiments abreast, only one battalion in division reserve, no interest in asking to earmark one of the Wildcat regiments for backup. But Geiger had arrived late in the planning process because of Guam's prolonged execution, and he had many other problems to overcome in a very short time.

Roy Geiger found shortcomings in amphibious intelligence, shipping, training, and naval gunfire support planning. Regarding combat intelligence, while the landing force benefited from the discovery on Saipan of the complete Order of Battle for the Peleliu garrison—who they were, how many shooters they had, what weapons—they had little evidence of

Nakagawa's revolutionary intentions. Geiger's force also had terrible maps, knew nothing about the convoluted high ground to the north, nor why the Japanese had been unable to finish that fighter strip on Ngesebus.

The prolonged fighting in the Marianas caused serious conflicts in ship scheduling and critical delays in delivery of combat equipment. Only at the absolute last minute did the 1st Marine Division receive new LVT-4s, flamethrowers, and armored amtracs. One provisional armored amphibian battalion could prepare for Peleliu only by studying blueprints of their new vehicles until their arrival just before embarkation. Because the Marines had to split the four available LSDs with the Army, the Old Breed had to leave sixteen of its forty-six Sherman tanks behind. Rupertus, attuned to jungle warfare, didn't fight very hard for his abridged tanks or tardy flamethrowers, both of which would be so critical in the Umurbrogal.

Final amphibious training, hurriedly conducted in congested areas, proved costly and frustrating. The 11th Marines had no place to conduct realistic artillery training on tiny Pavuvu. Said regimental operations officer (and future commandant) Lt. Col. Leonard F. Chapman Jr., "training was reduced to the pitiful expedient of firing into the water with the observers out in a boat or DUKW." Elsewhere, ships collided, landing craft swamped, men were injured. Rupertus broke an ankle dismounting from an LVT. He would go through the battle with a cane and in constant pain, never capable of observing battle conditions firsthand. Then came more bad news. The battleship *California* was so heavily damaged in a collision she would miss the campaign, a blow to the already sparse naval gunfire support available.

Inadequate preliminary naval gunfire would become one of the battle's low points. At Geiger's insistence, Rear Adm. George Fort extended the bombardment phase from two days to three, but he could do nothing to increase the original quantity of munitions. Peleliu in those three days would receive less weight of metal than Tarawa had received in its three hours. At one point, Rear Adm. Jesse B. Oldendorf, responsible for executing the bombardment, announced he had "run out of profitable targets." Oldendorf would become one of the landing force's most trusted bombardment commanders, but these words quickly came back to haunt him. The 1st Marines in particular were incensed to find "the Point" and a major blockhouse just inland of their left flank beach untouched by the bombardment—and delivering a murderous fire against the assault waves.

The Japanese also demonstrated a growing proficiency with mines and obstacles in defending Peleliu. UDT frogmen removed hundreds of antiboat obstacles from the approaches to the landing beaches during dangerous daylight operations. But Nakagawa had his own stealth swimmers. These he sent out the night before D-Day to plant rows of horned antiboat mines 150 yards from the beach. This was a stroke of brilliance, but it failed in execution because Nakagawa's swimmers in their haste neglected to pull the safety pins from most of the mines. Otherwise, the results could have been disastrous for the landing force. Postlanding sweeps found a large number of these powerful mines with their contact horns crushed by American LVTs, intact but harmless.

Nakagawa, alerted to the American's intended beaches by the UDT activity, endeavored to further disrupt the assault by stationing suicide teams in the water along the reef prepared to serve as "human bullets" against tanks and armored amphibians. He also tried to pre-position drums of fuel along the reef with which to ignite a wall of "fire along the seawater." None of these innovations worked, but Nakagawa's other plans for sacrificing one battalion to "bleed" the landing succeeded. Aircraft bombs planted vertically in the sand with special contact fuses served as awesome mines. His camouflaged positions of "passive defense" maintained their cover until the initial Marines had stormed inland—then emerged to shoot the next echelons in the back. All this—while Nakagawa's main force lay in deep shelter in the Umurbrogal.

"Moments are getting tense now that D-Day is near," admitted 1st Lt. Richard C. Kennard, an artillery forward observer, to his parents. "Will probably be a dirty little boy for a long time, as there is no water on this island, it being as flat as a pancake. The whole operation will be another Tarawa."

General Rupertus was more optimistic. "Rough but fast," he predicted to his subordinates and the handful of combat correspondents gathered on his flagship. "We'll be through in three days. It might take only two." Throughout the landing and the battle ashore Rupertus would exert unholy pressure on his regimental commanders for a speedy conquest. He expected a hot fight but assumed a steady offensive would crack the enemy's resolve, leading shortly to the traditional mass banzai charge and "open season" slaughter. Then it would be a simple matter of mopping up. The Army could do that.

The division commander's prediction spread false optimism among the troops. One man stated, "Hell, I can put up with anything for no

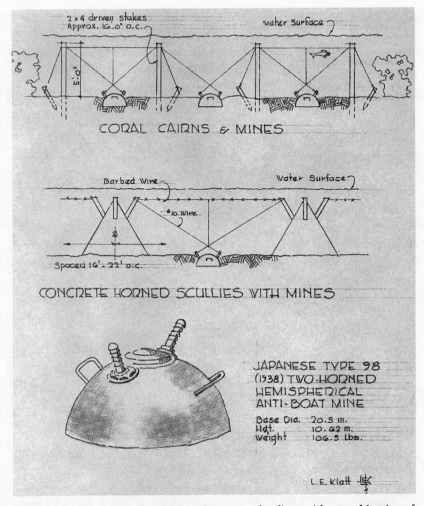

CORAL CAIRNS & MINES

CONCRETE HORNED SCULLIES WITH MINES

JAPANESE TYPE 98
(1938) TWO-HORNED
HEMISPHERICAL
ANTI-BOAT MINE

Base Dia. 20.5 in.
Hgt. 10.62 m.
Weight 106.5 lbs.

L.E. Klatt

The Japanese sought to disrupt American storm landings with a combination of antiboat mines tied to underwater obstacles in the shallows off likely landing beaches. This sketch reflects their use of coral for cairns and a continuing demand for cement and steel for "horned scullies." *(Larry E. Klatt)*

longer'n that." A veteran sergeant took the general's words to heart, telling his troops, "It's gonna be 'In-Again, Out-Again Finnegan!'" Said Rupertus: "Somebody bring me the Jap commander's dress sword." All this proved wishful thinking shortly after dawn on D-Day.

Peleliu was Pvt. Eugene B. Sledge's first action, and his subsequent book *With the Old Breed* has been appraised as the definitive enlisted man's account of World War II action. In a separate reflection on Peleliu's

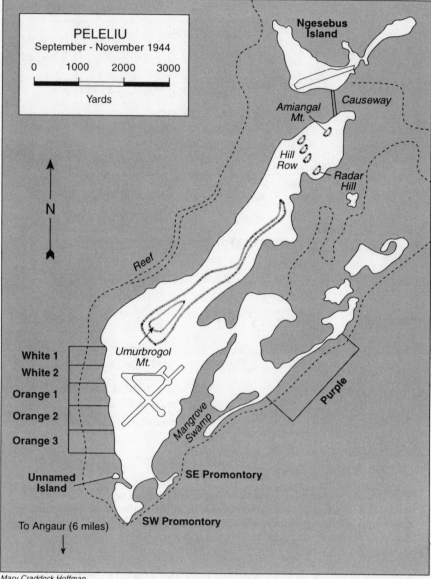

PELELIU
September - November 1944

0   1000   2000   3000
Yards

N

Ngesebus
Island

Causeway

Amiangal
Mt.

Hill
Row

Radar
Hill

Reef

Umurbrogol
Mt.

White 1
White 2
Orange 1
Orange 2
Orange 3

Purple

Mangrove
Swamp

Unnamed
Island

SE Promontory

SW Promontory

To Angaur (6 miles)

Mary Craddock Hoffman

Into the jaws of death. This was D-Day at Peleliu, the beginning of a murderous battle in one of the most obscure corners of the war. *(U.S. Naval Institute)*

fiftieth anniversary, Sledge described his experience in the assault waves on D-Day:

> The beach was a sheet of flame backed by a huge wall of black smoke, as though the island was on fire. . . . Every Marine in that amtrac was sickly white with terror. . . . Heavy Jap artillery and mortars were pounding the beach, and Marines were getting hit constantly. We piled out of our amtrac amid blue-white Japanese machine-gun tracers and raced inland. . . . Back on the reef I saw burning amtracs and struggling Marines. . . . A DUKW came in and stopped, to be hit almost immediately by a large shell that exploded dead center, engulfing it in thick black smoke. I didn't see anyone get out.

The Old Breed forced their tanks ashore early, less than five minutes after the last assault wave. Nakagawa had drilled discipline into his anti-tank gunners—remain under cover, ignore the amtracs, wait for the

unmistakable Shermans. Now they blazed away. They had the range—
but not the velocity. All but one of the eighteen Shermans assigned to support the 1st Marines received direct hits as they trundled over the reef—
some took four hits—but the Japanese gunners succeeded in knocking
out only three. Within the next eight months the Old Breed would feature
the most effective tank-infantry team in the Pacific. The teamwork the division exhibited getting their Shermans ashore at Peleliu—assigned infantry
close at hand, LVTs guiding the approach around submerged shell-holes,
each component in positive communications with the others—set the
foundation for that professional achievement.

Colonel Nakagawa had his own tank force, a dozen "tankettes" with
37-mm guns, and these he unleashed against the struggling beachhead at
midafternoon. A memorable melee followed. The Americans plastered
the lightly armored Japanese tanks with everything but the kitchen
sink—Sherman tanks, bazookas, mortars, point-blank artillery fire, even
a Navy dive-bomber. Two tanks penetrated to the shore, scaring hell out
of all hands in the vicinity, but soon they, too, lurched to a halt, burning
fiercely. It was a "use 'em or lose 'em" decision for Nakagawa—his tanks
had little value in the Umurbrogal defenses—and this vain charge certainly got the Americans' attention.

Getting ashore on D-Day was never rougher than on the extreme left
flank, where Capt. George P. Hunt led King Company, 3d Battalion, 1st
Marines, against a fortified promontory of coral and boulders, known
ever after as "the Point." Here Nakagawa had constructed five separate
pillboxes, four housing 20-mm machine cannons, the fifth a 47-mm antiboat gun—which took a heavy toll of LVTs by sustained enfilade fire
along the beachfront. Hunt found the promontory unassailable from the
sea; at best his Marines clutched at the rocky flanks, trying to root out
the Japanese literally face-to-face. Nor could the rest of Chesty Puller's
1st Marines lend a hand. They were fully embattled, and Hunt fought his
desperate saga for thirty hours in virtual isolation. At one point during
the night, Hunt's 230-man company was down to 18 Marines, desperately holding on to their small enclave with a captured machine gun and
an epic will to win. Those reinforcements who finally fought through to
the Point the next afternoon stared in horror. The shot-up bodies of both
sides scattered among the rocks resembled the graphic photographs of
Devil's Den at Gettysburg from the previous century.*

* The instructors at Marine Corps Schools in Quantico, Virginia, constructed an exact
replica of the Japanese defensive complex at "the Point" on a similar promontory in Lunga

Maj. Jonas M. Platt, operations officer for 3d Battalion, 1st Marines, was frustrated by his inability to relieve Hunt's isolated company any sooner. "It was a very, very hot beach," he recalled. Trying to direct naval gunfire against Japanese positions in the highlands, Platt kept getting interrupted by the destroyer skipper asking, "Can you observe? Can you observe?" "Hell, no," replied Platt, "we're taking grazing fire right over our hole."

No elements of the 1st Marine Division came ashore with impunity on D-Day. The 7th Marines on the right flank encountered an armed promontory of their own (Ngarmoked Island) and experienced great difficulty pushing across the southern end of Peleliu. Correspondent-artist Tom Lea landed with the 7th Marines and looked back at the beach: "Turning my head seaward I saw a direct center hit on an amtrac—pieces of iron and men seemed to sail slow-motion through the air."

The 5th Marines in the center escaped the worst of the enfilade fire going in, but then faced the open expanse of the airfield, swept by fire from the high ground, and took the brunt of the Japanese tank attack in the afternoon. Brig. Gen. Oliver P. Smith, assistant division commander, came ashore at noon, but by day's end there were insufficient LVTs left operational to land the reserves or General Rupertus and his full command group. Smith kept a calm hand on the throttle, accommodated General Geiger's surprise visit with aplomb, and succeeded late in the day in establishing communications with Puller, whose 1st Marines had suffered the most on D-Day. The Old Breed occupied a rather disappointing beachhead about three thousand yards long by five hundred yards at its deepest—plus George Hunt's isolated pocket to the north. Smith had eight infantry battalions ashore, plenty of tanks, and several batteries of 105-mm and 75-mm pack howitzers. All this came at the cost of eleven hundred casualties, including two hundred dead. The grim accounting measured worse than Guam and Tinian, but slightly better than Tarawa or Saipan—to this point.

Meanwhile, several hundred miles to the southeast, General Mac-Arthur watched with great interest as his 31st Division landed unopposed at Morotai, maintaining the promised "one-two punch" against the threat to his seaward flank. In scattered fighting ashore, the soldiers sustained a hundred casualties while killing or capturing an equal number of Japanese. Combat correspondents described MacArthur ashore

---

Reservoir, and for the next decade all second lieutenants undergoing Basic School had to formulate a tactical assault plan in field exercises.

looking over the horizon to the Philippines and remarking, "They are waiting for me there—it has been a long time."

The Americans on Peleliu would sustain the bulk of their casualties after D-Day in the northern highlands, beginning with the 1st Marines' assault on Bloody Nose Ridge on D+1 and continuing through the commitment of each Marine and Army regiment during the ensuing ten weeks. This savage fighting raged throughout a forbidding landscape—what one survivor described as "abominable terrain, a submerged reef suddenly thrust upward . . . with ridges as steep as the roof of a house." Shortly, each contested jumble earned troop nicknames: "the Five Sisters," "Dead Man's Curve," "the China Wall."

The real tragedy of Peleliu occurred during the first week, when General Rupertus and Colonel Puller believed they faced a linear defense along the perimeter of the nearest high ground, the kind of positions they could surely penetrate with just one more offensive push. As a result, for all their undeniable bravery, the 1st Marines sustained appalling casualties and had to be relieved by a regiment of Wildcats (at Geiger's insistence) six days after the landing. Maj. Ray Davis's 1st Battalion, 1st Marines, suffered most grievously, losing 70 percent of their number, their line companies reduced to a corporal's guard.*

Unable at first to dissuade Rupertus from his fixation with frontal assaults, Admirals Wilkinson and Fort and General Geiger made maximum use of their amphibious flexibility to achieve other campaign objectives at less cost. Deciding to bypass Babelthuap and Yap was provident—either could have been worse than Peleliu. On 17 September Wilkinson ordered General Mueller to land two regiments of Wildcats on Angaur. Wilkinson provided a commendable pounding of the small island by naval gunfire and carrier air strikes. Angaur, alone of all the Palaus, had no barrier reef, so Mueller had his pick of landing beaches. The Wildcats fought their way ashore convincingly, then spent three intense days fighting a veteran infantry battalion in heavy swamps and rain forests. Residual fighting would drag on a month, but Mueller shortly had the situation in hand well enough to accept Geiger's reassignment of one regiment to relieve the 1st Marines along Peleliu's Bloody

* In keeping with his aggressive nature, Colonel Puller maintained his regimental command post well forward; in fact, just behind his lead battalion. But Puller was slowed in this campaign by complications from his earlier wound at Guadalcanal. As Major Davis recalled: "I was always convinced that Lewie Puller would not have survived had he not been crippled. They were carrying him around on a stretcher. I was convinced if he had been able to walk around the way he was prone to do he was going to be killed."

Nose Ridge. On 23 September the 321st Regimental Combat Team switched from Angaur to Peleliu to relieve Puller's remnants.

Two days earlier, Wilkinson and Geiger landed Mueller's third regiment, RCT 323, at Ulithi Atoll. Here was the greatest strategic dividend of the campaign. While sparse in usable land areas, Ulithi's lagoon was deep and vast enough to provide a secure anchorage for up to six hundred warships. Ulithi would serve as a final marshaling yard for the great armadas preparing to assault Iwo Jima and Okinawa in the next several months. Ulithi also came at zero cost—the Wildcats lost not a man in this critical seizure.

On Peleliu, despite the bloodbath taking place in the hills and canyons, Admiral Fort stuck to the unglamorous work of improving the beaches, emplacing pontoon causeways, and completing the general offload of all combat cargo. SeaBees had the airfield ready for rough flight operations by D+3. On that day the first "Bird Dogs" of Capt. Wallace J. Slappey's Marine Observation Squadron Three landed on the airstrip and soon commenced providing air spot for artillery batteries and Navy gunships. Slappey's squadron would render enormous assistance to the Old Breed here, and again at Okinawa. So effective were the pilots and their observers that Japanese gun crews eventually ceased firing at the first sight of the Bird Dogs overhead, knowing from painful experience that accurate counterbattery fire would be called down on their heads in short order. The Marines loved these doughty little Piper Cubs, calling them "Piperschmidts" or "Messercubs."

On 26 September the troops in the lines cheered at the sight of gull-winged Marine Corps F4U Corsairs screeching overhead. Maj. Robert F. "Cowboy" Stout's Marine Fighter Squadron 114 (VMF-114) had arrived ashore, and henceforth both the Old Breed and the Wildcats would be receiving "personalized" close air support. Two days later Col. Caleb T. Bailey's Marine Air Group Eleven (MAG-11) came ashore and relieved the escort carriers of all further tactical support missions.

On 28 September Geiger and Rupertus put together a little jewel of a shore-to-shore amphibious assault against the islet of Ngesebus by the 5th Marines. The attackers made full use of their major weapons to support the assault: division and corps artillery, naval gunfire, close air support, armored amphibians blazing the way for troop-carrying LVTs. This widely observed assault afforded "Cowboy" Stout's Corsair pilots an opportunity to show their stuff. They performed spectacularly, roaring in at thirty feet off the deck, just ahead of the advancing LVT-As. A wounded

Japanese officer, captured in the ruins of the first line of blockhouses on the island, stated to his interrogator that the air strikes had been the most terrifying combat experience he had ever known—that the Marine riflemen were upon his position before his men could recover from the strafing.

The only disappointment at Ngesebus was the discovery that the island's soft, sandy soil would not support an airfield, which explained why the Japanese engineers had halted construction of their own fighter strip there. But U.S. engineers carving a new bomber strip out of Angaur's dense woodlands reported good progress, even while that battle lingered on. Given these reports, Wilkinson and Geiger concluded that they had fulfilled all the strategic objectives of Stalemate II. Ulithi represented a plum; Angaur would prove to be a better bomber field than Peleliu; and the Americans had succeeded in establishing an advance base at Peleliu despite the continuing horrors of the Umurbrogal.

Yet Colonel Nakagawa continued to rule the highlands, bloodying each American advance by day, deploying disciplined patrols of infiltrators to terrorize the enemy each night. He still had plenty of guns and ammo, including the lethal 150-mm heavy mortar, the biggest mortar the Marines had yet faced, an ideal weapon among the cliffs and crags of the Umurbrogals. The Japanese public followed reports of Nakagawa's extended resistance on Peleliu with patriotic intensity. Emperor Hirohito bestowed nine separate "decrees of praise" on the garrison during this time, an unprecedented expression of divine interest.

The pace of relentless close combat exacted a heavy toll among the Americans as well. "It was a young man's war," said Capt. John McLaughlin, a rifle company commander in the 5th Marines. "Only a young man could fight all night, then attack all day." Here was another forecast of the fighting to come on Iwo Jima and Okinawa. Two opposing armies; one aboveground, vulnerable, frustrated; the other almost entirely underground, living in relative comfort and safety, only briefly exposed while covering designated fields of fire. More than one U.S. commander exalted over finally winning a bitterly contested ridgetop—only to roar in anger at the smell of the Japanese cooking dinner in safe warrens hundreds of feet beneath the high ground.

Both sides resorted to ingenuity in the battle for the caves. U.S. troops often dangled a satchel charge at the end of a long rope down a cliff face, trying to swing the explosive pack into a cave mouth. Sometimes a Japanese soldier in a spider hole above the cave would lean out with a knife—sawing the rope in two just before the charge exploded.

General Geiger made sure that MAG-11 provided the kind of "flying artillery" that amphibious planners had envisioned before the war. This was close air support at its finest. Marine Corsairs would take off from Peleliu's airstrip and not even raise their landing wheels. In fifteen seconds they would be over the target, dropping their belly ordnance, then circling to land and rearm. Indeed, the first bomb delivered sprayed steel shrapnel onto the airfield, a mere thousand yards behind the point of impact.

Marine pilots used napalm bombs effectively at Peleliu, but the crazy-quilt front lines demanded special care in dropping these area weapons. In close quarters the pilots would drop the napalm tanks without detonators and merely dip their wings on pull-out to signal delivery. Nearby troops would then open fire with tracer rounds, igniting the napalm by "remote control." Reported the Japanese: "The enemy plan seems to be to burn down the central hills to ashes by dropping gasoline from airplanes."

By the end of September, Rupertus had suffered more than five thousand battle casualties in his division. The 1st Marines were so shot to pieces that Geiger ordered them evacuated to their base in the Russell Islands. Ironically, the survivors of this proud regiment had great difficulty leaving the grisly island to reembark their transports. Heavy seas swamped three DUKWs, spilling the troops in the water and requiring massive rescue efforts. Heartless Peleliu just wouldn't let go.

The protracted bloodbath on Peleliu received very little coverage in the States. The nation instead focused on war news from Europe—the dramatic Operation Market Garden in the Netherlands, American penetrations of the Siegfried Line, Russian thrusts into the Baltic. *Time* magazine barely mentioned Peleliu until five weeks after the assault began.

On 12 October Geiger declared the island secured and conducted a ceremonial flag-raising. Frontline troops snorted derisively at the news, but in truth the announcement merely signaled the end of the amphibious assault phase and the beginning of what the Army would call "Siege Warfare." Three days later the 81st Division relieved the Old Breed Marines and continued the battle another six weeks. On 20 October MacArthur indeed "returned" to the Philippines, landing in great strength on Leyte. On the next day, engineers completed Angaur's low-lying airfield. Yet another glitch materialized. The assigned Seventh Air Force bomber squadron had not completed its training qualifications. The first B-24 medium bombers did not take off on combat missions from the new field until 17 November, too late to contribute to the Leyte landing or subsequent beachhead breakout.

During the night of 24–25 November, Colonel Nakagawa sent his final message to Tokyo: "Our sword is broken and we have run out of spears." With that, he burned the regimental colors and shot himself.

Imperial Headquarters posthumously promoted the gifted colonel two grades to lieutenant general. One can only wonder why they waited, but the point is moot. Seventy-two days after D-Day, the long battle for Peleliu had ended.

Victory at Peleliu cost 9,600 American casualties—3,100 soldiers, 6,500 Marines. Nearly 1,200 died. Probably 16,000 Japanese died defending both Peleliu and Angaur. Logisticians calculated that the Americans fired an average of 1,589 rounds of all kinds of ammunition and ordnance to kill each enemy soldier.

Peleliu indeed left "a bad taste" with most survivors. As Eugene B. Sledge stated unequivocally on the battle's fiftieth anniversary: "I shall always harbor a deep sense of bitterness and grief over the suffering and loss of so many fine Marines on Peleliu for no good reason." Not every survivor agrees. Peleliu veteran Fred K. Fox reminds us that the 1st Marine Division once valued its alternate nickname as "MacArthur's Marines" and felt obligated to help the legendary general's return to the Philippines. In retrospect, the survivors among the Old Breed and the Wildcats have plenty of reason to view their combat performance at Peleliu with pride. Lacking the preponderance of numbers customarily required for amphibious assault, shortchanged by inadequate preliminary bombardment, the III Amphibious Force stormed ashore and prevailed against an enemy force that, man-for-man, represented the best fighters in the Japanese Empire. Peleliu's protracted, bloody, and frustrating battle became a convincing American victory.

Yet the perception of Peleliu as a wasteful campaign persists to some degree today. Historian Nathan Miller flatly states that Peleliu was "Nimitz's major mistake of the war." Advocates of fast carrier warfare have always asserted that Task Force 58 (or 38) could have neutralized Peleliu without having to invade the place. The argument certainly holds true in other bypassed islands like Truk, Marcus, and Wake. But there were major exceptions to airpower alone neutralizing a Japanese airfield. American medium and heavy bombers pulverized tiny Iwo Jima for one hundred straight days prior to that battle—yet every night the dump trucks loaded with "Keystone Kops" would come rumbling out of the caves to resurface the airstrips for flight operations. Sometimes these islands simply had to be subdued at bayonet point.

Star-crossed Operation Stalemate II produced certain strategic benefits. The former Japanese bastion in the western Carolines was now a center for U.S. long-range bombers and maritime patrol aircraft. The great natural anchorage of Ulithi would be of tremendous value in the campaigns to come. And the proud Japanese 14th Infantry Division, one of the empire's best, had been eliminated—killed at Peleliu and Angaur, or bottled-up and out of the war on Babelthuap and Yap. Taking Peleliu off the board also slammed the remaining door on the quarter of a million Imperial troops still at large in the Carolines.

Bad as it was, Peleliu provided the 1st Marine Division invaluable tactical experience for the near future. Of the six U.S. divisions engaged in the battle for Okinawa, none would surpass the Old Breed in their proficiency in tank-infantry coordination, use of close air support, and overall field savvy in cave warfare.

Regrettably—and almost inexplicably—the most useful lessons of Peleliu would not find their way in time to the troops who would need them most critically—the three divisions of Marines then preparing for the assault on Iwo Jima. Here again is evidence of an administrative oversight—or intracorps hubris—that should have been forcibly corrected by Holland Smith as commanding general of the Fleet Marine Forces, Pacific. Strange as it may seem, the Japanese were proving superior to their enemy in distributing tactical lessons learned from the epic amphibious battles of 1944. As a consequence, General Kuribayashi on Iwo Jima knew far more about the recent "antiamphibious struggles" at Biak and Peleliu than did his forthcoming enemy counterparts, Generals Holland Smith and Harry Schmidt.

Chapter Seven

Iwo Jima

Storming Sulfur Island

It was an operation of one phase and one tactic. From the time the engagement was joined until the mission was completed it was a matter of frontal assault maintained with relentless pressure.

Lt. Gen. Holland M. Smith, USMC
Commander, Expeditionary Troops, Iwo Jima
Task Force 56 Action Report,
March 1945

Iwo Jima was the most heavily fortified island the Americans would assault in World War II. The strategic benefits of acquiring airfields within fighter range of Tokyo would be significant—the risks in attacking that steep, volcanic fortress, "the Doorstep to Japan,"would be enormous. No U.S. amphibious force could have tackled this mission any earlier in the war. Seizing Iwo Jima would require full command of the air and sea, overwhelming firepower, imaginative naval campaign planning, seasoned shock troops, and violent, sustained amphibious execution.

Iwo Jima was a latecomer as a potential objective for U.S. amphibious forces. Many planners figured that the campaigns in the Philippines and Palaus would be followed by a combined operation against Formosa. Others, including Fifth Fleet Commander Raymond Spruance, believed the wiser choice would be to strike north-by-northwest against the Volcano and Ryukyu Islands. Seize Iwo Jima, he suggested, then Okinawa, in preparation for the final invasions of Kyūshū and Honshū.

Iwo Jima represented a major obstacle to the strategic bombing of mainland Japan by B-29s based in the Marianas. The island, lying about halfway between Saipan and Tokyo, contained an early warning radar system that provided Tokyo with an invaluable two-hour alert of each approaching B-29 raid. Further, Iwo-based fighters launched to intercept the incoming bombers, forcing them to fly a circuitous route, requiring more fuel and diminishing their payloads. Fighters on Honshū, alerted by Iwo Jima's radar, would be waiting for the American bombers, forcing them to fly at higher altitudes, further sacrificing bombing accuracy. After each mission, Iwo fighters sallied forth again to swarm around crippled U.S. Super-fortresses struggling to return to the Marianas. And Japanese medium bombers staged through Iwo for damaging raids on the U.S. air-fields on Saipan and Tinian, destroying more B-29s on the ground than Gen. Curtis E. LeMay's crews lost during their strike missions. The vaunted strategic bombing campaign had proven a bust so far. Iwo Jima had to go.

On 3 October 1944 the Joint Chiefs of Staff directed Nimitz to capture the ten-square-mile island. With Halsey still mired in the "tar pit" of Peleliu, Nimitz gave the newest tasking to Spruance. Reduced to its nub, the Fifth Fleet's mission was twofold: enhance the strategic bombing campaign; facilitate the ultimate invasion of the Japanese homeland. Nimitz emphasized speed of execution, as he had before Tarawa, saying: "It is a cardinal principle of amphibious operations that shipping be local-ized and exposed at the objective for the minimum possible time." This guidance would prove increasingly difficult to honor: seizing Iwo would take five full weeks; Okinawa, twice as long.

Operation Detachment, the campaign to seize Iwo Jima, became of necessity a stepchild wedged between the larger campaigns of Luzon and Okinawa. This narrow window of time dominated the planning for Detachment. Even as late as 1944–45 America lacked the resources to conduct two, simultaneous, full-scale amphibious operations in the Pacific. The JCS twice postponed D-Day for Iwo because slow progress in Luzon delayed the turnover of naval gunfire support ships and landing craft from MacArthur's forces to the Fifth Fleet. Nor was there any slack at the other end of the schedule. Spruance had to complete the seizure of Iwo Jima and reposition his amphibious forces to support the Okinawa campaign well before 1 April. That was the latest date Okinawa could be invaded without incurring undue risk from the summer typhoon season.

These time constraints did not unduly bother Spruance. He knew each of his principal task force commanders to be a veteran of urgent planning and hard campaigning in the Central Pacific. He led a seasoned, proven team. Marc Mitscher would again command the Fast Carrier Task Force (TF 58); Kelly "Terrible" Turner, the Joint Expeditionary Force; "Handsome Harry" Hill, the Attack Force. Rear Adm. W.H.P. "Spike" Blandy, highly regarded for his cool-headed handling of an amphibious group at Saipan and Tinian, would take command of the massive Amphibious Support Force (in effect, the "advance force commander").

Marine major general Harry Schmidt would command V Amphibious Corps as he had done so ably at Tinian. Schmidt would have the distinction at Iwo Jima of commanding the largest force of Marines ever committed to a single battle: a three-division landing force numbering seventy thousand men. But Spruance and Turner (to the displeasure of Nimitz) complicated the command structure by inviting Lt. Gen. Holland Smith along for one last campaign. Smith would serve as commanding general of "expeditionary troops," a contrived billet in this case where one amphibious corps attacked one island. Smith knew this, and endeavored to keep out of the Corps commander's way, but Schmidt would forever be resentful of Smith "stealing his thunder."

Smith actually contributed significantly at the highest echelons to the success of the campaign. By serving as the eminently quotable Marine spokesman for the media—and by "baby-sitting" VIP visitors like Navy Secretary James Forrestal—Smith allowed Schmidt to fight the tactical battle without distraction. And it would be Holland Smith's role to provide a necessary "reality check" for the combat correspondents gathered on the flagship before D-Day. "This is going to be a rough one," he predicted, "we could suffer as many as fifteen thousand casualties here." Few believed him.

Aside from aerial photography (and periscope photographs from the submarine *Spearfish*), American intelligence collection and analysis prior to Iwo Jima proved less effective than most preceding amphibious campaigns. Analysts looked at the island's severe water shortage and concluded that no more than thirteen thousand troops could be accommodated there, a 40 percent shortfall. Analysts also believed the senior officer on the island to be Maj. Gen. Kotono Osuga, assuming incorrectly that little-known Lt. Gen. Tadamichi Kuribayashi maintained his headquarters on Chichi Jima, 140 miles away. Planners underestimated the proliferation of Japanese major weapons. "The Japs had more heavy guns than we expected," admitted Kelly Turner to a *New York Times* reporter during the battle.

Nor did Turner, Smith, or Schmidt pay much attention to the evidence of the transformation in Japanese antiamphibious tactics manifested at Biak and Peleliu. They expected another Saipan, another General Obata. They anticipated a vigorous defense along the perimeter, followed by a massive banzai attack the first night. "We welcome a counterattack," growled Smith. "That's when we break their backs." A revealing 5 January 1945 intelligence report that forecast a radically different Iwo defense organized in depth along the lines of Peleliu attracted little top-level attention.

Iwo Jima represents a paradox in American naval history. The battle resulted in total victory, acquisition of strategic airfields virtually on Japanese territory, and an enduring symbolic legacy. Yet Iwo Jima also became the bloodiest battle in the history of the U.S. Marine Corps, the only major Pacific assault where the landing force sustained higher casualties than they inflicted on the Japanese garrison. As Smith would shortly be forced to admit, "This is the toughest fight in the 169 years of our Corps." Why such a surprise this late in the war? What made "Sulfur Island" such a tough nut to crack?

The Americans at first believed the Japanese had spent years preparing Iwo's intricate, mutually supporting defenses. They would be surprised to learn later that the fortifications they encountered in February 1945 had largely resulted from a crash construction program completed barely a week before the invasion. As late as February 1944 only fifteen hundred troops occupied the unfortified site. It took Nimitz's Central Pacific drive to alert IGHQ to Iwo Jima's strategic vulnerability. But it would take a strong-willed, imaginative commander to reverse the rigidity of service politics and the Bushido code and turn the island into the most formidable fortress in the Pacific.

Imperial Headquarters in 1944 created a new subtheater, the Ogasawara Area, which included islands of that name, plus the neighboring Bonin and Volcano Islands—to which they assigned a freshly formed, patched-together command designated as the 29th Division. Many of these soldiers would be assigned to Iwo Jima. Navy forces on the island were encouraged to "cooperate" with the area-division commander. Neither the subtheater nor the division reflected inspired staff work. The critical difference would lie in the personality of the newly designated commander, Lt. Gen. Tadamichi Kuribayashi.

Kuribayashi may have been a stranger to the Americans in mid-1944, but by the following March certain Marine riflemen were calling him "the best damned general on this stinking island." Kuribayashi was fifty-three years old, tall and portly, a native of Nagano Prefecture in central Honshū, and a descendent of samurai ancestors. A 1914 graduate of the Military Academy, he served the ensuing thirty-one years as a cavalry officer. With the outbreak of war in Asia, Kuribayashi commanded a cavalry regiment in Manchuria, a brigade in China. He participated in the capture of Hong Kong in December 1941 as chief of staff, 23d Army. With the emperor's approval, he took command of the Imperial Guard Division in Tokyo. From this post in late May 1944 Prime Minister Hideki Tojo selected him to command the suddenly vital island called Iwo Jima (literally "Sulfur Island" in Japanese).

Kuribayashi's military record provides few clues as to what made him such a formidable commander at Iwo Jima. His experience commanding men in combat represents an asset, but this pales against the combat record of his contemporaries who fought in the tougher battles in Malaya, the Philippines, or New Guinea. He was an unreconstructed cavalryman, refusing to "transition" into tanks and armored warfare, and therefore of diminishing tactical value to his service. As a colonel assigned to the Ministry of the Army in 1937, for example, he served as head of equestrian affairs in the logistics branch—more concerned with forage and farriers than the more central issues of war plans or mobilization.

Given this unremarkable record, it is no wonder American intelligence analysts failed to predict Kuribayashi's tactical brilliance. Iwo Jima somehow invoked a metamorphosis for Kuribayashi. In his final command he proved to be tough, cool-headed, pragmatic, innovative, and fearless—a warrior in the best definition of any nation's army. Holland Smith's grudging postwar assessment summed it all up: "Of all our adversaries in the Pacific, Kuribayashi was the most redoubtable."

General Kuribayashi came to Iwo Jima during the second week of June 1944 and found the small garrison ill-prepared for war, a hodgepodge of squabbling units at each other's throats. Several disasters occurred in short order. On 15 and 24 June, Rear Adm. Joseph J. "Jocko" Clark's fast carrier task group struck Iwo hard, sweeping away the inexperienced Japanese aircraft and bombing the island with impunity. Then during 4–5 July, American battleships and cruisers bombarded the island at leisure. Recorded one member of the Japanese garrison: "For two days we cowered like rats."

Relief came from an unexpected quarter. The U.S. decision to tackle the Palaus after the Marianas provided the Japanese a half-year grace period in which to fortify Iwo Jima. Kuribayashi took full advantage of this lull. With the fall of Saipan, IGHQ diverted the veteran 145th Infantry Regiment, earmarked to reinforce the Marianas, to Iwo Jima for duty. This was a windfall. Although numerically small, the ranks of the 145th were filled with men from Kagoshima, renowned fighters, commanded by Col. Masuo Ikeda. Kuribayashi would build his defense with this regiment at its core; he would die with Ikeda at his side. In early August, Rear Adm. Toshinosuke Ichimaru reported to Iwo for duty, a legendary naval aviator, long crippled, hungry for a fight. The next week Maj. Gen. Joichiro Sanada, operations chief of the Army General Staff, visited the island. Like Kuribayashi, he was appalled by the unpreparedness he saw. As he recorded in his diary, "Kuribayashi warns that if an American task force of the size of the July 4th fleet returns with a division and a half of troops he could sustain the defense for at best a week to ten days." Sanada had great influence in Tokyo. Soon, more troops, weapons, and ammo began flowing to Iwo Jima.

As Kuribayashi studied the topography of the Volcano and Bonin Islands, he concluded that Iwo Jima was the only one with the potential for a bomber strip. This would inevitably attract the Americans. Kuribayashi saw the paradox. Iwo Jima served only a limited tactical advantage to the Japanese as an early warning site and fighter-interceptor base. On the larger scale, the island was a strategic liability to the Japanese. American seizure of Iwo would be catastrophic to the Japanese war effort, bringing the home islands within range of medium bombers and fighter escorts to augment the B-29s. Sensing this, Kuribayashi spent weeks determining whether the Japanese would be better off simply blowing the island up—or at least sinking the central plateau into the sea. Some demolition experts came down from Tokyo, examined the volcanic rock, and said it could not be done.

Kuribayashi then took a long look at the defensive tactics recently employed by Japanese commanders defending Biak, Peleliu, Angaur, and Luzon. In each case the Japanese provided only minimal resistance at the point of landing but established interior positions in depth. While the Americans at Peleliu had scoffed at these tactics as "the Cornered Rat defense," their ultimate victory had come only at a very high cost in casualties and after an unexpectedly protracted campaign. Kuribayashi concluded that this was the best he could expect to accomplish: fortify the interior of the island so expertly that the Americans would take exorbitant casualties and perhaps lose heart. If all else failed, a prolonged and lethal defense of Iwo Jima might make the American public have second thoughts about invading the Japanese home islands.

Kuribayashi then announced his decisions. He would establish the headquarters of his 109th Division on Iwo Jima, not on the larger, safer, more comfortable island of Chichi Jima. He ordered the evacuation of all civilians from the island, including the "comfort girls." He abolished all booze. He ordered all facilities moved underground. Finally, and most controversial of all, he stated his plan to concede the amphibious landing and instead concentrate his defenses in depth among the broken terrain of the central and northern highlands. Further, he forbade any large-scale banzai attacks. Counterattacks would only be launched by small units and for limited tactical objectives. He would make maximum use of the night, sending out "prowling wolves," small groups of marauders to gather intelligence, destroy enemy crew-served weapons, or kill sentries.

Kuribayashi's difficulties in enforcing these unpopular decisions were compounded by the duality in service command lines that continued to fracture Japanese operations. He was clearly senior to Admiral Ichimaru (and the two actually got along well), but Ichimaru felt pressured by some of his own hot-headed officers and the Navy General Staff to argue for beachfront defenses. Against his better judgment Kuribayashi agreed to a compromise. He would permit construction of 135 pillboxes along the obvious landing beaches in the southern part of the island. The project took three months; the Americans would overrun all of them in the battle's first three hours.

General Sanada continued to ramrod support for Kuribayashi from the Army General Staff. Surprisingly, Kuribayashi did not ask for more troops. The earlier arrival of the 26th Tank Regiment commanded by the colorful Baron Takeichi Nishi, added to Ikeda's troops, gave Kuribayashi a solid core of veterans. Many of the newly formed battalions in the 2d Independent Mixed Brigade contained little more than raw recruits, more liabilities than assets. Kuribayashi wanted neither to saturate his defenses nor to overwhelm the island's meager water supplies. He had the guns and the shooters; now he needed fortification specialists. Sanada quickly provided mining engineers, quarry experts, fortress units, and labor battalions. The island's volcanic ash lent itself to efficient cement mix; its soft interior rock yielded to thousands of picks and spades.

Kuribayashi kept his training simple: antitank defenses, night infiltrations, marksmanship. Each man's defensive position was to be his grave, his military shrine. Knowing how isolated the battlefield would quickly

From Peleliu on, Japanese island commanders placed top priority on training their troops in antitank tactics. Their Model 1 (1941) 47-mm gun, small enough to be manhandled quickly in and out of caves, proved heavy enough to knock out U.S. medium tanks at ranges up to a thousand yards, especially against the Sherman tank's lightly armored sides and rear. *(Larry E. Klatt)*

become, the general posted "Courageous Battle Vows" in each bunker. If each man took ten American lives for his own, he told them, Japan could win a glorious victory.

An assessment of the Japanese garrison on the eve of the battle reveals a checkered mix of strengths and weaknesses. On the plus side, Kuribayashi had transformed the divided, dispirited garrison into a force imbued with readiness to remain in prepared positions and inflict maximum casualties. The borrowed engineers had created a masterpiece of defensive works, particularly in the main belt that crossed the island just north of the second airfield. In the 145th Infantry Regiment, the 26th Tank Regiment, and some of the artillery units Kuribayashi had first-rate troops, a credit to any armed force. In Col. Chosaku Kaido, commanding the composite artillery brigade, Kuribayashi had one of the finest gunners in the empire.

On the negative side, the 109th Division was hardly one of the empire's best—certainly not one of the vaunted Manchukuoan outfits from the Kwantung Army. Moreover, Kuribayashi did not even have his entire division at hand. His second independent mixed brigade was scattered to the north, defending places like Chichi Jima and Marcus Island. Nor could the 109th Division ever expect to match in open combat the task organization, firepower, and unit integrity of any one of the three U.S. Marine Corps divisions steaming toward Iwo. Further, while Kuribayashi had been able to stockpile plenty of food and weapons in advance, he did not have that luxury in terms of artillery, mortar, and rocket ammunition. Only on D-Day would his gunners enjoy unrestricted firing. The very proliferation of types and calibers of major weapons would further complicate ammunition supply and distribution. Some weapons were simply inappropriate. The enormous Japanese 320-mm spigot mortars would scare hell out of the Marines, but their 675-pound shells would often prove more hazardous to the handling crews; the launchers had an operating life of only five to six rounds.

Kuribayashi seemed to accept all this. When Japanese scout planes reported the departure of hundreds of American ships from Ulithi and Saipan on 13 February, the general ordered his men into their final bunkers and moved into his command post in the Motoyama highlands. "I pray for a heroic fight," he said.

Kelly Turner's joint expeditionary force approached Iwo Jima with 495 ships—including 125 amphibians and 75 seagoing landing craft—a force ten times the size he had led against Guadalcanal thirty months earlier. Only one useful piece of intelligence had filtered to the landing force from the unsavory Peleliu experience. A captured Japanese message from Peleliu recommended that drums of fuel be placed along the obvious landing beaches for remote ignition during the height of the American's ship-to-shore assault. The latest aerial photos of Iwo showed a suspicious line of fifty-five-gallon drums positioned at close intervals along the beaches. Schmidt's Marines in the first waves would therefore land wearing fire-retardant grease on their exposed skin.

Holland Smith and Harry Schmidt were more concerned with an acrimonious dispute with the Navy over the extent of preliminary bombardment allotted to Iwo. The Marines, sensing the difficulty of seizing this godforsaken rock, asked for ten days—but got three. The Navy saw a greater need to orchestrate tactical surprise, coordinate the bombardment with strikes against Honshū by Mitscher's fast carriers, and guard against an incursion by the remnants of the Combined Fleet. Logistic restraints also served to limit bombardment. The Pacific Fleet had not yet mastered the art of underway replenishment of major-caliber ammunition (8-inch and larger); those ships would have to retire to a distant anchorage to rearm for any prolonged bombardment. There was also concern for conserving ammunition for the pending, larger invasion of Okinawa. The arguments became rancorous. Blandy's gunships would deliver four times

The maestro. Lt. Gen. Holland M. "Howlin' Mad" Smith, USMC *(foreground),* **surveys storm damage to landing craft on Iwo Jima's steep beaches. No one contributed more to the development of U.S. amphibious assault prowess than Smith, especially during the critical period 1938 to 1944.** *(U.S. Naval Institute)*

the shelling Tarawa received and one and a half times the prep fires at Saipan. Yet the Marines argued that prolonged, deliberate fire—repeated hits on hard targets—was more critical than gross tonnage delivered.

There is little doubt that a greater preliminary bombardment would have saved Marine lives. The heart of Kuribayashi's defenses in the Motoyama plateau remained essentially unscathed during the three days before D-Day. On the other hand, most of Kuribayashi's emplacements in the north were so skillfully camouflaged, his men so deeply entrenched, that they probably would have remained impervious to any extended shelling. They had already withstood ten weeks of daily pounding by Seventh Air Force bombers without substantial damage. Suspending the naval shelling each night provided further respite to the subterranean garrison. As 1st Lt. Kinryu Sugihara, a member of the 11th Antitank Battalion on Iwo Jima, recorded in his diary for the night of 17 February: "Our units are taking advantage of the slackening of the bombardment during the night and are strengthening their positions, repairing fortifications, and hauling food and ammunition to the different positions. They worked all night in preparation for tomorrow."

Landing force planners knew in advance that Iwo's steep beach and loose volcanic sand would complicate the movement of vehicles from landing craft to the high-water mark. Admiral Hill and his chief beachmaster, Capt. Carl E. "Squeaky" Anderson, had worked furiously to devise means of improving beach trafficability. Bulldozers would be in high demand along the beach on D-Day; Hill and Anderson fabricated armored shields to protect the operators from sniper fire. The two officers also developed sand sleds and "Marston matting," folded, hinged metal mats intended to surface an expeditionary airfield, modified so they could be payed out from a tracked vehicle to lay an improvised "road" over the soft sand as a beach exit. Hill said the task force brought eight miles of hinged matting to Iwo.

Marine planners looked beyond the beach, noting the heights on either flank, sensing how Mount Suribachi and the Rock Quarry would afford the enemy deadly fields of fire. Said Maj. Gen. Clifton B. Cates, commanding the 4th Marine Division and a veteran of Belleau Wood, Guadalcanal, and Tinian: "I didn't like the idea of landing in a bight, where you were flanked on both sides."

Iwo Jima would be the fourth assault landing in thirteen months for the 4th Marine Division. The 3d Division, scheduled initially in a reserve role, had defeated the Japanese at Bougainville and Guam. The 5th Division was brand new, but former Raiders and paratroopers with combat experience in the Solomons led most of its rifle companies. Moreover, the training focus for each division was right on target for Iwo: small-unit tactics, assaults on fortified positions, coordinated use of combined arms. Collectively, this was a tough, combat-savvy landing force, as lethal an amphibious spearhead as the Marine Corps ever fielded.

Embarking the huge landing force uncovered frustrating problems. The newly modified M4A3 Sherman tanks were now too heavy to be safely transported in standard LCM-3 tank lighters and had to be loaded, five at a time, on medium landing ships (LSMs), which in turn skewed landing plans at the last minute. Commanders and cannoneers worried about their 105-mm howitzers preloaded in DUKWs. Iwo was known to have rough

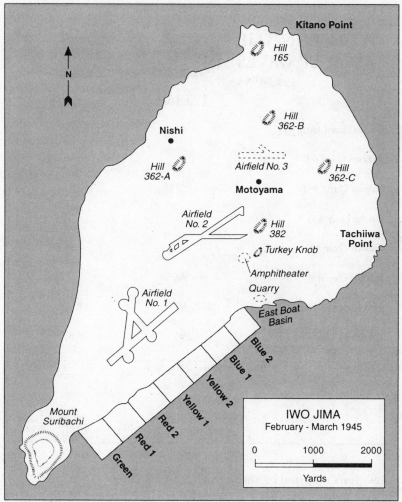

Mary Craddock Hoffman

seas. The weight of the field piece equaled the DUKW's maximum payload; there would be precious little freeboard. Amphibious rehearsals reflected the recurring problem of geographic separation of key task groups. Most amphibian tractor (LVT) units did not get the chance to rehearse with the LSTs, many of them new to the ship-to-shore business.

Although the Japanese knew of their approach, the Fifth Fleet quickly established near-total dominance over the air, sea, and underwater approaches to the island. The most spectacular exchange of heavy gunfire

LVTs IN THE ASSAULT WAVES
1942-1945

	LVT (A)s	LVTs
Guadalcanal (Aug 42)	0	0
Tarawa (Nov 43)	0	87
Saipan (June 44)	138*	594*
Guam (July 44)	75	381
Tinian (July 44)	66*	453*
Peleliu (Sep 44)	72	223
Iwo Jima (Feb 45)	68	380
Okinawa (Apr 45)	290*	872*

*Includes US Army vehicles by type

at Iwo Jima occurred on the morning of 17 February, D-minus-2, during the conduct of the beach reconnaissance by Navy and Marine swimmers. These were men of the Navy Combat Demolitions Unit, augmented by reconnaissance Marines, collectively called "frogmen" (also, "half fish, half crazy"). Many were veterans of stealthy reconnaissance missions in the Marshalls, Marianas, and Palaus, but there would be nothing covert about this operation: a direct approach into "the bight" in broad daylight. This was a mission of tremendous risk, reflecting the critical shortage of information on the landing beaches.

A dozen LCI-G gunboats comprised the first line of fire support for the frogmen, closely followed by several destroyers. The sight of this miniarmada approaching the most obvious beach made General Kuribayashi believe the main landing was at hand, and he authorized his local commanders to open fire from their concealed coast-defense batteries along the eastern slopes of Suribachi and the Rock Quarry. The tiny LCI-Gs were shot to pieces: one sank, all others badly damaged, two hundred casualties.

To the rescue came a dozen destroyers and cruisers, moving close ashore to engage the enemy batteries one-on-one, both sides catching hell and delivering same. Incredibly, the swimmers accomplished their mission despite the cannonade, even braving Japanese rifle fire to gather samples of beach sand.* They found only one mine, no obstacles, no natural barriers to the approach—then retracted, bearing their precious vials of sand, with the loss of a single man.

The swimmer mission, accomplished at great risk and acceptable cost, thus served the more valuable function as an inadvertent amphibious feint, causing the enemy to play his hand prematurely. Kuribayashi, facing his first amphibious landing, had even radioed Tokyo that his forces had repulsed a major landing. But Blandy's gun crews had a field day the next thirty-six hours, systematically taking out the big guns overlooking the beaches that the Japanese had unwisely revealed. This factor, a tactical disaster for the Japanese—and Kuribayashi's only major mistake of the battle—surely saved a thousand American lives on D-Day morning.

Kelly Turner hoped for three days of good weather in which to conduct the landing. He got less than one. D-Day morning was nigh perfect. At 0645 Turner signaled "land the landing force." The now-familiar choreography began, the process that proved so difficult at Tulagi or Tarawa now ticking like a Swiss clock. To some observers the ship-to-shore assault against Iwo Jima's southeast coast resembled the third day at Gettysburg: hundreds of thousands of men of both sides watching the panorama of ten thousand shock troops in disciplined alignment charging the center. "The landing was a magnificent sight to see," said Marine lieutenant colonel Robert H. Williams. "So the real landing has come at last!" recorded Lieutenant Sugihara, as he cleansed himself for death in combat.

Mitscher's Task Force 58 returned from raiding Honshū in time to add to the fireworks. Among other assets, this provided the landing force with the temporary support of eight carrier-based Marine fighter squadrons, each well trained in close air support. The troops cheered as the Corsairs with USMC markings roared down the beaches ahead of the landing.

* Fine-grained sand would indicate favorable trafficability; these samples contained large grains, confirming the problems to be encountered on D-Day.

The ship-to-shore movement at Tarawa fifteen months earlier had featured a convoluted ten-mile trek that took hours and left the LVTs dangerously low on fuel. Worse, the only senior control officer in the lagoon was the skipper of the minesweeper marking the line of departure, a brave man but inexperienced in amphibious execution and unassisted by any Marines. At Iwo Jima, the LVTs had an easy thirty-minute run to the beach, and the assistant commanders of the assault divisions, both brigadier generals, took station on the control vessels marking each end of the line of departure.

Nor were there any deadly lapses in naval gunfire support as the assault waves of LVTs approached the beach. Navy and Marine fighters made one final screeching sweep along the coastline, then the ships commenced a carefully regulated "rolling barrage" to provide a moving curtain of heavy explosives just ahead of the disembarking troops. This complex procedure worked to perfection, reflecting the cumulative experience and painstaking planning of the amphibious task force. The torrent of explosives vaporized the worrisome line of fuel drums and demolished many of the Imperial Navy's vaunted gun positions. A Japanese naval officer observing all this from a cave on Mount Suribachi could hardly believe his eyes: "At nine o'clock in the morning several hundred landing craft with amphibious tanks in the lead rushed ashore like an enormous tidal wave."

This was the ultimate storm landing of the Pacific War. Okinawa would be bigger but unopposed. At Iwo Jima eight thousand Marines raced ashore in the first few minutes. Within ninety minutes some of these men cut the lower part of the island in two. By dusk, when Lieutenant Sugihara guessed that "enemy strength [ashore] is approximately two thousand men and eighty tanks," General Schmidt had actually landed thirty thousand men, the better part of two divisions, each with their own tank battalions and most of their organic field artillery. There would still be hell to pay, but the V Amphibious Corps had stormed ashore in great strength and good order. Kuribayashi was already in grave danger—abruptly he was outnumbered.

The first enemy encountered by the landing force on Iwo Jima was the island's damnable hydrography. Even in mild weather the steep beach featured a constantly plunging surf and a vicious undertow. Time and again the surf would first broach, then shatter the Higgins boats, reducing them to shards and splinters, further fouling a beach that soon resembled a demolition yard. For those vehicles that made it ashore, trafficability proved worse than expected. "Squeaky" Anderson's experimental Marston matting worked well at first but soon became chewed to pieces by hundreds of tracked vehicles desperately trying to negotiate the steep terraces under fire. And while the Japanese had not mined the precipitous offshore approaches, they had spared no effort in mining beach exits. Many Sherman tanks and LVTs came to grief in a deadly field of horned antitank mines, inverted depth charges, and naval torpedoes buried vertically beneath pressure detonators.

Like Colonel Nakagawa at Peleliu, Kuribayashi decided to expend one infantry battalion in the vicinity of the beaches to disrupt the landings. The Americans' "rolling barrage" made mincemeat out of most of these men, but those who survived maintained a hot fire. "Crossing that second terrace the fire from automatic weapons was coming from all over," said one Marine battalion commander. "You could've held up a cigarette and lit it on the stuff going by." This was simply the beginning.

While the assault forces maneuvered in the soft sand to overcome the local defenders they failed to notice an almost imperceptible stirring among the rocks and crevices of the interior highlands. With grim anticipation, Kuribayashi's gunners began unmasking their big weapons—the heavy artillery, giant mortars, and naval rockets held under tight discipline for this precise moment. Kuribayashi had patiently waited until the beaches and terraces were clogged with troops and material. His gun crews knew the range and deflection to each preregistered target. At Kuribayashi's signal, these hundreds of weapons opened fire. It was shortly after 1015.

The ensuing bombardment was as deadly and terrifying as any of the Marines had ever experienced. There seemed to be no cover at all. Explosions blanketed every corner of the three-thousand-yard beachfront. Large-caliber coast-defense guns and antiaircraft guns firing horizontally added their deadly scissors of direct fire from high ground on both flanks. Landing force casualties mounted appallingly. As the Japanese fire reached a crescendo, the four assault regiments radioed dire reports to the flagship:

1036: (From 25th Marines): "Catching all hell from the quarry. Heavy mortar fire."

1039: (From 23d Marines): "Taking heavy casualties and can't move. Mortars killing us."

1042: (From 27th Marines): "All units pinned down by artillery and mortars. Casualties heavy."

1046: (From 28th Marines): "Taking heavy fire, forward movement stopped. Machine gun and artillery fire heaviest ever seen."

Veteran combat correspondent Robert Sherrod spent D-Day morning with General Cates on the troop transport *Bayfield,* flagship for the 4th

Marine Division. Cates watched the fighting ashore through binoculars and agonized over the pounding of his troops. "Look at that goddamned murderous fire on our Yellow beaches," he exclaimed to Sherrod, adding, "There goes another hit square on a tank—burned him up!"

The landing force suffered and bled but did not panic. The profusion of combat veterans in the ranks helped steady the rookies. Communications remained effective. Keen-eyed aerial observers spotted some of the now-exposed Japanese gun positions and directed naval gunfire effectively. Carrier planes swooped in low to drop napalm canisters. The heavy Japanese fire would continue to take an awful toll throughout the first day and night, but it would never again be so murderous as that first unholy hour.

Robert Sherrod went ashore in the late afternoon, but even his previous experiences during D-Day landings with the Marines at Tarawa and Saipan had not prepared him for the carnage he encountered. "Whether the dead were Japs or Americans, they had one thing in common," he reported, "they had died with the greatest possible violence. Nowhere in the Pacific War had I seen such badly mangled bodies. Many were cut squarely in half. Legs and arms lay fifty feet from the nearest cluster of dead."

By day's end General Schmidt counted twenty-four hundred casualties among the landing force, a stiff price for the beachhead—comparable to losses of the U.S. V Corps at Normandy's Omaha Beach on D-Day—but still proportionally better than the first night at either Tarawa or Saipan. Schmidt began to sense he was facing a formidable opponent, although it would be days before his staff could confirm that Kuribayashi had in fact been present on Iwo Jima from the start.

Bad weather the next day severely hampered unloading operations. Even the larger landing ships, LSTs and LSMs, had difficulty maintaining position when beached. Stern anchors rarely held. Forward cables to "deadmen" (usually wrecked tanks or LVTs on the beach) snapped under the strain. Smaller craft played hell getting ashore. One artillery battalion commander, Lt. Col. Carl A. Youngdale, watched in helpless horror as twelve of his fourteen 105-mm guns went down in deep water, one by one, when their DUKWs swamped in the choppy seas.

Schmidt's desire to land a regimental combat team from the 3d Marine Division, the corps reserve, on D+1 could not be met. The troops debarked in a series of hair-raising net-to-boat episodes, then circled for hours, desperately seasick, waiting for the pounding surf to abate on the beach. It never did. The troops had to struggle back on board their transports and wait another day. Hill's efforts to land heavy equipment by pontoon causeway sections also proved disastrous.

At this point, the inexperience of some of the LST crews and the absence of any opportunity to rehearse with LVT and DUKW units proved costly. Because of the high surf, wounded Marines could only be evacuated from the island during the first several days by these amphibian vehicles, often just at dusk to avoid enemy fire. All too frequently, however, the green LSTs refused to accommodate any unfamiliar craft appearing close aboard out of the darkness. When pleas and curses failed to work, the small vehicles could only move further out to sea in hopes of finding a more receptive ship. Too often this resulted in LVTs and DUKWs foundering in high seas at night, usually with a dozen wounded men on board. The landing force lost eighty-eight LVTs to noncombat sinkings during the campaign, most of them under such circumstances during the confusion of the first several nights.

Kelly Turner's naval officers at Iwo Jima included an unusually high percentage of newcomers to combat. While in due time they would become seasoned, valuable veterans, their first days were filled with a mixture of awe and distress. Future Hollywood producer David H. Susskind recorded his emotions on D-Day at Iwo Jima as a fresh-caught lieutenant on board the troop transport *Mellette:* "Iwo Jima was not all flaming spectacle and harrowing death. For this ship and this crew—for me—it was the end of one world and the beginning of the other. . . . We were 'young-in-war' and everything ahead would be the first for most of us."

Fully effective naval support for the Marines ashore remained hostage to the treacherous surf and the looming presence of Japanese-held Mount Suribachi. The 556-foot volcanic cone—honeycombed with its Fukkaku caves and firing ports—became the objective of the 28th Marines. Kuribayashi knew his southern sector could not hold Suribachi-yama indefinitely, but he expected them to resist for two weeks. He was stunned when the Marine regiment took the pinnacle in four days. "Hot damn!" exclaimed Navy pilot David Conroy over the air control net as he flew past the summit and saw the first flag go up. "All hands look at Suribachi!" bellowed "Squeaky" Anderson over his beachmaster's bullhorn. "There goes our flag!"

The Suribachi flag-raisings have taken on a life of their own in the ensuing half century—to the point that many modern readers express surprise that the events occurred on the battle's fourth day, not the thirty-sixth.

Seizing Suribachi was essential to prosecuting the rest of the battle and enabling the logisticians to get on with the mammoth buildup ashore, but the spectacular flag-raisings signaled "the end of the beginning"— hardly the end of the battle. Ahead lay a full month of combat as savage and relentless as the Marines would ever face.

Kuribayashi rued the precipitate loss of the highest peak on the island, but he knew the Americans had yet to encounter his real defensive masterpiece in the central highlands. That battle commenced directly with three Marine divisions attacking abreast. Each would pay dearly for every yard, every redoubt. Throughout this period the Marines rarely saw a live Japanese soldier in the daytime. Nights were marked by desperate struggles between small groups of shadowy men slashing and stabbing with knives and bayonets. The VAC would average a thousand casualties a day during the first three weeks of the assault.

Nowhere was the Navy's role in the Iwo Jima battle more crucial than in sustained medical support. Surgical teams operated around the clock in field hospitals barely two miles behind the lines. A dozen women, Navy flight nurses, served aboard DC-3s making daily runs from Guam to Iwo and back during the fighting to help evacuate nearly twenty-five hundred critically wounded men. Former flight nurse Norma Crotty recalls holding many a desperate hand on the return flights to Guam, murmuring, "Hold on, son, just hold on." The DC-3s inbound to Iwo also delivered priceless cases of whole blood to battlefield surgeons. And every boat or LVT or DUKW that delivered supplies ashore returned to hospital ships at sea with another load of wounded Marines.

This was an extremely costly battle for the surgeons and corpsmen who accompanied Marine units. Exactly 850 of these men were killed or wounded at Iwo Jima, twice the rate for bloody Saipan. The bond between Marines and their corpsmen was never more profound than during the protracted, point-blank combat on Iwo. The pressures on these young medical technicians were enormous. Corpsman Stanley Dabrowski recalls "being up to my elbows in grime, dirt, and blood, and you're constantly asking yourself, 'Am I doing the right thing? Am I doing enough?'" Four of the seven Congressional Medals of Honor awarded to Navy corpsmen during World War II originated at Iwo Jima.*

Kuribayashi's field medical service suffered by comparison. Often the only "cure" for a wounded Japanese was for his companions to leave him a

---

* Twenty-two Marines received the Medal of Honor for Iwo; half were awarded posthumously.

hand grenade with which to end it all. The subterranean caverns soon
filled with dead and dying men. And despite their "Courageous Battle
Vows," the Imperial troops failed to exact the ten-to-one kill ratio sought
by their commander. They died by the thousands, many sealed up in caves
and tunnels by armored bulldozers, or burned alive by flame-throwing
tanks.* They had not anticipated the Americans' proficiency in combined arms, small-unit leadership, field expedience—nor their undeniable individual courage. And nothing in the combat experience of
Kuribayashi or his other veterans had prepared them for the intensity of
American firepower, delivered day after day from ships, planes, artillery
pieces, and rocket trucks. "We need to reconsider the power of bombardment from ships," he telegraphed the chief of the general staff. "The
violence of the enemy's bombardments are far beyond description. . . .
The power of the American warships and aircraft makes every landing
operation possible to whatever beachhead they like."

With Suribachi in American hands, Admiral Hill opened up beaches
on both sides of the southern coast. The 3d Marine Division (less the 3d
Marines, withheld as Expeditionary Troops reserve in a controversial
decision by Holland Smith) streamed ashore and shouldered into line
between the 4th and 5th Divisions in the attack north.† Navy SeaBees
landed in force, an entire brigade of them, and began rebuilding Iwo's
vital airfields under scattered fire. Army antiaircraft units moved their
big guns ashore to provide a high-velocity land-based punch to counter
the expected air raids from the Japanese home islands. An Army Air
Forces P-51 Mustang fighter group flew ashore, providing superb close-
air support and a lethal interception force.

At Iwo Jima, however, the Fifth Fleet's picket screens and combat air
patrols experienced few difficulties in intercepting aerial counterattack-
ers. There were two exceptions. The night before D-Day a pair of Japanese bombers penetrated the task force and struck the transport *Blessman*.
Ironically, this was the mother ship for the Navy combat demolition
teams, the men who had just executed their bold mission so successfully

* The 4th and 5th Marine Divisions each deployed four Sherman tanks modified with the
"POA-CWS-H1" flamethrower mounted in the turret and fired through a salvaged 75-
mm gun tube. They could fire a 6 percent napalm solution eighty yards and proved invaluable in Iwo's "Jungle of Stone." All were hit; none were lost.

† Although pilloried by officers ashore for this decision, Smith probably made the right
choice here. As CG, Fleet Marine Force, Pacific, he well knew he would have to rebuild
these shattered forces quickly in time for the scheduled invasion of Kyūshū in November.
The 3d Marines would have been his nucleus.

along Iwo's beaches. The ship survived the attack—the bomb just missed the after hold where the frogmen stored their TNT—but the unit lost more of its members in this one fiery instant than the total of all their combat operations in the Pacific.

At twilight on D+2, a flight of fifty kamikaze planes penetrated the fleet screen. In desperate action that foreshadowed the Okinawan campaign the ships managed to down all fifty planes, but not before some crashed aboard the escort carrier *Bismarck Sea,* sinking her, and the old warhorse *Saratoga,* damaging her enough to send her back to Hawaii. There were no other breakdowns in air defense.

Japanese attempts at aerial resupply proved ludicrous. According to Imperial Navy chief petty officer Kei Kanai, one of the few Iwo survivors, a plane flew over Japanese positions in the north one night and dropped packages for the garrison—filled solely with bamboo spears.

Nor did the once-mighty Combined Fleet make any serious move toward disrupting the Iwo landing. In operational terms, the Japanese Navy's only contribution was the dispatch of several *kaitan* "human torpedoes" embarked on fleet submarines. Three of these subs left Kure for Iwo during 22–23 February, followed by two more on 2 March. None got through.

By 4 March, the end of the second week of fighting ashore, the Marines had suffered thirteen thousand casualties, and the end seemed nowhere in sight. Yet at that point the first crippled B-29 landed on Iwo's main runway, a great boost to American morale. Thirty-five more of the silver war birds, damaged in Tokyo raids, would land successfully on Iwo during the battle. The troops cheered each one. "We knew where they'd been!" said one rifleman.

This was the beginning of the end for the Japanese garrison. Unknown to the Marines, they had now pierced the main defensive belt, killed as many Japanese as their own casualty total, and forced Kuribayashi that very day to abandon his forward command post and seek shelter in a cave near Kitano Point, prepared to make his last stand. "Send me air and naval support and I will hold the island," he radioed Tokyo; "without these things I cannot hold." On the following day a heavy American bombardment killed Colonel Kaido in his artillery command post at Turkey Knob.

In Kuribayashi's absence from the central highlands, the infantry brigade commander in the eastern sector disobeyed his standing orders and launched an all-out, traditional banzai charge against the 4th

Marine Division. Many of these Marines were veterans of larger counterattacks at Saipan and Tinian; once again they stayed low, aimed carefully, and scored devastating hits against the charging Japanese, backlit
by a thousand flares. Morning revealed rows of dead Imperial troops,
fully eight hundred of them. The 4th Marine Division, their back-breaking
burden suddenly lightened by this turn of events, then made such rapid
progress they secured the entire coast in their sector in five days. The 3d
Marine Division, fighting ferociously, sent Schmidt a canteen of seawater from the northeast coast.

The next day, 17 March, the 5th Marine Division swept over Hill
165, trapping the remnants of Kuribayashi's forces in what would be
called "the Bloody Gorge." Colonel Ikeda burned his regimental colors.
Fleet Admiral Nimitz declared victory. Kuribayashi bade an emotional
farewell to the people of Japan. That evening Prime Minister Kuniaki
Koiso made an unprecedented announcement over Radio Tokyo to a
shocked nation: Iwo had fallen.

General Kuribayashi and several hundred survivors actually held out
another nine days, making the 5th Marine Division bleed for every bitter
yard in the Gorge. His body was never identified. Some survivors
claimed he led the final, savage, "all-out-attack" against the American
bivouac at airfield number 2 during the predawn of 26 March, the last
day of the battle. Whatever his final end, Kuribayashi fought a good
fight and died. So did 22,000 other Japanese. Yet Kuribayashi's imaginative and radical defensive plans achieved little more than inflicting
24,053 casualties upon the attacking Marines and prolonging the campaign for five weeks.

In the context of the great sweep of forces converging on Japan by the
spring of 1945, such heroic sacrifices stood for little. The Americans had
gained operational use of airfields on Japanese territory within the first
two weeks of the battle. Already Curtis LeMay's B-29s were enjoying an
elevenfold increase in bombing effectiveness; a total of 24,761 crewmen
from crippled bombers would owe their lives to the Marine seizure of
Iwo in the months ahead. And the Joint Chiefs' master plan remained
fully intact. Iwo Jima officially ended on 26 March. On that same date—
right on schedule—Raymond Spruance and Kelly Turner kicked off
Operation Iceberg in the waters off Okinawa.

Kuribayashi's principal contribution to the Pacific War was the por-
tent he provided the world of what to expect should the Japanese home
islands be invaded: savage, no-quarter fighting on a massive, protracted

scale. On the other hand, Iwo Jima's inexorable loss sobered the Japanese high command. The Americans had seized one of the most heavily defended islands in the world, conquered it in spite of the bravery and ingenuity of Kuribayashi and his men, and achieved this in the face of daunting losses. The Americans, it was quite clear, had the ways and means—and will—to inflict their storm landings against any defended shore.

Chapter Eight

Okinawa

Amphibious Capstone

The approaching landing waves possessed something of the color and pageantry of medieval warfare, advancing relentlessly with banners flying.

Commander, Task Force 54
Okinawa Action Report,
5 May 1945

The three-month-long battle of Okinawa covered a seven-hundred-mile arc from Formosa to Kyūshū and involved a million combatants—Americans, Japanese, British, and native Okinawans. With a magnitude that rivaled the Normandy invasion the previous June, the battle of Okinawa was the biggest and costliest single operation of the Pacific War.

Okinawa would become the U.S. Navy's greatest operational challenge: protecting an enormous amphibious task force in orbit around its beachhead against the ungodliest of furies, the Japanese kamikazes. Equally, Okinawa would test whether U.S. amphibious power projection had truly come of age—whether Americans in the Pacific Theater could execute a massive assault against a large, heavily defended landmass, integrate the capabilities of all services, fend off every imaginable form of counterattack, and maintain tactical momentum ashore.

Okinawa, the largest of the Ryukyu Islands, sits at the apex of a triangle almost equidistant to strategic areas. Kyūshū is 350 miles to the north;

Formosa 330 miles to the southwest; Shanghai 450 miles to the west. The island has a peaceful heritage, but geography ruled its destiny in 1945. Okinawa's proximity to Japan—well within medium bomber and fighter escort range—and its militarily useful ports, airfields, anchorages, and training areas made the skinny island an imperative objective for the Americans, eclipsing their earlier plans for the seizure of Formosa for that purpose.

As with Peleliu and Iwo Jima, the Japanese did little to fortify Okinawa until the shocking news of the fall of Saipan. At that point, IGHQ established a heavily armed field force on Okinawa, the 32d Army, and began to funnel trained components to it from Japan's great armed perimeter in China, Manchuria, or the home islands.*

Admiral Nimitz turned once again to his most veteran commanders to execute Operation Iceberg, the forcible seizure of Okinawa: Raymond Spruance to command the U.S. Fifth Fleet, Kelly Turner to command all amphibious forces under Spruance. But Turner's military counterpart would no longer be the familiar old Marine warhorse, Holland Smith. Iwo Jima had been "Howlin' Mad" Smith's last fight. Army lieutenant general Simon Bolivar Buckner Jr., the son of a Confederate general who fought against Ulysses S. Grant at Fort Donelson in the American Civil War, would command the newly created U.S Tenth Army, the first field army to arise in Nimitz's command.

Six veteran divisions—four Army, two Marine—would comprise Buckner's landing force, with a division from each service marked for reserve duty. Here was another indication of the growth of U.S. amphibious power in the Pacific. Earlier, the Americans had forcibly landed one infantry division at Guadalcanal, two each in the Gilberts, Marshalls, and Palaus, and three each at Saipan and Iwo. By spring 1945 Turner and Buckner could count on eight experienced divisions.

Buckner's Tenth Army had three major components. Army major general John R. Hodge commanded the XXIV Corps, comprised of the 7th, 77th, and 96th Infantry Divisions, with the 27th Infantry Division in floating reserve, and the 81st Infantry Division in area reserve.† Marine major general Roy S. Geiger, veteran of Guadalcanal, Guam, and Peleliu,

---

* On 29 June 1944, the USS *Sturgeon* torpedoed the transport *Toyama Maru* and sank her with the loss of fifty-six hundred troops of the 44th Independent Brigade, bound for Okinawa.

† XXIV Corps, reprieved at the last minute from the Palaus, had gained valuable amphibious campaign experience in Leyte under MacArthur.

commanded the III Amphibious Corps (IIIAC), comprised of the 1st and 6th Marine Divisions, with the 2d Marine Division in floating reserve. The third major component of Buckner's staff was the Tactical Air Force, commanded by Marine major general Francis P. Mulcahy.

The 1st Marine Division, now commanded by Maj. Gen. Pedro A. del Valle, had returned from Peleliu to "pitiful Pavuvu" in the Russell Islands to prepare for the next campaign. Del Valle, a consummate artillery officer who had proven his combat worth earlier at Guadalcanal, insisted upon tank-infantry training under the protective umbrella of supporting howitzer fires. The 6th Marine Division became the only division to be formed overseas in the war when Maj. Gen. Lemuel C. Shepherd activated the colors and assumed command in Guadalcanal in September 1944. The unit may have been new, but veterans of hard campaigning in the Solomons, Marshalls, and Marianas provided the grit and gristle of this enterprising outfit. Looking ahead to Okinawa, Shepherd emphasized tactical mobility, large-scale combined-arms operations, and combat in built-up areas.

The Marine divisions preparing to assault Okinawa experienced yet another organizational change, the fourth of the war. The overall size of each division increased from 17,465 to 19,176. This growth reflected the addition of an assault signal company, a rocket platoon (the "Buck Rogers Men"), a war dog platoon, and—significantly—a 55-man assault platoon in each regimental headquarters. The most timely weapons change occurred with the replacement of the 75-mm "half-tracks" with the newly developed M-7 105-mm self-propelled howitzers—four to each regiment. Purists in the artillery regiments tended to sniff at these weapons, deployed by the infantry not as massed howitzers but rather as direct-fire, open-sights "siege guns" against Okinawa's thousands of fortified caves, but the riflemen soon swore by them.

General Buckner assumed command of the Tenth Army in August 1944, the same time that Lt. Gen. Mitsuru Ushijima took command of the Japanese 32d Army on Okinawa. Ironically, both senior generals had commanded their respective national military academies, Buckner at West Point, Ushijima at Zama. Both would die in the battle, three days apart and within five miles of each other.

General Ushijima's 32d Army represented an amalgam of Manchurian-theater veterans, new recruits, and native Okinawan levees, reinforced by an unusual quantity of field artillery and heavy mortar units, originally destined for the Philippines. Imperial General Headquarters made one

critical mistake in their preparations for the coming invasion. Still unsure of
the main American thrust in November 1944, the high command stripped
Ushijima of his most valuable force, the veteran 9th Division, sending it
south to oblivion in Formosa. Ushijima could only shake his head at this
top-level folly and make the most of his remaining 110,000 troops.

Without the 9th Division, Ushijima had insufficient forces to guard
Okinawa's extended coastline. Instead, he would go to ground in the
broken jumble of ridges in the southern third of the sixty-mile-long
island, building a concentric ring of fortifications centered on the ancient
Ryukyuan fortress of Shuri Castle. While this meant yielding the critical
airfields of Kadena and Yontan along the East China Sea, Ushijima took
comfort in the fact that his fields of fire from the Shuri complex would
prevent American use of the port of Naha for any major buildup of combat power ashore.

Throughout the war the Americans failed to appreciate or anticipate the
digging ability of the common Japanese soldier. While not a factor at Betio
(shallow water table) or Saipan (beachfront defense philosophy), this
propensity for rapid burrowing underground would produce startling
results in the cave warfare battles that followed. At Okinawa, the 32d
Army achieved a masterpiece in less than seven months. Working entirely
with hand tools—there was not a single bulldozer on the island!—the garrison dug miles of underground fighting positions and "fire port caves," literally honeycombing southern Okinawa's ridges and draws. Staff officers
stocked each successive position with reserves of ammunition, food, water,
and medical supplies. Okinawa would be the supreme Fukkaku defense.

General Ushijima's objective became simply this: to engage the U.S.
landing force in a costly, protracted battle of attrition while Japanese air
power savaged the Fifth Fleet. The battle would thus feature the unique
integration of a near-passive island defense with a violent air offensive
using suicide tactics on a totally unprecedented scale.

American forces by now were familiar with the enemy's propensity for
individual suicide measures—kamikaze pilots in the Philippines, antishipping swimmers in the waters off Iwo Jima, "human bullet" antitank
demolitionists at Peleliu. These reappeared in large numbers during Okinawa. But Imperial General Headquarters introduced something terrify-
ingly new in the Ryukyus: the *kikusui*, the "floating chrysanthemum"
mass kamikaze flights, hundreds of suicidal planes, attacking in waves.
The Japanese would launch ten separate kikusui during the battle, always
in conjunction with conventional air strikes and often coordinated with

tactical offensives, like the massive ground counterattack during 12–13 April, or the sacrificial sortie of the battleship *Yamato*.

Surprisingly, for an operation preceded by near-continuous ULTRA decryption intercepts and aerial photography, U.S. intelligence failed to pinpoint either the location of Ushijima's major fortifications or his likely tactical intentions. Spruance, Turner, and Buckner anticipated a stiff defense of the western airfields and therefore stockpiled a huge amount of shells for the preliminary naval bombardment—at the considerable expense of the bombardment more critically needed at Iwo Jima a few weeks earlier. Assault troops in the 1st Marine Division were warned to expect "80–85 percent casualties."

The Tenth Army plan of attack called for a massive four-division assault over the Hagushi beaches (the Marines of IIIAC on the north, the soldiers of XXIV Corps on the south). Meanwhile, the 2d Marine Division with a separate naval task unit would endeavor to duplicate its successful amphibious feint off Tinian by demonstrating opposite the Minatoga beaches on Okinawa's southeast coast. Love-Day (selected from the existing phonetic alphabet in order to avoid confusion with Iwo Jima's D-Day) would occur on 1 April 1945. Hardly a man failed to comment on the obvious irony: it was April Fool's Day and Easter Sunday—which would prevail?

Rear Adm. W.H.P. Blandy would command the "amphibious support force" at Okinawa and be given a full eight days to execute his missions. This would forfeit surprise (although after Saipan that hardly mattered any more) in exchange for life-saving, time-saving preparation of the objective for the main assault.

Blandy deployed the 77th Division to launch Operation Iceberg with a skillful seizure of the Kerama-rettō Islands, a move that surprised the Japanese and produced great operational dividends. Admiral Turner now had a series of sheltered anchorages to repair ships damaged by Japanese kamikazes, already exacting a toll. The soldiers also captured the main cache of Japanese suicide boats, nearly three hundred power boats equipped with high-explosive rams intended to sink troop transports as they approached their assault anchorages. The Fleet Marine Force, Pacific, Force Reconnaissance ("Force Reconn") Battalion, commanded by Maj. James L. Jones, preceded each Army landing with stealthy nocturnal patrols and also scouted the barren sand spits of Keise Shima, seven miles off the southwest coast of Okinawa, finding them undefended. With that welcome news, the Army landed a battery of 155-mm

"Long Toms" on the islets, soon adding their high-velocity punch to the naval bombardment of Okinawa's main landing beaches.

The relative shallowness of the East China Sea afforded the Japanese the opportunity to sow an unusually high number of antishipping mines. One sank a U.S. destroyer in a matter of minutes. Blandy's minesweepers had their hands full clearing approach lanes to the Hagushi beaches. Navy underwater demolition teams, augmented by Marines, searched for man-made obstacles in the shallows. And in a full week of preliminary bombardment, the fire support ships delivered more than twenty-five thousand rounds of 5-inch shells or larger. The shelling produced more spectacle than destruction, however, because the invaders still believed Ushijima's forces would be arrayed around the beaches and airfields. A bombardment of that scale and duration would have saved many lives at Iwo Jima or Peleliu; at Okinawa this precious ordnance produced few tangible results.

Operation Iceberg nonetheless got off to a roaring start on Love-Day. The enormous armada, assembled from ports all over the Pacific, now stood coiled to project its landing force over the beach. This would be the ultimate seaborne forcible entry, the epitome of all the amphibious lessons learned so painstakingly from the crude beginnings at Guadalcanal and North Africa.

Kelly Turner made his final review of weather conditions, marveling at his recent good fortune. As at Iwo Jima, the amphibians would be blessed with good weather on the critical first day of the landing. Skies would be cloudy to clear, winds moderate east to northeast, a decent surf. At 0406 Turner announced, "land the landing force." Combat troops already manning the rails of their transports then witnessed an unforgettable display of naval power—the sustained bombardment by shells and rockets from hundreds of ships, alternating with formations of attack aircraft streaking low over the beaches, bombing and strafing at will. Spruance and Turner had concentrated thirteen hundred ships offshore—the sense of raw dominance was tangible.

Historians Jeter A. Isely and Philip A. Crowl captured the moment nicely in this passage written six years after Love-Day at Okinawa:

> Through the din and smoke, vessels carrying the first waves of landing troops slowly felt their way to their assigned positions, dropped their stern anchors, and came to rest fronting a shore line more than seven

miles in length. These were strange craft that would have shocked any honest sailor ten years before—ungainly, flat-bottomed, scrofulous with varicolored camouflage paint. They were the tank landing ships (LSTs) . . . with double doors fitted into their bows almost flush with the water line. As the doors swung open, out swarmed hordes of another singular craft, the tracked landing vehicle (LVT), one of the few truly amphibian vehicles of the war.

Turner confirmed H-Hour at 0830. Now came the turn of the 2d Marine Division and the ships of the diversionary force to decoy the Japanese with a feint landing on the opposite coast. The ersatz amphibious force steamed into position, launched LVTs and Higgins boats loaded conspicuously with combat-equipped Marines, then dispatched them toward Minatoga in seven waves. Paying careful attention to the clock, the fourth wave commander crossed the line of departure exactly at 0830, the time of the real H-Hour on the west coast. The landing craft then turned sharply away and returned to the transports, mission accomplished.

There is little doubt that the diversionary landing (and a repeat performance the following day) achieved its purpose. In fact, Ushijima retained frontline infantry and artillery units in the Minatoga area for weeks thereafter as a contingency against the secondary landing he fully anticipated.

Yet the deception proved too successful. Japanese air units, convinced that this was the main landing, vectored a flight of kamikazes against the small force, seriously damaging the transport *Hinsdale* and LST 844. The 3d Battalion, 2d Marines, and the 2d Amphibian Tractor Battalion suffered nearly fifty casualties; the two ships lost an equal number of sailors. Ironically, the division expected to have the least exposure in the L-Day battle lost more men than any other division in the Tenth Army that day.

On the southwest approaches, the main body experienced no such interference. An extensive coral reef provided an offshore barrier to the Hagushi beaches, but by 1945 reefs no longer posed a problem to the landing force. Unlike Tarawa, where the reef dominated the tactical development of the battle, at Okinawa General Buckner had more than 1,400 LVTs to transport his assault echelons from ship to shore without hesitation. These long lines of LVTs now extended nearly seven miles as they churned across the line of departure on the heels of 360 armored LVT-As, whose turret-mounted, snub-nosed 75-mm howitzers blasted away at the beach as they advanced the final four thousand yards.

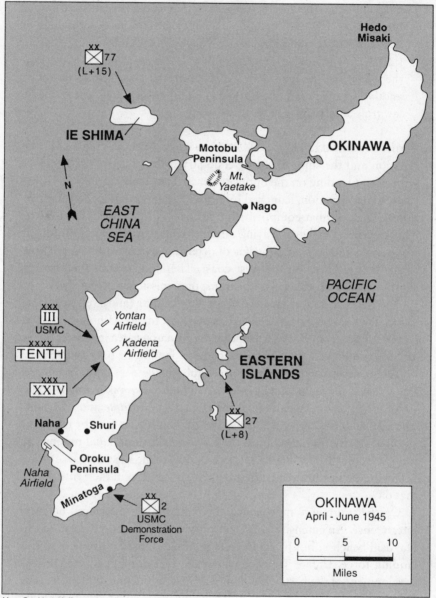

Hedo
Misaki

XX
77
(L+15)

IE SHIMA

OKINAWA

Motobu
Peninsula

Mt.
Yaetake

N

EAST
CHINA
SEA

Nago

PACIFIC
OCEAN

XXX
III
USMC

Yontan
Airfield

Kadena
Airfield

XXXX
TENTH

EASTERN
ISLANDS

XXX
XXIV

XX
27
(L+8)

Naha

Shuri

Oroku
Peninsula

Naha
Airfield

Minatoga

XX
2
USMC
Demonstration
Force

OKINAWA
April - June 1945

0   5   10

Miles

Mary Craddock Hoffman

Marine Corps LVTA-5 armored amphibians lead the massive assault ashore at Okinawa on Love-Day, 1 April 1945. The landing swept across a seven-mile beach and succeeded in putting sixty thousand men ashore by nightfall. *(U.S. Naval Institute)*

Behind the LVTs came nearly 700 DUKWs bearing the first of the direct support artillery battalions.

The horizon behind the DUKWs seemed filled with lines of landing boats. These would pause at the reef to marry with outward bound LVTs. Soldiers and Marines alike had rehearsed transfer line operations exhaustively. There would be no break in the assault's momentum this day.

"My amphibian tractor passed right between two huge battleships that were so close together I could have thrown a ball to the sailors," wrote Lieutenant Kennard, the forward observer from the 11th Marines. "You should have seen the way they cheered us Marines on as we went by."

The first assault wave touched down within three minutes of the designated H-Hour. Infantrymen stormed out of their LVTs, swarmed over the berms and seawalls, and entered the great unknown. The forcible invasion of Okinawa had begun. Within the first hour the Tenth Army projected sixteen thousand combat troops ashore—in order, unscathed, a cakewalk at last.

The morning continued to offer pleasant surprises to the invaders. They found no mines along the beaches, discovered the main bridge over the Bishi River still intact and—wonder of wonders—both airfields relatively undefended. The 6th Marine Division seized Yontan Airfield by 1300; the 7th Division had no problems securing nearby Kadena.

The rapid clearance of the immediate beaches by the assault units left plenty of room for follow-on forces, and the division commanders accelerated the landing of tanks, artillery battalions, and reserves. The mammoth buildup proceeded with only a few glitches. Four artillery pieces went down when their DUKWs foundered along the reef. Several Sherman tanks grounded on the reef. And the 3d Battalion, 1st Marines, had to spend an uncomfortable night in their boats when sufficient LVTs could not be mustered for transfer line operations along the reef at sunset.

These were minor inconveniences. Incredibly, by day's end Turner and Buckner had sixty thousand troops ashore, occupying an expanded beachhead eight miles long and two miles deep. Losses in the entire Tenth Army, even including the hard-luck 2d Marine Division, amounted to 28 killed, 104 wounded, and 27 missing on L-Day. This represented barely 10 percent of the casualties sustained the first day on Iwo Jima.

Nor did the momentum of the assault slow appreciably after the Tenth Army broke out of the beachhead. The 7th Division reached the east coast on the second day. On the third day, the 1st Marine Division seized the Katchin Peninsula, effectively cutting the island in two. Raymond Spruance exalted in this progress in a letter to his wife, then added—likely as a warning to himself: "But there are many thousands of Japs on Okinawa and undoubtedly they will put up a stiff fight and have to be killed."

The soldiers of XXIV Corps would be the first to encounter Ushijima's prepared defenses along the northern edge of the Shuri complex, but the first several days ashore seemed idyllic to the veteran landing force. Their immediate problems stemmed from a sluggish supply system, still being processed over the beach. The reef-side transfer line worked well for troops but poorly for cargo. While Navy beachmasters labored to construct an elaborate causeway to the reef, the 1st Marine Division demonstrated some of its amphibious logistics prowess learned at Peleliu. The Old Breed brought with them to Okinawa a number of swinging cranes mounted on powered causeways; these they launched on call, securing them along the seaward side of the reef. As boats would pull alongside in deep water the cranes would transfer nets full of combat cargo into the open hatches of a DUKW or LVT waiting on the shoreward side of the

This is just one corner of the logistical masterpiece under way along Okinawa's beaches to sustain the 180,000-man landing force of the U.S. Tenth Army in its protracted battle. *(U.S. Naval Institute)*

reef for the final run to the beach. This procedure worked so well that the Tenth Army made the division share these jury-rigged assets with the other units, a backhanded compliment.

Beach congestion also slowed the process. Both Marine divisions resorted to using their replacement drafts as shore party teams. The inexperience of these men in this unglamorous but vital work, combined with the constant call for groups as replacements, created turmoil—traffic mayhem, haphazard supply dump development, rampant pilferage. The rapidly advancing assault divisions had an unexpected and soon-critical need for motor transport vehicles and bulk fuel, but these proved slow to land and distribute. Okinawa's rudimentary road network further compounded the situation. In all, there were enough problems building up sustainability without the customary interference from enemy action or bad weather.

General Mulcahy did not hesitate to move the command post of the Tactical Air Force ashore as early as L+1. Operating from crude quarters between Yontan and Kadena, Mulcahy kept a close eye on the progress being made by the SeaBees (and Army and Marine engineers) in repairing both captured airfields. The first American aircraft, a Marine observation plane, landed on 2 April. Two days later the fields were ready to accept fighters. By the eighth day, Mulcahy could accommodate medium bombers and announced to the Fifth Fleet his assumption of control of all aircraft ashore. By then his fighter arm, the Air Defense Command, had been established ashore nearby under the leadership of Marine brigadier general William J. Wallace. With that, the F4U Corsairs of Col. John C. Munn's MAG-31 and Col. Ward E. Dickey's MAG-33 flew ashore from their escort carriers. Wallace immediately tasked them to fly Combat Air Patrols (CAP) over the fleet, already seriously embattled by massed kamikaze attacks.

Other air units poured ashore as well: air warning squadrons, night fighters, torpedo bombers, and an Army Air Forces fighter wing. While neither Yontan or Kadena were exactly safe havens—each received nightly artillery shelling and long-range bombing for the first full month ashore—the two fields remained in operation around the clock, an invaluable asset to both Spruance and Buckner.

General Geiger unleased the 6th Marine Division to sweep north in pursuit of a regiment of Japanese defenders. These were heady days for General Shepherd's troops: riflemen clustered topside on tanks and self-propelled guns, streaming northward against an elusive foe. Not since Tinian had Marines enjoyed such exhilarating mobility. By 7 April the division had seized Nago, the largest town in northern Okinawa, and the Navy obligingly swept for mines and employed UDT to breach obstacles in order to open the port for direct, seaborne delivery of critical supplies. The 22d Marines continued north through broken country, reaching the far end of the island on L+12, having covered fifty-five miles from the Hagushi landing beaches.

Things took a serious turn for the balance of the division when the two thousand members of the Kunigami Detachment went to ground in prepared positions atop twelve-hundred-foot Mount Yae Take on the Motobu Peninsula. Rooting out these tenacious soldiers took the division six days of stiff fighting and nearly a thousand casualties, but in this process the new unit came of age. Shepherd and his colorful operations officer, Lt. Col. Victor H. "Brute" Krulak, already demonstrated great prowess with supporting arms. On 17 April, as one result, the 29th Marines found their assault on the deadly mountain eased considerably by exceptional fire support from the 14-inch guns of the old battleship *Tennessee* and low-level, in-your-pocket bombing from the Corsairs of Marine Fighting Squadron 322.

During the battle for Motobu Peninsula, the 77th Division again displayed its amphibious virtuosity by landing on the island of Ie Shima to seize its airfields. Major Jones's Force Reconn Battalion helped pave the way by seizing a tiny islet six thousand yards from Ie Shima. Here the soldiers positioned a 105-mm battery as a fire support base to bolster the assault. The 77th needed plenty of fire support. Nearly five thousand Japanese defended the island. The soldiers overwhelmed them in six days of very hard fighting at a cost of eleven hundred casualties. One of these was the popular war correspondent Ernie Pyle, shot in the head by a Japanese Nambu gunner. Pyle was beloved of enlisted infantrymen in all theaters of World War II. Soldiers and Marines alike on Okinawa grieved his death. Six days earlier they had dealt with the news of Pres. Franklin D. Roosevelt's passing.

The war in southern Okinawa had already turned ugly. Within the first week the soldiers of the 7th and 96th Divisions had answered the riddle of "Where are the Japs?" By the second week, both Buckner and Hodge were painfully aware of Ushijima's intentions and the depth of his defensive positions. The Americans were entering killing zones of savage lethality.

These early U.S. assaults set the pattern to be encountered for the duration of the campaign in the south. Buckner committed the 27th Division, the XXIV Corps reserve, to the southern front, but it took time to readjust the front lines and build up adequate units of fire for field artillery to support the mammoth, three-division offensive the Tenth Army envisioned. After a week of intense staff activity (and troop inactivity), the offensive began on 19 April, preceded by the ungodliest preliminary bombardment of the ground war, a heralded "typhoon of steel" delivered by artillery, ships, and up to 650 aircraft. But the Japanese simply burrowed deeper into their underground fortifications and waited for the infernal pounding to cease. The XXIV Corps executed the assault with great valor, made some gains, then were thrown back with heavy casualties. The Japanese also exacted a heavy toll on U.S. tanks supporting the 27th Division in the fighting around Kakazu Ridge. In that battle, the Japanese separated the tanks from their supporting infantry by fire, then blew up twenty-two of the thirty Shermans with everything from mines to 47-mm guns to hand-delivered satchel charges.

The cakewalk had ended. Overcoming the concentric Japanese defenses around Shuri was going to require several divisions, massive firepower, and time—perhaps a very long time. Buckner needed immediate help. His operations officer directed General Geiger to provide the 1st Tank Battalion to the 27th Division. Neither Geiger nor del Valle would countenance the breakup of the 1st Marine Division's veteran tank-infantry team. Geiger appealed to Buckner to refrain from piecemeal commitment of his Marines. Buckner agreed, then ordered Geiger to provide del Valle's entire division.

During the next three days the 1st Marine Division moved south to relieve the now shot-up 27th Division on the western flank of the lines. The 6th Marine Division received a warning order to prepare for a similar mission in the south. The long battle for Okinawa's southern highlands had shifted into high gear.

Meanwhile, throughout April and with unprecedented ferocity, the Japanese kamikazes had punished the ships of the Fifth Fleet supporting the operation. So intense had the aerial battles become that the western beaches, so beguilingly harmless on L-Day, became positively deadly each night with the steady rain of shrapnel from thousands of antiaircraft guns in the fleet. Ashore or afloat, there were no more safe havens.

The swarming kamikazes had bedeviled the Fifth Fleet from the time the advance force first steamed into Ryukyuan waters. No one had imagined the devastation these inexperienced pilots in their ramshackle, one-way planes would create. Spruance's task forces, after all, contained the most effective combination of fighter-interceptors and antiaircraft batteries in the naval world. Indeed, only a few of the 2,373 kamikazes launched against the American fleet off Okinawa ever reached a target. But those "special attack unit" pilots who somehow survived the air and surface screens inflicted grievous damage. By the end of the campaign, the Fifth Fleet would suffer 34 ships and craft sunk, 368 damaged, and over 9,000 casualties—the greatest losses ever sustained by the U.S. Navy in a single battle.

The Japanese also attacked the Fifth Fleet off Okinawa with their newest weapon, the "Baku bomb," a manned, solid-fuel rocket packed with forty-four hundred pounds of explosives, launched at ships from the belly of a twin-engine bomber. The Baku bombs became in effect the first antiship guided missiles, screaming toward the target at an-unheard-of five hundred knots. One such weapon blew the destroyer *Manert L.*

Abele out of the water. Fortunately for dozens of other U.S. ships, most Bakus missed their targets, the missiles proving simply too fast for the inexperienced pilots to control in their few dizzy seconds of glory.

The ultimate suicide attack was the final sortie of the superbattleship *Yamato,* the last of the world's great dreadnoughts, whose feared 18.1-inch guns could outrange the biggest and newest U.S. battleships. Imperial General Headquarters dispatched *Yamato* on her last mission, a bizarre scheme by western standards—no air cover, a handful of surface escorts, only enough fuel for a one-way trip. She was to distract the American carriers to allow a simultaneous kikusui attack against the remainder of the fleet. Achieving this, *Yamato* would beach herself directly on Okinawa's west coast, using her big guns to shoot up the nearby amphibious ships and the landing force ashore.

In earlier years of the war the sortie of this mammoth warship would have caused consternation among the U.S. fleet protecting an amphibious beachhead. Not now. Patrolling U.S. submarines gave Spruance early warning of *Yamato*'s departure from Japanese waters. "Shall I take them or will you?" asked Marc Mitscher, commanding the fast carriers of Task Force 58. Interesting choice. Spruance knew his battleship force yearned for a surface engagement to avenge their losses at Pearl Harbor, but this was no time for sentiment. "You take them," he signaled. With that, Mitscher's Hellcats and Avengers roared aloft, intercepted *Yamato* a hundred miles from the beachhead and sank her with ridiculous ease. The cost: eight U.S. planes, a dozen men.

Another bizarre Japanese suicide mission proved more effective. On the night of 24–25 May, six transport planes loaded with *Giretsu,* Japanese paratroop commandos, approached the U.S. airbase at Yontan. Alert antiaircraft gunners flamed five. The surviving plane made a wheels-up, belly landing on the airstrip, discharging troops as she slid in a shower of sparks along the tarmac. The scrambling commandos dispersed in the darkness, blew up eight U.S. planes, damaged twice as many more, set fire to seventy thousand gallons of aviation gasoline, and raised hell throughout the night. Jittery aviation and security troops fired at shadows, injuring their own men more than the Japanese. It took twelve hours to hunt down and kill the last raider.

Spruance at sea and Mulcahy ashore exerted herculean efforts to reduce the effectiveness of this air offensive. American and British carriers struck the heavily camouflaged Japanese airfields in Kyūshū and Formosa time and again. Small landing parties of soldiers and Marines seized outlying islands in the Ryukyus to establish early warning and fighter direction outposts. And fighter planes from all three services took to the air to intercept the intermittent waves of enemy planes.

Not all the Japanese air strikes were kamikazes. An equal number of fighters and bombers accompanied each raid to guide the suiciders to their victims and attack other American targets by conventional means. Some of these included late-model fighters like the Nakajima "Frank." Deadly air-to-air duels took place over hundreds of miles of ocean expanse. The CAP planes ran a double risk. Dueling a Japanese fighter often took both planes within range of nervous shipboard AA gunners who sometimes unwittingly downed both antagonists.

Even without the mass kikusui attacks, small groups of suiciders appeared every night. The fleet seemed particularly vulnerable during the full moon. One naval officer described the nighttime raiders as "witches on broomsticks." More often than not, the victims of these nocturnal attacks were the "small boys," the picket ships and diminutive amphibs. Nineteen-year-old Signalman 3/c Nick Floros manned a 20-mm gun mount on tiny *LSM-120* one midnight when a kamikaze appeared "out of nowhere, gliding in low with its engine cut off—like a giant bat." The plane struck the adjacent LSM with a terrific explosion before anyone could fire a shot.

The Japanese high command, accepting as always the inflated claims of observers accompanying the kikusui attacks, believed their suicidal air offensive had fatally crippled the U.S. armada. This was wishful thinking. The kamikazes had stressed and battered the Fifth Fleet, but Spruance's force was simply too huge to be deterred. The fleet withstood the worst of these seemingly endless air attacks without for a moment forsaking its primary mission of supporting the amphibious assault on Okinawa. Naval gunfire support, for example, had never been so thoroughly effective, beginning with the thirty-eight hundred tons of explosive fire delivered on L-Day.

Similarly, even during the most intense of the kikusui attacks of 1–16 April, the fleet unloaded an astonishing 557,000 tons of supplies over the Hagushi beaches to support the Tenth Army, executed the division-level assault on Ie Shima, and cleared mines and obstacles under fire to open the port of Nago. The only direct effect the mass kamikaze raids ever had on the conduct of Tenth Army operations ashore was the sinking on 6 April of the ammunition ships *Logan Victory* and *Hobbs Victory*. The subsequent shortage of 105-mm and 155-mm artillery ammunition delayed

General Buckner's first great offensive against the outer Shuri defenses by about three days. In all respects, the Fifth Fleet deserved its media sobriquet as "the Fleet That Came to Stay."

But as April dragged toward May, and the Tenth Army seemed bogged down in unimaginative frontal attacks along the Shuri line, Spruance and Turner began to press Buckner to accelerate his tactics in order to decrease the vulnerability of the fleet. Admiral Nimitz, quite concerned, flew to Okinawa to counsel Buckner. "I'm losing a ship and a half each day out here," Nimitz said. "You've got to get this thing moving." Buckner bristled at this criticism of his tactics, and Nimitz threatened to relieve him—but nothing came of the confrontation.

The senior Marines urged Buckner to "play the amphib card," to execute a major landing on the southeast coast, preferably along the alternate beaches at Minatoga, in order to turn the Japanese right flank. Several Army generals, who already perceived what a meat-grinder the frontal assaults along the Shuri line would become, joined in this recommendation. The Commandant of the Marine Corps, Gen. Alexander A. Vandegrift, visited the island and seconded these suggestions to Buckner. After all, Vandegrift observed, Buckner still had control of the 2d Marine Division, a veteran amphibious outfit that had demonstrated effectively against the Minatoga beaches on L-Day. Buckner had subsequently returned the embarked division to Saipan to reduce its vulnerability to kamikaze attacks, but the unit still had their assigned ships at hand, still combat loaded.

General Buckner was a popular, competent commander, but his experience with amphibious warfare had been limited to observing the Aleutian landings. He also had a conservative nature. His staff warned of logistics problems involved in a second front. His intelligence advisers predicted stiff enemy resistance around Minatoga. Buckner had also heard enough of the costly Anzio operation in Italy to be leery of any landing executed too far from the main effort. He honestly believed the Japanese manning the Shuri defenses would soon crack under his massed firepower. Buckner therefore rejected the amphibious option out of hand.

Surprisingly, Nimitz and his operations officer, Rear Adm. Forrest Sherman, agreed. Not so Spruance and Turner or the Marines. As Spruance later admitted, "There are times when I get impatient for some of Holland Smith's drive." General Shepherd noted, "General Buckner did not cotton to amphibious operations." Even Col. Hiromichi Yahara, operations officer for General Ushijima, admitted under interrogation that he had been baffled by the American's adherence to a purely frontal assault from north to south. "The absence of a landing [in the south] puzzled the 32d Army Staff," he said, "particularly after the beginning of May when it became impossible to put up more than a token resistance in the south."

By then the 2d Marine Division was beginning to feel like a yo-yo. Lt. Col. Samuel Taxis, Division G-3, remained unforgiving of Buckner's decision. "I will always feel," he stated after the war, "that the Tenth Army should have been prepared the instant they found they were bogged down; they should have thrown a left hook down there in the southern beaches. . . . They had a hell of a powerful reinforced division, trained to a gnat's whisker."

Buckner stood by his decision. There would be no "left hook." Instead, both the 1st and the 6th Marine Divisions would slog toward Shuri as infantry divisions under the Tenth Army. The 2d Marine Division, less one reinforced regimental landing team (the 8th Marines), would languish back in Saipan. Then came Okinawa's incessant spring rains.

The bitterest fighting of the campaign took place within an extremely compressed battlefield. The linear distance from Yonabaru on the east coast to the bridge over the Asa River above Naha on the opposite side of the island measured barely nine thousand yards. By 8 May General Buckner had four divisions on this line: two Army divisions on the east, two Marine divisions on the west. Each division would fight its own desperate, costly battles against disciplined Japanese soldiers defending elaborately fortified terrain features. The funneling effects of the region's cliffs and draws reduced most attacks to brutal frontal assaults by fully exposed tank-infantry-engineer teams. Tactical efforts to conquer features like the Awacha Pocket, Conical Hill, Wana Draw, or the Sugar Loaf complex were each protracted, point-blank, bloody battles fought under unspeakable conditions of mud, filth, and death.

General Buckner captured the fancy of the media with his metaphor about the "blowtorch and corkscrew" tactics needed for effective cave warfare, but this was simply stating the obvious to the Army veterans of Biak and the Marine veterans of Peleliu. Flamethrowers represented the blowtorch, demolitions the corkscrew—but both weapons had to be delivered from close range by tanks and their exposed riflemen.

The nature of this deliberate attrition warfare made Okinawa the biggest battle of the war for artillery outfits. Tenth Army artillery units

The Okinawa campaign finally brought Marine Corps aviation and ground units into synchronized alignment. Here a Landing Force Air Support Control Unit operations officer briefs pilots of a TBM squadron on a bombing mission in support of the III Amphibious Corps. *(U.S. Marine Corps)*

would fire 2,046,930 rounds down range—in addition to 707,500 rockets, mortars, and shells of 5-inch or larger from naval gunfire support. Marine lieutenant colonel Frederick P. Henderson described this combination of fire support: "Not many people realize that the artillery in Tenth Army, plus the LVT-As and naval gunfire equivalents, gave us a guns-per-mile-of-front ratio on Okinawa that was higher than any U.S. effort in World War II, similar to the Russian front."

The landing force also made great strides toward refining supporting arms coordination during the battle. Commanders established Target Information Centers (TICs) at every level from Tenth Army down to battalion. Each TIC provided a centralized target information and weapons assignment system responsive to both assigned targets and targets of opportunity. Finally, all three component liaison officers—artillery, air, and naval gunfire—were aligned with target intelligence information officers. Simple as it may sound, it took virtually the entire war to work out such an arrangement.

Close air support coordination also greatly improved in this battle. Air liaison parties accompanied frontline divisions to request close air support and direct (but not *control*—the front was too narrow) aircraft to the target. Coordination of lower-echelon air requests became the province of three Marine Landing Force Air Support Control Units, one representing Tenth Army to the fleet commander, the others responsive to the Army XXIV Corps and IIIAC. This technique further refined the experiments instigated a few weeks earlier at Iwo Jima. In most cases, close air support to the infantry proved exceptionally effective. Some units reported prompt, safe delivery of ordnance on target within a hundred yards. In other instances there were inordinate delays or mind-numbing accidents, usually where the front lines were too intermingled to distinguish the muddy antagonists from the air.

Once again the fragile little observation "Grasshoppers" proved their great value, flying 3,486 missions of artillery spotting, photoreconnaissance, and medical evacuation.[*] One senior artillery officer described the VMO (observation) pilots as "the unsung heroes of Marine aviation. . . . Often they would fly past cave openings at the same level so they could look in and see if there was a gun there." Colonel Yahara complained that his artillery units knew from bitter experience that the presence of an improbable Piper Cub overhead presaged quick retribution for any Japanese gun that fired.

In sum, each supporting arm surpassed itself in providing improved relief to the foot-slogging infantry. As one rifle battalion commander remarked, "It was not uncommon for a battleship, tanks, artillery, and aircraft to be supporting the efforts of a platoon of infantry during the reduction of the Shuri position."

Shuri Castle fell to the 1st Battalion, 5th Marines, on 29 May, but it was a hollow victory. Ushijima had skillfully withdrawn most of his forces during the torrential rains. Now his remnants occupied prepared positions along a series of forbidding cross ridges, "sticking out like bones from the spine of a fish." Behind them lay the rocky southern coast. Frontally attacking these final eight miles would cost Buckner three more weeks of frightful casualties—and his own life.

---

[*] During the battle for Kunishi Ridge, "Grasshopper" pilots from VMO-3 and VMO-7 reduced casualty evacuation times to rear-area hospitals from a half-day by jeep ambulance to eight minutes by direct flight from an improvised dirt strip near Itoman. This was the dawn of tactical air MedEvacs, which would save so many lives in subsequent Asian wars. In eleven days, these doughty pilots safely flew 641 badly wounded Marines to first-class medical treatment in field hospitals.

General Shepherd, despairing of Buckner's endless meat-grinder and appreciative of the vast amphibious resources still available offshore, decided to inject tactical mobility and surprise into the sluggish campaign. In order for the 6th Marine Division to reach Naha Airfield, Shepherd first had to overwhelm the forbidding Oroku Peninsula. Shepherd could do this the hard way, attacking from the base of the peninsula and scratching seaward—or he could launch a shore-to-shore amphibious assault across the estuary to catch the defenders in their flank. The answer seemed obvious to Shepherd. Buckner agreed without enthusiasm, but gave the 6th Division barely thirty-six hours to plan and launch a division-level amphibious assault.

Shepherd and Krulak nevertheless proceeded with relish. Scouts from Maj. Anthony "Cold Steel" Walker's 6th Reconnaissance Company stole across the estuary at night and confirmed the existence on the peninsula of a cobbled force of Imperial Japanese Navy units under an old adversary from the Solomons. Fittingly, this final opposed amphibious landing of the war would be launched against the last surviving Japanese rikusentai commander, Rear Adm. Minoru Ota.

Despite heavy rains on 4 June, Shepherd kicked off the assault on schedule. The peninsula erupted in flame under the pounding of hundreds of naval guns, artillery batteries, and aerial bombs. Major Walker's scouts seized Ono Yama Island, the 4th Marines swept across the estuary, and LCMs and LCIs loaded with tanks appeared from "Loomis Harbor" to the north. The first waves of troops scrambled ashore and into the brush quickly. Too many worn-out LVTs broke down en route, causing uncomfortable delays, but enemy fire proved intermittent, and empty LVTs from the first waves quickly returned to transfer the stranded troops. Shepherd, the future commandant, had attained both tactical surprise and operational momentum against an enemy who more than any other Japanese commander on the island should have known to protect his flanks from the sea.

Admiral Ota, aroused and enraged, struck back savagely. His spirited sailors fought with elan, and they were very heavily armed. No similar-size force on Okinawa possessed as many automatic weapons or employed mines so effectively. The attacking Marines also encountered some awesome weapons at very short range—8-inch coast-defense guns that swiveled inland and rail-mounted 8-inch rocket launchers that fired the dreaded Screaming Mimi's. Wresting the Oroku Peninsula from Ota's death grasp took Shepherd ten days and cost 1,608 casualties and thirty tanks. In the end, the 6th Marine Division had slain 5,000 Japanese sailors, forced the ritual suicide of the last rikusentai (Ota's final message: "Enemy tank groups are now attacking our cave headquarters; the Naval Base Force is dying gloriously"), and opened up unopposed naval resupply to the nearly starving troops along the southwest coast. General Buckner was impressed.

On 18 June, Buckner climbed a ridge to watch the newly arrived 8th Marines advance along the valley floor. Japanese gunners on the opposite ridge saw the official party and opened up. Shells struck a nearby coral outcrop, driving a lethal splinter into the general's chest. He died in ten minutes, the highest-ranking U.S. officer to be killed in action throughout World War II.

As previously arranged, Roy Geiger assumed command. Geiger had already been selected for promotion; his third star became effective immediately. The Tenth Army remained in capable hands. Geiger became the only Marine—and the only aviator of any service—to command a field army. The soldiers on Okinawa had no qualms about this. Senior Army echelons elsewhere did. Army general Joseph Stillwell received urgent orders to Okinawa. Five days later he relieved Geiger, but by then the battle was over.

Okinawa proved extremely costly to all participants. Well over 100,000 Japanese died defending the island. Native Okinawans endured the worst, suffering as many as 150,000 deaths, a figure representing one-third of the island's population. The Tenth Army sustained nearly 40,000 combat casualties, including more than 7,000 Americans killed. An additional 26,000 nonbattle casualties occurred, mainly combat fatigue and accidents.*

Admiral Spruance described the battle of Okinawa as "a bloody, hellish prelude to the invasion of Japan." As protracted a nightmare as Okinawa had been, every survivor knew in his heart that the next battles in Kyūshū and Honshū would be incalculably worse. Everyone knew that plans for invading Japan specified the Kyūshū landings would be executed by the surviving veterans of Iwo Jima and Luzon; the reward of the Okinawa survivors would be the landing on the main island of Honshū.

* Marine Corps casualties overall—ground, air, ships' detachments—exceeded 19,500. In addition, there were 560 casualties among the Navy Medical Corps organic to Marine units. Thirteen of the 18 infantry battalion commanders in IIIAC who landed on L-Day were killed or wounded in the campaign.

By coincidence, the enormous and virtually flawless amphibious assault on Okinawa occurred thirty years to the month after Gallipoli's colossal disaster in World War I. By 1945 the Americans had refined this difficult naval mission into an art form. Spruance had every possible advantage in place for Okinawa—a proven doctrine, specialized ships and landing craft, mission-oriented weapons systems, trained shock troops, flexible logistics, unity of command. Everything clicked. The massive projection of sixty thousand combat troops ashore on L-Day and the subsequent series of smaller landings on the surrounding islands fully justified a doctrine earlier considered ill-advised, harebrained, or downright suicidal.

Yet the Tenth Army squandered several opportunities for surprise and maneuver available in the amphibious task force. An unimaginative reliance on firepower and siege tactics played to the strength of the Japanese defenders, prolonged the fighting, and increased the costs. The landings on Ie Shima and Oroku Peninsula, despite their successful executions, comprised the only division-level amphibious assaults undertaken in the ten weeks after L-Day. How discouraging it must have seemed to the veteran amphibians to have reached the very pinnacle of strategic and operational offensive power, only to fritter away the advantage by unenlightened tactical rigidity.

There remained at least one favorable aspect. If nothing else, the amphibious seizure of Okinawa represented joint service cooperation at its finest. This was General Buckner's greatest achievement, and Roy Geiger continued the sense of teamwork after Buckner's death. In terms of interservice cooperation alone, the Central Pacific Forces were now fully ready for an all-out amphibious assault on the Japanese home islands.

Chapter Nine

Collision Course

The Planned Invasion of Kyūshū

There comes a time in every combat unit's experience when it
no longer brags about the extent of its losses.

Gen. Merrill B. Twining, USMC (Ret.)
From *No Bended Knee,*
1996

hree and a half years of increasingly vicious fighting between
the United States and Japan across the breadth of the Pacific had
led to the ultimate showdown in the Imperial homeland itself.
The two antagonists now stood toe-to-toe: unblinking, gasping,
bleeding—one dying on his feet, still snarling in defiance. "The Japanese
are defeated," observed one American officer, "but we have not yet won
the victory."

Once again enormous amphibious assault forces began to concentrate
in the great lagoons of the Central Pacific; once again legions of Japanese
defenders began digging coastal fortifications and assembling suicide
attack forces. Both sides fully realized that this coming storm landing
would dwarf all others in scale and savagery.

At the end, the Japanese high command could only seek to buy time,
blindly hoping for some reversal of fortune—the unraveling of the Western Alliance, perhaps, or another killer typhoon to destroy the enemy fleet
as it had against Mongol invaders in the thirteenth century (the original

"divine wind"). Most of all, the Imperial General Headquarters clung to the belief that the will of the American public would not endure a protracted war in the Pacific—that having defeated their principal villain, Adolph Hitler, the Americans would not accept the high casualties required for a direct assault on the Japanese home islands. Surely, they reasoned, another campaign as prolonged and costly to the Americans as Okinawa had been would cause the U.S. government to abandon its odious "unconditional surrender" demands and negotiate an armistice, a ceasefire in place. Then, for Japan, there would be no invasion, occupation, loss of overseas "possessions," war crimes trials—no global humiliation.

The principal Japanese war aim had thus devolved into simply hanging on, inflicting maximum casualties, and waiting for "war weariness" to force the Americans to lose heart. The Japanese took some encouragement that their old nemesis, Pres. Franklin D. Roosevelt, the author of the "unconditional surrender" demands, had died at the onset of the Okinawa campaign, and his replacement, Harry S. Truman, lacked experience in international affairs.

Truman, derided by many of his own countrymen as "the Accidental President," had grit and common sense. He had also experienced combat as an artillery officer in World War I. Truman swiftly reaffirmed the objective of Japan's unconditional surrender. He concluded that starving the Japanese into submission by means of naval and air blockade would take too long. The fearsome new bomb being developed by the Manhattan Project might not be ready in time, might not even work.

Truman exacted a promise from Soviet marshall Joseph Stalin that the Red Army would enter the war against Japan within three months from the surrender of Germany. He encouraged British Prime Minister Winston Churchill to launch Operation Zipper to recapture Singapore. These two initiatives would preoccupy the sizable Japanese Army forces in mainland Asia. But Truman also sensed that an American invasion of Japan was inescapable. On 18 June 1945 he asked the Joint Chiefs of Staff for a detailed briefing on Operation Downfall.

Operation Downfall, the planned two-phased invasion of Japan, had staggering dimensions. More than 5 million troops (mostly American, some British, Canadian, and Australian) would conduct the two largest amphibious assaults in history—surpassing completely the earlier landings at Normandy, Okinawa, and Luzon. The two phases of Downfall had the code names of Olympic and Coronet. Operation Olympic was the first step, the seizure of Kyūshū by fourteen divisions of the U.S. Sixth

Army on X-Day, 1 November 1945. Forcible seizure of the region's many airfields, seaports, harbors, and staging areas would enable the subsequent buildup and launching of Operation Coronet, the amphibious assault against Honshū's Kanto Plain and seizure of the Tokyo-Yokohama region by twenty-five divisions on Y-Day, 1 March 1946.

Truman listened to the ambitious invasion plans with a heavy heart. He had assumed the presidency at a time when the rate of American casualties had reached their highest levels of the war—nearly nine hundred a day being reported from both theaters. Truman was particularly bothered by the casualties incurred throughout the Okinawa campaign, which paralleled the first ten weeks of his presidency. "I don't want you to conduct another Okinawa from one end of Japan to the other," he instructed his service chiefs. Yet even their conservative casualty estimates for Olympic upset the president: he could expect to suffer sixty thousand battle casualties on Kyūshū in the first two months alone, the chiefs told him. Of these, fifteen thousand Americans would likely die.

Truman approved the Joint Chiefs' plans, but expressly reserved for himself the right to issue the execution order for Olympic. His interim decision coincided with a special report of the death in combat on Okinawa of Gen. Simon B. Buckner, commanding the U.S. Tenth Army.

Planning the ultimate invasion of Japan made the Joint Chiefs confront the long-deferred selection of the supreme Allied commander in the Pacific. Operation Olympic would for the first time concentrate all Pacific resources in a single campaign. Dividing the Pacific between General of the Army Douglas MacArthur and Fleet Admiral Chester Nimitz could no longer be sensibly justified. On the surface, the solution appeared obvious. Nimitz had no aspirations to command ground forces in a protracted campaign ashore in Kyūshū; this was clearly MacArthur's role. But getting the troops ashore involved a massive amphibious operation—and therein lay the rub.

Beginning with Tarawa, Nimitz and his tactical commanders in the Central Pacific had paid scrupulous attention to the issue of unity of command in amphibious warfare. As evolved in practice and codified in doctrine, the naval attack force commander retained operational authority over his embarked landing force until such time as his counterpart ground commander had gone ashore and announced his readiness to assume full responsibilities for subsequent operations.

This was not the case in MacArthur's Southwest Pacific Area. Vice Adm. Dan E. Barbey's role more closely resembled a modern "component commander"—he commanded his ships but never MacArthur's embarked troops. And for MacArthur, finally on the cusp of becoming supreme Allied commander in the Pacific, the notion of yielding temporary command of his landing force to a Navy admiral until such time as the amphibious beachhead could be secured was anathema. Resolving this amphibious doctrinal issue took the Joint Chiefs much of a bitter winter and spring of 1945, leading to a series of very sharp exchanges between George Marshall and Ernest King. Finally, JCS Paper No. 1331/3 of 25 May ("Directive for Operation Olympic") put the issue to rest— somewhat. MacArthur would take the lead in planning Olympic and command all Allied forces, except during the amphibious phase when his landing forces would serve under the temporary command of the attack force commander—unless an undefined "exigency" arose, at which point MacArthur would assume full command authority.

Such stratospheric debates among five-star flag officers had little impact on most of the rank and file of assault forces being assembled in the Western Pacific. The summer equinox brought the region's typhoon season into full fury. Veterans of earlier amphibious campaigns knew these conditions would prevail for the next four months, restricting large-scale offensive campaigning. October would bring better weather and the so-called invasion window. Olympic planning continued with heightened urgency.

The assault divisions of the U.S. Sixth Army preparing for the invasion of Kyūshū had already seen plenty of fighting in the Pacific. Olympic would occur too soon for the recycled combat divisions from the European Theater to arrive following their elaborate screening, retraining, and transshipment process. Further along, ten infantry divisions and an airborne division from Europe would comprise follow-on forces for the invasion of Honshū. For now, however, it was business as usual for the old Pacific hands.

The tactical commanders selected for Olympic likewise reflected a lineup of men who had proven themselves in a series of trials by fire across the Pacific. Adm. Raymond Spruance would exercise overall naval command, but for the first time both the Third and Fifth Fleets would participate in the same operation, bringing Admirals William "Bull" Halsey and Spruance together. Adm. Richmond Kelly Turner would command the largest amphibious armada in history, over 2,700 specialized ships and craft from all three Pacific amphibious forces (compared with a bare-bones total of 51 amphibs at Guadalcanal three years earlier). Army lieutenant general Walter Krueger would command the Sixth

Army, 650,000 strong, arguably as tough and seasoned a force of GIs and Leathernecks as any yet assembled.

MacArthur's mission, with Nimitz's specified assistance, was to isolate Kyūshū, destroy Japanese forces ashore, and seize airfields, ports, and staging bases to support the subsequent invasion of Honshū.

Kyūshū, the southernmost island of Japan, resembles a gnarled, open hand, its fingers extending invitingly toward Okinawa, 350 miles to the south. Kyūshū is three times the length and much fatter than Okinawa. The strategic jewel of the island, to American planners, was Kagoshima Bay in the south, a huge, natural harbor. Significantly for the landing force, the island had plenty of beaches and no barrier reef. But Kyūshū also featured an abundance of mountains, steep ravines, narrow streambeds, and natural caves—truly a Japanese defender's dream.

General MacArthur's operational genius surfaced early in the planning. Realizing that his mission did not require the Sixth Army to seize all of Kyūshū, he designated a ninety-mile diagonal line across the lower third of the island, from Sendai in the west to Tsuno in the east, the line roughly following the southern slope of the central mountain range. His troops would secure Kagoshima Bay and all other ports and airfields below this line, then bottle up Japanese troops in the north by plugging the mountain passes.

In support of this strategy, Admiral Turner would execute three, near-simultaneous, corps-size landings:

• Vice Adm. Barbey's VII Amphibious Force to deliver Maj. Gen. I. P. Swift's I Corps (25th, 33d, and 41st Divisions) against the Miyazaki beaches below Tsuno on the east coast;

• Vice Adm. Theodore S. Wilkinson's III Amphibious Force to land Lt. Gen. Charles P. Hall's XI Corps (1st Cavalry, Americal, and 43d Divisions) in Ariaka Bay in the southeast;

• Vice Adm. Harry W. Hill's V Amphibious Force to land Maj. Gen. Harry Schmidt's V Amphibious Corps (2d, 3d, and 5th Marine Divisions) along the Satsuma Peninsula on Kyūshū's southwestern coast.

Amphibious planning for the Kyūshū assaults reflected the cumulative experience gleaned in scores of earlier landings. Deception operations received major emphasis. The Americans used bogus radio traffic and

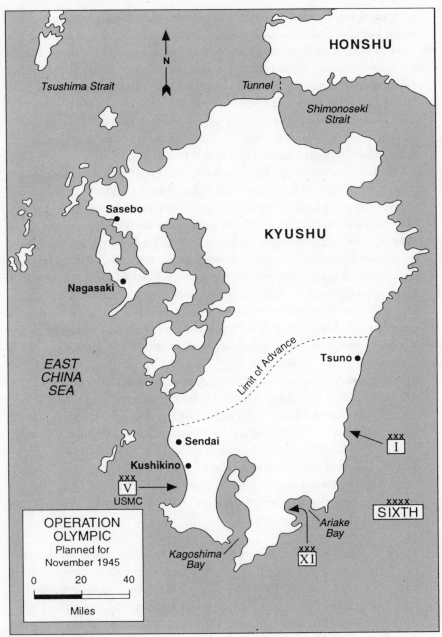

HONSHU

Tsushima Strait

N

Tunnel

Shimonoseki Strait

Sasebo

KYUSHU

Nagasaki

EAST CHINA SEA

Limit of Advance

Tsuno •

XXX
I

Sendai

Kushikino

XXX
V
USMC

XXXX
SIXTH

Ariake Bay

XXX
XI

Kagoshima Bay

OPERATION OLYMPIC
Planned for
November 1945

0   20   40

Miles

Mary Craddock Hoffman

misleading intelligence overflights to indicate the strategic target would be the island of Shikoku vice Kyūshū. Tactically, U.S. intelligence officers went to great lengths to create the perception among the Japanese that the next campaign would feature a massive reliance on airborne and glider assault units—even though only one airborne division existed in the Pacific at the time and there were no plans to drop paratroopers in the Olympic landings.* Conspicuous airborne rehearsals and use of dummy gliders, however, forced Japanese planners to earmark mobile forces inland to guard against this new threat.

Advance seizure of the Kerama Retto Islands in the Okinawa campaign had proven so beneficial that Kelly Turner sought to repeat the maneuver as part of the preliminary operations for Olympic. Rear Adm. G. B. Davis's Western Attack Force would land the 40th Division in the Koshiki Retto off the southwest tip of Kyūshū on X-Day-minus-5. The same force would seize seven other offshore islands in the ensuing forty-eight hours. American possession of these islands would reduce the threat of suicide boat attacks, provide secure anchorages for damaged ships, help clear the approach lanes to the landing beaches, and give the fleet commander additional early warning and fighter direction capabilities against kamikaze attacks. In addition, the 158th Regimental Combat Team stood ready to seize the large island of Tanega Shima should it prove necessary to protect the minesweepers at work in the waters nearby.

Turner picked Vice Adm. Jesse B. Oldendorf to command Task Force 54, the Gunfire and Covering Force. The naval gunfire commanders under Oldendorf reflected the level of experience being brought to bear on this first landing on the Japanese homeland: Rear Adms. Jerauld Wright, Ingolf N. Kiland, and Richard L. "Close-In" Conolly. Between them, these bombardment commanders would distribute the fires of thirteen battleships, twenty-four cruisers, and thirty-eight destroyers against the principal landing beaches.

Many members of the same Navy–Marine Corps team that prevailed at Iwo Jima would reunite for the forcible seizure of the Kushikino beachhead on X-Day. Adm. "Handsome Harry" Hill would again command the V Amphibious Force from his flagship *Auburn*. Hill's considerable ego sometimes prevented him from listening to the advice of his staff or the entreaties of his landing force counterpart, but he was man enough

---

* MacArthur assigned the 11th Airborne Division as Sixth Army reserve afloat for Olympic.

to admit his mistakes, and he had certainly learned his profession first-hand, having commanded major attack forces in every amphibious campaign across the Central Pacific, from Tarawa to Okinawa—missing only Peleliu. Personally brave and intellectually creative, Hill had become Kelly Turner's principal subordinate commander. Significantly, he also got along well with VAC commander Harry Schmidt. The cooperation and frank exchanges between these two veterans throughout Tinian and Iwo Jima had provided the foundation for success in both campaigns.

Maj. Gen. Harry "the Dutchman" Schmidt had commanded the 4th Marine Division at Roi-Namur and Saipan, before relieving Holland Smith in command of VAC before Tinian. Smith had left the war zone after Iwo, having left his unmistakable mark on the Pacific War. Schmidt was colorless but competent. His rock-steady control of three fiercely independent division commanders throughout the Iwo Jima battle exemplified the most desirable traits of a Corps commander. Indeed, Schmidt and Roy Geiger both deserve special laurels for difficult command of enormous forces of Marines under absolutely hellish conditions. Schmidt would have served well the seventy-five thousand men of VAC earmarked for Operation Olympic.

The mission of Schmidt's Marines would be to land south of Kushikino, fight their way across the dozen miles of the Satsuma Peninsula to Kagoshima Bay, block reinforcements from boiling out of the mountains to the north, and link up with Army troops coming from the east. Significant Japanese coast-defense batteries at Noma Misaki and Hashima Saki would receive early attention from Wright's battleships. When aerial photographs revealed a steady proliferation of other enemy gun positions further inland, the Marines were told that the heavy bombers of the Far East Air Force would pound them into oblivion in advance. Hearing this drew jeers from the Iwo Jima veterans, recalling the ten weeks of preliminary bombing of that sulfuric rock, which did little more than drive the enemy deeper underground.

General Schmidt reported to the Sixth Army for planning purposes on 31 May, barely two months after leaving Iwo. His staff already had a landing plan in the works. Basically, the 2d and 3d Marine Divisions would land abreast, with the 5th Marine Division in reserve.

These three divisions had already experienced much of the roughest fighting in the Pacific to this point: the 2d Division at Guadalcanal, Tarawa, Saipan, Tinian, and Okinawa; the 3d Division at Bougainville, Guam, and Iwo Jima; and the 5th Division, whose single, terrible battle had been all thirty-six days of Iwo. According to military historian Richard B. Frank, the three Marine divisions by August 1945 had suffered the combined loss of 32,759 battle casualties in the Pacific, including 7,580 deaths.

Maj. Gen. Graves B. Erskine still commanded the 3d Marine Division, which left Iwo Jima for Guam, the island they had recaptured so convincingly the previous summer. Nearby, the 2d Marine Division, which had paid an unexpectedly high price for a series of demonstration landings off Okinawa, returned to Saipan. Maj. Gen. Leroy P. Hunt took command. Both divisions began conducting progressive training, which stressed integrated assault teams attacking bunkers and caves. Southern Kyūshū seemed to offer the same deadly fortified terrain as Iwo and Okinawa.

Maj. Gen. Thomas E. Bourke, who had commanded Julian Smith's artillery at Tarawa, now commanded the 5th Marine Division. Not knowing what tactical missions to expect in his capacity as corps reserve, Bourke organized nine separate battalion landing teams, each configured for limited independent operations. His division, extremely glad to be back in their familiar camp on the friendly island of Hawaii, integrated thousands of replacements and began applying the combat lessons they had learned at such a cost on the slopes of Suribachi and along the entire western coast of Sulfur Island. All three divisions resumed amphibious refresher training, pointing toward full-scale rehearsals with the V Amphibious Force, scheduled for August in the Marianas.

Marine Corps aviation figured to play a major role in Olympic. Three of the four air wings in the Pacific would participate: 1st MAW from captured airfields in southern Kyūshū, 2d MAW from Okinawa fields, 3d MAW distributed among eight carrier groups on CVEs. Earlier, Admiral Nimitz transferred two of these escort carriers, *Block Island* and *Gilbert Islands*, with their Marine squadrons, from the Okinawa campaign to the Dutch East Indies. There, beginning 1 July 1945, the Marine pilots provided close air support to the Australian 7th Division during their landing on Balikpapan on the east coast of Borneo.* Significantly, on that same date, Marine Corsairs from the Tenth Army's Tactical Air Force on Okinawa escorted Army Air Forces B-25s on the first medium bomber attack on the Japanese homeland since the Doolittle Raid of April 1942. These experiences, combined with an exceptional record of close air support to

---

* For the Balikpapan landing, Allied cruisers provided sixteen days of preliminary saturation shelling, the longest sustained naval bombardment of the war.

Army units in the Philippines, brought Marine aviation close to its potential as a unique expeditionary combat element.

American air strikes in fact had become too effective in one critical area. Intelligence staffs serving both MacArthur and Nimitz had come to rely increasingly on their ability to decipher Japanese coded messages by the ULTRA system, as well as a growing proficiency in radio traffic analysis. The Joint Chiefs had to remind the theater commanders not to target Japanese radio stations and communications centers for bombing missions lest the volume of radio traffic be inadvertently diminished beyond use.

The theater commanders may have pooh-poohed these strictures, but the truth was, ULTRA intercepts had become more and more critical as an indication of Japanese strength on Kyūshū—as well as a barometer of that nation's will to keep on fighting indefinitely.

If the Americans could somehow have mustered the forces to attack Kyūshū immediately following Okinawa, the island might have been taken at a bargain-rate level of casualties. Only three to four divisions patrolled the entire fifteen-thousand-square-mile landmass; minimal fortifications existed. Unfortunately, an offensive of this scale was beyond the grasp of either MacArthur or Nimitz at the time. The Fifth Fleet had taken an awful pounding from Japanese kamikazes at Okinawa; the typhoon season was in full swing; and the shot-up divisions from Iwo Jima and Luzon needed time to recover and reorganize.

The Japanese meanwhile were not blind to the likely next strategic moves of their relentless opponents. By now, IGHQ had become keenly aware of the Americans' propensity for going after existing ports and airfields, particularly those within the protective range of land-based air support. Kyūshū would be the obvious next target, and the south of Kyūshū—fully in range of tactical aircraft from both Okinawa and Iwo Jima—offered every feature the Americans would need to stage the enormous forces and supplies required to launch the final assault on the main island of Honshū. In a masterpiece of intelligence interpretation and analysis, IGHQ predicted the theater, forces, mission, timing, and likely landing beaches for Operation Olympic. So effective was the Japanese anticipation and precise buildup that MacArthur's staff began to suspect that enemy spies had infiltrated their very headquarters.

American commanders were also astounded at the speed with which IGHQ could conscript, organize, train, equip, and deploy new combat units for service in southern Kyūshū. Nor were these inconsequential forces. Indeed, IGHQ mobilized and deployed at least eight brand-new infantry divisions and several independent mixed brigades to Kyūshū within a matter of weeks. That all of this was accomplished under the smothering intrusion of American air and sea superiority is all the more remarkable. These were by no means first-rate troops, but Japanese field commanders had always been proficient in motivating and training raw levees into decent fighters in an implausibly short time.

Reorganizing to deal with the Allied threat to the homeland, IGHQ created the Second General Army under Field Marshall Shunroku Hata, who established his headquarters in Hiroshima. Hata coordinated two area armies, one in the Osaka area of Honshū, the other, larger, in Kyūshū. This became the Sixteenth Area Army, commanded by Lt. Gen. Isamu Yokoyama, a fifty-six-year-old infantry officer who had distinguished himself in China the previous two years. Yokoyama established his headquarters in Fukuoka on northern Kyūshū, but his attention remained focused southward.

Imperial General Headquarters also redeployed two veteran divisions (the 25th and 57th) from the Kwantung Army to Kyūshū. Yokoyama welcomed these seasoned units, but he also realized no more could be spared. Japanese forces guarding the Manchurian border now faced their most critical threat of the past seven years in the alarming buildup of the Soviet Red Banner Army. The steady draw-down of veteran units of the Kwantung Army to reinforce Pacific islands since the fall of Saipan had taken a toll on the once-formidable force in Manchuria. Yokoyama used his experienced veterans to help train and motivate the hundreds of thousands of conscripts. The new soldiers soon found themselves undergoing the same exhausting routine of their predecessors in Okinawa, Iwo Jima, Peleliu, and Tarawa: training all day, digging fortifications half the night.

General MacArthur's ULTRA cryptologists could hardly believe their translations. Every week, it seemed, a new Japanese division or brigade materialized on Kyūshū. The Sixth Air Army under Lt. Gen. Michio Sugawara became operational in Fukuoka. An amphibious brigade arrived from the Kuriles. In swift succession, cryptologists identified three field armies, two of them—the 57th and the 40th—in the field in the south.* Between April and August the number of infantry divisions on Kyūshū increased from four to fourteen. American analysts located at least eight

* The 40th Army redeployed from Formosa to the Ijuin area of southwestern Kyūshū in May–June 1945.

divisions in the south; the two Manchukuoan divisions, retained under Yokoyama's direct control, seemed poised to deploy in either direction. On 6 August, the same day the first atom bomb fell on Japan, MacArthur's intelligence analysts reported over six hundred thousand Japanese troops on Kyūshū, mostly in the south. Even assuming a leveling off in Japanese mobilization, the U.S. Sixth Army would have been forced to land with nowhere near the three-to-one superiority in numbers over the defenders. There would be near parity between the antagonists.

Numbers themselves fail to tell the story. The Japanese on Kyūshū may have been imbued with the warrior spirit, but their arms and equipment would have been significantly deficient in the projected battle. The American blockade and bombing program had seriously crippled Japanese production and distribution of war materials. Fuel—a luxury for both Army and Navy as early as 1943—became extremely rare by mid-1945. Experiments with pine root fuel alternatives failed to solve the crisis. Yokoyama could expect precious little fuel for his trucks to distribute the required calibers and levels of ammo for his uneven assortment of field guns, rockets, and mortars.

Other logistical constraints became evident. Documents captured on Okinawa revealed Japanese intentions of constructing "deliberate field fortifications" in the homeland of stronger proportions than employed in the outer islands, specifying walls and ceilings up to "3.5 meters thick for machine gun pillboxes and rapid-fire gun casemates." But Kyūshū was nearly devoid of concrete and steel reinforcing rods—once again it would be sturdy men with picks and shovels carving out another Fukkaku defensive network.

Interestingly, the Japanese had war-gamed the "hypothetical defense of Kyūshū" as early as January 1944. At that point, just after Tarawa and before the Marshalls campaign, the IGHQ defensive policy remained perimeter-oriented: "destroy the enemy at the water's edge. . . . Deliver swift, decisive counterattacks on land and sea. . . . Use amphibious forces and airborne raiding forces to conduct counterlanding combat operations."

Japanese message traffic in the spring of 1945 reflected the desperation with which IGHQ tried to produce a viable defense against the American amphibious juggernaut. Defending their island fortresses in the Central Pacific at the water's edge had failed under the terrible pounding of naval gunfire. Conceding the landings and reverting to positional attrition warfare in the Schoutens, Palaus, Philippines, Iwo Jima, and Okinawa had prolonged the campaigns and inflicted high casualties on the invaders—but still failed. From April through June, IGHQ released tactical guidance that placed maximum emphasis on the use of special attack forces (suicide units) and seemed to revert to the original perimeter defense policies. Defending the sacred homeland required extraordinary measures. A new field manual issued in early June contained this exhortation: "We should be determined to destroy the enemy landing forces at the water's edge by conducting an all-out decisive battle there using suicide attacks against the enemy."

Here would lie the principal difference between the assault on Kyūshū and the earlier landings at Tarawa, Saipan, Guam, Peleliu—even Iwo Jima. General Yokoyama and his air counterpart, General Sugawara, would stake their defense on massive, coordinated suicide strikes against the amphibious task forces at their point of greatest vulnerability—the approach to the island and launching of the ship-to-shore assault. Tarawa and the others had been savage enough. Iwo Jima's horrors had been magnified by a single evening's kamikaze attack that sank an escort carrier and knocked a fleet carrier out of the war. Okinawa had demonstrated how massed suicide strikes could jeopardize an entire amphibious campaign. The Japanese defense of Kyūshū would seek to integrate every possible special attack asset. Of these, there were legion.

MacArthur's intelligence staff, making fruitful use of ULTRA decryption intercepts, became well aware of the emphasis the Kyūshū defenders would place on using suicide forces against the invasion force. Foremost of these efforts would be massed kamikaze attacks by as many as 6,000 aircraft against the U.S. fleet. In a significant departure from tactics employed at Okinawa, the kamikaze pilots in the battle for Kyūshū would ignore the carriers and other warships and target exclusively the troop transports in the amphibious task force. These would be attacked in waves of 200 to 300 aircraft every hour as soon as they came within range. The kamikazes would include more of the self-guided Baku bombs. Conventional aircraft would also target the troop transports: the Imperial Navy earmarked some 3,725 "anticonvoy bombers." The Navy selected other pilots to crash their float planes into American landing craft as they crossed the line of departure. The whole air campaign evolved under the code name *Ketsu-Go.*

The Japanese also planned to take advantage of Kyūshū's irregular shoreline to launch thousands of suicide boats, each mounted with contact depth charges, against the transport anchorage. In addition, the defenders planned to deploy midget submarines and suicide guided

The 50-mm "knee mortar" was more accurately a "grenade discharger," but Japanese naval infantrymen were extremely adept at dropping rounds into approaching landing craft. As the American amphibious forces began to encounter veteran Imperial Army units closer to Japan itself, they also experienced the unwelcome fire of medium- and large-caliber mortars like the 120-mm and 150-mm shown. They were deadly weapons. *(Larry E. Klatt)*

torpedoes against the American amphibs. Weighing the entirety of these efforts, the Japanese estimated they could sink 35 percent of the troop ships, greatly disrupting the landing before the first waves ever touched the sacred soil. The deputy chief of the Army General Staff in a top-level conference in June described these integrated suicide operations as "the key to success" in defending the homeland. Other senior officers of both services expressed similar optimism. The Americans, they said, would find Kyūshū much different from far-off Guadalcanal or New Guinea.

Assessing the likely outcome of this climactic-but-canceled amphibious showdown from the vantage of hindsight provides little to affirm the rosy predictions of the Japanese commanders. The cumulative combat experience of the American invasion force would have constituted an overwhelming tactical advantage over the Japanese defenders, despite their numbers and motivation. By 1945 even the most experienced Manchukuoan division could hardly compare with their U.S. counterparts, the veterans of Biak, Saipan, Iwo Jima, or Leyte. In truth, American GIs and Marines had already taken the measure of some of the best military forces in the Empire.

Nor did the Japanese defending Kyūshū enjoy any advantages in leadership. Field Marshall Hata and General Yokoyama had credible military experience in China, but neither could compare with MacArthur or Krueger. Nor could Yokoyama's three field army commanders hope to match the experience of the U.S. corps commanders—Swift, Hall, and Schmidt—arrayed against them. One had been recalled from retirement; the other two had spent the heart of the war in staff or training billets. American amphibious forces had already faced—and defeated—exceptional Japanese commanders like Generals Ushijima and Kuribayashi, Admiral Shibasaki, and Colonel Nakagawa. No Japanese field commander in Kyūshū would have proven half as redoubtable as these fallen leaders of the Japanese garrisons on Okinawa, Iwo, Tarawa, and Peleliu.

While the 16th Area Army on Kyūshū had plenty of major-caliber guns and rockets with which to pound the invaders, they lacked the brilliance of the artillery commanders who fought and died at Iwo Jima, Okinawa, and the Philippines. There comes a point as well when the very proliferation of big guns becomes much more a logistical problem than a tactical advantage. Yokoyama's fuel shortages and the vulnerability of his limited motor transport assets to enemy air interdiction would have seriously crimped ammo resupply operations after the battle was joined.

Ironically, at a time when Japanese garrisons were just beginning to demonstrate a proficiency in laying minefields—both along beach approaches and inland—the supply of suitable mines dried up. American UDT teams and combat engineers were preparing for a mammoth mine-clearing effort in Olympic until radio intercepts revealed the Japanese had experienced major shortfalls in producing and distributing these munitions.

The Japanese would have fought this battle under still another disadvantage. Imperial General Headquarters had failed to resolve the longstanding, acrimonious rivalry between the Army and Navy. Nothing in the captured or intercepted documents indicates any improvement in interservice cooperation—even for defending the motherland.

In the final analysis, the salient strengths of the 16th Area Army defending Kyūshū included two familiar elements—tenacity and topography—and two enhanced or new elements—great numbers (six times the size of the Okinawa garrison) and a concentrated, integrated Special Attack Force, as embodied by the Ketsu-Go plan.

By comparison, the U.S. Sixth Army had the leadership, experience, joint service integration, doctrine, command and control, logistic support, and weaponry to assault successfully even this large and daunting objective. The war in Europe was over and won. American factories, shipyards, and proving grounds, operating at full bore around the clock, were pouring new ships, planes, tanks, and guns into the Pacific at a mind-boggling rate. Krueger's forces would have landed on Kyūshū equipped with new Pershing tanks, improved and more numerous flame tanks, night-optics "snooper-scopes," and bunker-busting recoilless rifles up to 75mm in size. The familiar "blowtorch and corkscrew" assault tactics would be applied against Kyūshū's many caves with postgraduate proficiency.

If there was one factor that would have mitigated against Krueger's overwhelming combat superiority in 1945, it would have been a cumulative "war-weariness" among the many veterans in his ranks. The survivors of Iwo Jima and Leyte could hardly have viewed their next assignment with anything but resigned fatalism. No man could rightfully expect the gods of war to allow him to endure a second—even greater—bloodbath unscathed.

Part of this malaise reflected the fact that only a handful of American combat divisions carried the entire load of the Pacific War for the duration. There simply were not enough Army or Marine divisions available to provide suitable recovery and retraining periods between hellish assault landings. Richard B. Frank's research indicates the fourteen divisions assigned to the Sixth Army for Olympic had already sustained 74,239 battle casualties (including 17,861 deaths) in the Pacific. Of these, the 2d Marine Division had the lugubrious distinction of having suffered the most: 12,770 battle casualties by mid-1945.

Typically, the bulk of these casualties occurred in the rifle companies of each division. The ensuing half-century of "limited war" may have inoculated subsequent practitioners of the military art to the real costs of close, unrestricted combat. Two examples from Iwo Jima may prove illuminating. Capt. William T. Ketcham's Item Company, 3d Battalion, 24th Marines, stormed ashore on D-Day with 133 Marines in its three rifle platoons. Twenty-six days later, when the 4th Marine Division back-loaded its ships, only 9 of these riflemen were still on their feet. Capt. Frank C. Caldwell's Fox Company, 2d Battalion, 26th Marines, fought the battle for thirty-six consecutive days. Caldwell somehow survived, but he lost all his platoon commanders and 221 men.

Repeated exposure to such horrors over time led to a marked increase in psychoneurosis cases, or "combat fatigue." Tarawa's brief savagery had produced few identifiable cases, but each longer campaign produced its significant share. The 43d Division suffered 2,500 cases of combat fatigue in the jungles of New Georgia; the I Marine Amphibious Corps, 749 at Bougainville; the 4th Marine Division, 414 at Saipan. Iwo Jima cost the V Amphibious Corps more than 2,600 cases, including 99 during the Japanese bombardment on D-Day alone. The protracted hell of Okinawa produced a record 26,221 cases. Dr. Michael F. Keleher, a battalion surgeon in the 25th Marines at Saipan, Tinian, and Iwo Jima, recalled two kinds of combat fatigue: "We all had battle fatigue to a degree; we were numb, fatalistic, exhausted, but some men simply crossed the line, could no longer function in a combat zone. Some would even hallucinate at night, open fire on imaginary enemy troops, exposing our own men. We had to get them out of there."

Most infantrymen developed an abiding fear of mutilation by exploding shells or mines. Recalled Lt. Col. Robert E. Cushman Jr., a battalion commander at Guam and Iwo, and later commandant: "I always had fear. I hated high explosives. Its effects are so terrible."

The Navy had been particularly traumatized by relentless kamikaze and conventional air attacks throughout the Okinawa campaign. Sleeplessness and fear took its toll. Officers with a driven personality like Kelly Turner found little time to recuperate. "When I came back from the Marshalls, I was dead tired," he said. "I stayed dead tired for the rest of the war."

This is revealing, because Turner's amphibs in Task Force 40 would have borne the brunt of the Ketsu-Go attacks. The battle for Kyūshū would to considerable extent depend on how proficiently the U.S. Navy had learned to deal with massed suicide attacks—the whole panoply of fleet air defense, including early detection, vectoring of combat air patrols for interception, evasive action, antiaircraft fire, and damage control. Whether Japan's numerous but increasingly younger and "aviationally challenged" kamikaze pilots could have stayed the course through all these obstacles with sufficient presence of mind to identify troop transports from the hundreds of other ships filling the horizon and the requisite skill to press the attack successfully home remains conjecture.

Based on the Okinawa experience, it appears likely that enough kamikazes would have survived the entire air defense gauntlet to hit and sink up to two dozen troop transports en route to the objective. Assigning an arbitrary loss rate of 40 percent (about four hundred men) per sunken ship presents a grim projection of ninety-six hundred deaths among the landing force before the first soldier or Marine ever hit the beach. In that regard, Ketsu-Go may have proven to be the best possible answer to Japan's war-long search for an effective antidote to American storm landings.

It still would not have been sufficient. Cumulative war weariness and heavy losses to mass kamikaze attacks would not have been enough to prevent the U.S. Sixth Army from landing in force on southern Kyūshū and—in probably ninety days of methodical killing—the American invaders would have secured the southern third of the island. Uprooting and killing six hundred thousand Japanese in that type of terrain would have proven costly, however—and in the political sense, dangerously costly. The forcible seizure of southern Kyūshū could well have cost the Sixth Army more than seventy-five thousand battle casualties. Couple this projection with preliminary losses among the transports en route and the inevitable nonbattle accidents and combat fatigue cases (not to mention the certain "collateral damage" deaths to easily half a million civilians), and the American public might indeed have grown discouraged about launching an even greater bloodbath against Honshū. This is strictly conjectural, of course, but one fact is certain: the Joint Chiefs of Staff read the ULTRA reports of the Japanese buildup in Kyūshū—and within southern Kyūshū, along the exact beaches to be assaulted—with mounting concern as July turned to August.

The situation grew worrisome enough for the Joint Chiefs to give consideration to employing special weapons to reduce American casualties. These ranged the gamut of creativity, from reverse-engineered German V-2 rockets to "war-weary" B-17s loaded with TNT or napalm that would be "aimed" at Kyūshū by special crews before they bailed out to safety. The most likely candidate was poison gas.

The Joint Chiefs had considered this option earlier for Iwo Jima. Neither Japan nor the United States had signed the prewar international accord banning the use of poison gas. General Kuribayashi had evacuated Iwo Jima's few civilians before the battle. The United States had sufficient stocks of mustard-gas munitions in the Pacific at the time to deliver a lethal dose against an island that small. Aware of the political sensitivity of the issue, the JCS in 1944 assigned the project to the Office for Strategic Service (OSS). An OSS agent visited Chester Nimitz in 1944 to discuss the possible use of gas at Iwo. The plan had Orwellian overtones: jam all Japanese transmitters; change the tell-tale color-coded markings on the munitions to keep American crewmen unaware of the mission. Nimitz agreed in principal, but the process was academic. Only President Roosevelt could authorize such a plan, and FDR flatly opposed any use of gas. When the OSS recommendations reached his desk in late 1944, the president gave it short shrift: "All prior endorsements denied, Franklin D. Roosevelt, Commander in Chief."

With Truman in the White House—acutely concerned about American casualties—and Kyūshū appearing more formidable every week, Army Chief of Staff George Marshall resurrected the idea to support Olympic. To Marshall, the offensive use of lethal gas made sense—it was hardly more inhumane than napalm or white phosphorous, and its use would decidedly save many U.S. lives. According to military historian John Ray Skates, the Army's Chemical Warfare Service conducted tests of poison gases against caves and underground fortifications at Dugway Proving Ground, Utah, in 1945. Three agents proved highly effective: mustard, cyanogen chloride, and phosgene. "Preparations for the use of gas were built into the Olympic plans," concluded Skates. On 6 July 1945 General MacArthur reported to Marshall his readiness to use gas offensively. Assault troops would have landed wearing gas masks and full suits of protective clothing.

General Marshall took his concern for the anticipated casualties at Kyūshū a notch higher. During the critical two-day period in August when the Japanese government seemed unresponsive to the atomic bombs, Marshall concluded that the invasion would still have to go. He then asked the Manhattan Project scientists whether atomic bombs could be downsized for tactical application against Japanese defenses on Kyūshū. The answer came swiftly: nine "tactical nukes" could be produced in time for the 1 November landings—and they could be profitably used against military targets on Kyūshū. The Japanese surrender announcement the next day, however, put a quick end to these deliberations.

The Marines of the V Amphibious Corps knew little of these high-level proceedings. They knew enough to expect the bloodiest landing of the war. Their intelligence officers reported that VAC's three divisions would be landing in the teeth of the Japanese 40th Army, four divisions under the overall command of Lt. Gen. Mitsuo Nakazawa. The Marines would first encounter the newly created 146th Division, formed to defend the Satsuma beaches with little mobility or firepower ("human breakwaters" in the apt description of Edward J. Drea). Next would come the heavier, more combat-effective 206th Division, which contained its own heavy artillery, mortars, and engineer units. The Marines expected the 77th Division in Kagoshima and the 303d Division in Sendai to constitute a counterattacking mobile reserve in their sector.

The VAC beaches were narrow, dominated by dunes, and fully exposed to observation and direct fire from a line of six-hundred-foot hills less than a kilometer away. The Marines would also have to force a crossing of the Ozato River, which flowed parallel to the beach about five hundred yards inland. The Japanese had a number of high-velocity, direct-fire guns mounted on rails behind steel doors in hidden caves in this part of the island. They also had plenty of their 120-mm mortars and Nambu machine guns on hand.

When Col. Samuel G. Taxis, D-3 of the 2d Marine Division, landed on Kyūshū during the postsurrender occupation, he made a point of walking the ground his division would have had to take by force of arms. "We would've faced a very difficult landing against vicious opposition— all in all, it looked pretty tough," he reported. "It could have been a lot worse than anyone figured." Most Marines sensed this. Even those units on Okinawa, earmarked for Coronet, grew uneasy about Olympic. Said Col. Wilburt S. Brown, commanding the artillery regiment in the 1st Marine Division, "I was scared to death that the Tenth Army would have been called on to relieve or augment the Sixth Army in Kyūshū."

Emperor Hirohito's decision to accept unconditional surrender after the second atomic bomb attack immediately relegated Olympic to the historical dustbin. In truth, however, it was the combination of pressures on Japan that did the job—the bombs, certainly, but also the Soviet invasion of Manchuria (and very-near amphibious assault of Hokkaido), the sustained conventional bombing and submarine strangulation, and the very real threat of a massive invasion of the home islands.

Ironically for the Marines, their actual first landing in Japan turned out to more closely resemble the 1853 landing of Commodore Matthew C. Perry and his Fleet Marine Officer, Brevet Maj. Jacob Zeilin, than any vestige of a twentieth-century storm landing. On 30 August, Brig. Gen.

Infantrymen of the 6th Marine Division enjoy a rare free ride on a north-bound Sherman tank in early action in central Okinawa. Kyūshū would have been big enough to permit opportunities for maneuver warfare, but the presence of half a million Japanese troops in the vicinity would probably have caused another meat-grinder campaign like southern Okinawa. *(U.S. Marine Corps)*

William T. Clement led ashore the Third Fleet Marine Landing Force, which included a company of bluejackets from the fleet (as well as a combined force of Royal Marines and Royal Navy seamen) at Yoko-suka, Japan. Clement's main body consisted of the veteran 4th Marines, fresh from victory in Okinawa and loaded for bear, but the landing was bloodless, unopposed. The war had truly ended.

Few of the men of the U.S. Sixth Army ever expressed any regret that Truman's decision to drop the atomic bombs eliminated the requirement to forcibly seize Kyūshū against the Ketsu-Go. The words of one Army veteran spared from that ordeal likely reflect the reaction of all hands at the time: "When word got around that the bombs had forced the Japanese surrender, we knelt in the sand and cried. For all our manhood, we cried. We were going to live. We were going to grow up to adulthood after all."

Epilogue

Parting Shots

The outstanding achievement of this war, in the field of joint undertakings, was the perfection of amphibious operations, the most difficult of all operations in modern warfare.

Fleet Adm. Ernest J. King, USN
Commander in Chief, U.S. Fleet
War Reports, 1947

n the late summer of 1941 the Honorable Frank Knox, forty-seventh secretary of the Navy, traveled to Parris Island, South Carolina, to observe a demonstration amphibious landing conducted by a rifle platoon of the 2d Battalion, 7th Marines. At a given signal, the Leathernecks paddled ashore in half a dozen inflatable rubber boats. Secretary Knox then met with the Marines on the beach, commending them on their amphibious prowess.

The Marines and the Gator Navy of mid-1941 had developed more sophisticated means of executing the ship-to-shore movement, to be sure, but only rubber rafts were available to show the secretary of the Navy that day. The Marines had to rely on "paddle power," just as their forebears had in the Vera Cruz landing of 1847, just as some of their immediate successors would during the second day at Tarawa in 1943.

By early 1945, however, the scope and scale of amphibious warfare had changed almost beyond comparison. To cite one example, the 5th Marine Division executed its storm landing at D-Day on Iwo Jima by means of this

U.S. NAVY AMPHIBIOUS TASK FORCES
Evolutionary Changes, 1942-44

	Guadalcanal August 1942	Tarawa* Nov 1943	Saipan** June 1944	Okinawa Apr 1945
Amphibious Command Ships (AGC)	0	0	2	6
Battleships (OBB)	0	3	6	10
Cruisers (CA/CL)	8	4	11	13
Escort Carriers (CVE)	0	5	7	21
Attack Transports (APA/AP)	13	13	25	130
Attack Cargo Ships (AKA/AK)	5	3	8	54
Dock Landing Ships (LSD)	0	1	5	6
Tank Landing Ships (LST)	0	3	53	187
Mine Sweepers (DMS/AM/YMS)	5	2	21	96

*Tarawa reflects Task Force 53 only   **Saipan reflects Task Force 52 only

abundance of specialized craft: 1 dock landing ship, 19 tank landing ships, 12 medium landing ships, 7 tank landing craft, 72 medium landing craft, 339 Higgins boats, 204 LVTs, 36 LVT-As, and 100 DUKWS.

The designated Navy wave guide for the night landing at Tanambogo in August 1942 was a ship's dentist, a brave officer but totally unskilled in his duties. Assault waves at Saipan and the Philippines would be led across the line of departure by highly trained crews manning specialized, thirty-ton landing craft control boats (LCCs).

The Japanese considered the initial American landings on Tulagi and Guadalcanal in 1942 such an operational fluke that Prime Minister Tojo did not even mention them in his nightly radio report to the Japanese public. Less than three years later the entire Japanese nation would listen breathlessly to every radio dispatch from their embattled garrisons at

Iwo Jima and Okinawa as U.S. amphibious forces inexorably squeezed them into oblivion.

Marine colonel Alan Shapley's Pacific War began when Japanese dive-bombers blew him off the battleship *Arizona* at Pearl Harbor; by 1945 he had led Raider battalions and the 4th Marines ashore in the Solomons, Marshalls, Guam, and Okinawa. Recalling this "rags to riches" theme in the emergence of American amphibious might, Shapley said: "We were getting powerful. . . . You just can't [envision]—nobody can unless they can see an invasion force. Eniwetok anchorage as far as you could see, nothing but ships of all kinds and thousands and thousands and thousands of men. It will never happen in this world again. Never. We were unstoppable."

The development of storm landings as the embodiment of an assault launched from the sea against defended beaches accelerated the Allied victory in the Pacific and constituted a major factor—admittedly one of several—in convincing the Japanese to surrender unconditionally. Amphibious forces, having earned their spurs so convincingly in both theaters of the war, went on to make significant contributions to national security throughout the Cold War, covering the spectrum of conflict, from major opposed landings like Inchon (1950); to unopposed landings in force in Lebanon (1958), DaNang (1965), Dominican Republic (1965); to the mere threat of a storm landing (Cuba 1963, the Gulf War 1991). The abiding principles of unity of command, parallel and concurrent planning, detailed coordination of supporting arms, and flexible execution stood the tests of time and technology.

The handful of Marine Corps and Navy pioneers who sat down in Quantico in the early 1930s to produce a viable offensive amphibious doctrine from the ruins of Gallipoli had proven themselves men of exceptional vision and common sense. Their concept, boiled down to the bare bones, was simply this:

•Attain at least temporary air, sea, and surface superiority over the enemy in the objective area to enable the execution of a full-scale ship-to-shore assault at acceptable cost.

•Develop the control measures and landing craft needed to project the landing force ashore rapidly, in the desired tactical formation, with full unit integrity, on the right beach, at the right time.

• Maintain unity of command in a seamless passage of control from sea to shore as the tactical situation permits.

• Achieve these objectives in the minimum time possible in order to reduce the great vulnerability of the amphibious task force to enemy interdiction by air, surface, subsurface, and counterlanding attacks.

Amphibious techniques, tactics, and hardware changed throughout the war—and indeed ever since—but these primal concepts have remained constant. In 1992 the Joint Chiefs of Staff produced Joint Publication 3-02, *Joint Doctrine for Amphibious Operations,* one more milestone in the lineage that began with publication of *Tentative Manual for Landing Operations* in 1935. The newest authority's basic tenets would be familiar to the Quantico pioneers of sixty years earlier. An amphibious operation is now defined as "a military operation launched from the sea by naval and landing forces embarked in ships or craft involving a landing on a hostile or potentially hostile shore." The "essential usefulness" of an amphibious operation "stems from its mobility and flexibility." And this reminder appears early: "The salient requirement of an amphibious assault . . . is the necessity for swift, uninterrupted buildup of sufficient combat power ashore from an initial zero capability to full coordinated striking power."

Three other components of amphibious warfare need special emphasis in this survey of storm landings in the Central Pacific: leadership, logistics, and tactical mobility.

Executing an opposed landing on a hostile shore exerts special demands on combat leadership. In the words of Joint Pub 3-02: "The complexity of amphibious operations and the vulnerability of forces engaged in these operations require an exceptional degree of unity of effort and operational coherence." Both the amphibious task force commander and the landing force commander must "gain and maintain exceptional situational awareness." Chronic communications failures during the first thirty hours of Tarawa kept Harry Hill and Julian Smith completely in the dark regarding the situation ashore. Fifteen months later, Kelly Turner and Harry Schmidt maintained such "exceptional situational awareness" of conditions along the beaches and terraces at Iwo Jima on D-Day that they could accurately direct the massive flow of reinforcements and supporting arms ashore.

That's one kind of leadership. When "situational awareness" on the flagship failed at Tarawa, the battle would be won or lost on the raw courage of the men on the scene, officers like David Shoup, Mike Ryan, Alexander Bonnyman, Deane Hawkins, or staff noncommissioned officers like William Bordelon. Tactical success in each case required the leader to inspire small groups of disorganized men to overcome two inevitable characteristics of the assault beachhead—chaos and inertia. "Chaos reigned" reported the landing force commander after the 1924 Fleet Problem in the Caribbean—and in fact chaos reappeared to some degree in every subsequent landing in the Pacific, even Tinian. Inertia surfaced among those who survived a particularly harrowing ship-to-shore movement, as at Tarawa or Peleliu. At Betio, getting the masses of exhausted, demoralized troops huddled against the seawall to resume the offensive took incredible leadership. Some leaders like Shoup and Henry Crowe got results literally by "kicking ass." Others—Bordelon, Bonnyman, Hawkins—set a personal, sacrificial example. Mike Ryan seemed to combine the two styles. Men such as these won that pivotal battle by surpassing themselves and motivating others.

Logistics dominates amphibious operations from concept to consolidation. No aspect of military art requires such a fine balance between the "broad-arrow operators" and the "stubby-pencil logisticians." The most exquisite landing plan will quickly come to grief unless the ships are combat loaded with such excruciating forethought as to support each aspect of the scheme of maneuver ashore. Successful embarkation required detailed knowledge of both combat cargo and the characteristics of all types of amphibious and merchant ships—a rare blend of arcane skills.

Unloading the stuff took less mental acumen but much more manpower. General Geiger had to deploy nearly one-fifth of his III Amphibious Corps as shore party and shipboard working parties at Guam. Here again, leadership—or the lack of it—dominated. While the Navy produced legendary logistics specialists like Commodore Carl E. "Squeaky" Anderson, the Marines too often regarded their own shore party as a transient brigade for combat replacements. A few brilliant logisticians emerged in the Fleet Marine Force—Col. Francis B. Loomis Jr. of IIIAC, Col. Earl S. Piper of the 5th Marine Division, Lt. Col. James D. Hittle of the 3d Marine Division—but shore party support of the landing force evolved only fitfully throughout the war. Some of the problems were organizational. The Marine divisions lacked sufficient vehicles and personnel to support advancing troops fully during an extended campaign over considerable distances, as at Okinawa (or, by projection, Kyūshū).

Col. Robert Debs Heinl, veteran artillery officer and colorful historian of the Corps, described the "entire roll of Central Pacific battles, from Tarawa to Iwo Jima [as] amphibious warfare *a l'outrance* [to the utmost]."

The key ingredient for this formula lay in the realm of tactical mobility, the means of rapid projection of the landing force ashore with sufficient acceleration to overrun the defenders. Amphibian tractors (LVTs), DUKWs, and Higgins boats (LCVPs) eventually constituted the trinity of the ship-to-shore assault, and the combination proved effective. But each type of craft held disadvantages for the landing force: in the aggregate they were slow, rough-riding, and vulnerably exposed. Not even the LVTs were well-suited for tactical assault beyond the high-water mark, as Saipan and Iwo Jima showed.

Certain officers in the postwar period considered the vulnerability of the ship-to-shore movement to be the last unresolved problem of amphibious assault. In 1951 Col. Lewis W. Walt, a highly decorated veteran of the Solomons and Peleliu, wrote: "The time is past when assault infantry can be placed as helpless victims aboard slow-moving landing craft, several miles from shore, and expect a sufficient number of them will reach a defended beach to initiate an attack."

Such concerns led eventually to the development of alternate, faster means of getting men and combat equipment ashore: transport helicopters, air-cushioned landing craft, tilt-rotor aircraft, and the "moonstone" of engineering development, an armored, assault amphibian fully capable of transitioning into an infantry fighting vehicle ashore. Reducing the chronic vulnerability of the surface assault remained for decades the one lingering shortfall from the Pacific War.

Storm landings in the Central Pacific were therefore both effective and dangerous. The United States resorted to frontal, daylight attacks because we lacked the command, control, and navigational capabilities to execute massive night landings—and because of our inability to observe and adjust preliminary naval bombardment in darkness.

The unbroken string of victories in the Central Pacific exacted a heavy toll. For the Marines and their organic Navy personnel alone, storming the fortified islands of Tarawa, Saipan, Guam, Tinian, Peleliu, Iwo Jima, and Okinawa cost a total of 74,805 combat casualties. Losses among participating Army and offshore Navy units in these same operations would spike the total close to 100,000 men.

Reflect on this for a moment. Consider both the sacrifices and the achievements of these men and their surviving counterparts in fighting their way across five thousand miles of hostile ocean under conditions that are almost beyond modern comprehension. We today might well feel constrained to ask the same question Lt. Col. Donn J. Robertson

Combat artist Kerr Eby captured the grim cost of storm landings in his etching titled "Ebb Tide" and rendered on Tarawa. *(U.S. Navy Combat Art Collection)*

asked himself after watching the lead elements of his 3d Battalion, 27th Marines, storm ashore during the worst of Japanese shelling at Iwo Jima: "What impels a young guy landing on a beach from the very first craft in the face of fire ?"

Veteran combat correspondent Robert Sherrod put it this way: "It is true, by and large, that the United States won the Pacific war through its massive industrial power, which the Japanese could never expect to match—and it is easy to say so. But no man who saw Tarawa, Saipan, Iwo Jima, or Okinawa would agree that all the American steel was in the guns and bombs. There was a lot, also, in the hearts of the men who stormed the beaches."

And each of those soldiers, sailors, airmen, Coast Guardsmen, and Marines who did so—on our behalf—left us a national heritage, a legacy of saltwater, and coral sand, and young blood.

Semper Fidelis

Appendix

Ten Unforgettable Amphibians

The legendary amphibians of the Pacific War included great commanders with
colorful nicknames— "Terrible" Turner, "Howlin' Mad" Smith, "Handsome
Harry" Hill, "Close-In" Conolly—as well as their less-flamboyant counterparts
like Roy Geiger, Harry Schmidt, Simon Buckner, and Julian Smith. Yet tens of
thousands of "lesser lights" executed these seven storm landings—or defended
against them—and rarely received their due credit.

Here is a sampling of ten of these men: six U.S. Marines, three U.S. Navy, one
Imperial Japanese Navy. The sample includes a fighter pilot, a beachmaster, a
SeaBee, a battalion surgeon, a rikusentai, a rifleman. Their personal contribu-
tions helped make the storm landings so memorable in our history.

Carl E. "Squeaky" Anderson, Navy Beachmaster. In amphibious operations, the critical "blue-green" seam between the Navy and the landing force exists along the
high-water mark of the beach. Navy beachmasters control the boats; shore party
units hump the cargo clear of the beach. Here chaos often reigns. Indeed, a vital
lesson learned from Tarawa concerned the need for a "fully qualified beachmaster arriving early to take charge of the entire unloading situation." "Squeaky"
Anderson filled that vacuum. (The nickname came from his use of bullhorns on
the beach to exert his will.) His commanding presence at Iwo Jima impressed a

Royal Navy liaison officer: "On the beach was an extraordinary character, almost as wide as he was tall, delivering his commands in amazingly blasphemous language with a strong Scandinavian accent. He managed to get things done." Anderson, a native of Jansberg, Sweden, came to the United States in 1909, served in the Navy in World War I, then worked as a master mariner in Alaskan waters. Returning to active duty in 1940, he served in the Aleutians, then joined Adm. Harry Hill's staff in the Central Pacific. His ability to unload critical cargo over unlikely beaches at Apamama, Eniwetok, Saipan, and Tinian proved invaluable. Iwo Jima presented the greatest challenge. Anderson, then fifty-seven, developed hinged Marston matting, armored bulldozers, and sand sledges in advance to move cargo over the soft-sand beaches. Yet, once ashore, even Anderson had to admit "this is the toughest beach I have ever seen." When asked by reporters how he had managed to keep supplies flowing in, casualties flowing out, he replied, "I get so much hell from the Admiral I yust pass it on. Then we get things done." Anderson ended the war as force beachmaster on Hill's staff.

Thomas Jack Colley, Marine Combat Intelligence Officer. Storm landings would demand exceptional tactical intelligence. As staff intelligence officer for the 2d Marine Division at Tarawa, Saipan, and Tinian, Jack Colley pioneered new ground and set tough professional standards. Colley was thirty-four at Tarawa, a Naval Academy graduate with field experience in China, Iceland, and Guadalcanal. Planning the Tarawa assault became his greatest challenge. He and his free-spirited staff integrated information from ULTRA intercepts, aerial and submarine periscope photographs, interviews with former Gilbertese, and their own judgment to produce an astonishingly accurate intelligence estimate. Indeed, the D-2 situation map of Betio became a collector's item before the year was out, a model of painstaking analysis and careful artwork. Neither Colley nor anyone else in 1943 had knowledge of the "apogean neap tide"—his field notebook for D-Day at Betio contains the carefully penciled expectation of high tide at 1009 at five feet even, an otherwise accurate forecast. Colley went ashore on D+3 with Julian Smith, both officers having to bail out when Japanese fire from "the Pocket" disabled their LVT. Colley respected the rikusentai. "These people here were Jap marines," he wrote his parents, "and were highly selected, trained, and dead-eye Dicks with their weapons." He also bristled at media efforts to blame Tarawa's casualties on poor intelligence. "Actually," he wrote, "and you can paste this in your hat, nobody in authority was very much surprised at that Battle—I know I wasn't." At Saipan, Colley's interrogation of his captured Japanese counterpart provided a chilling, early forecast of the extent of civilian resistance to be expected should the Allies invade Japan proper.

Robert E. Galer, Marine Aviator. Bob Galer's war against the Japanese ran the gamut from Pearl Harbor to Okinawa. Although he would never forget the outrage of the preemptive Japanese air raid, Galer attained early vengeance. As a twenty-nine-year-old major, he commanded Marine Fighting Squadron 224 during the early, desperate months at Guadalcanal. Flying from Henderson Field, Galer became one of the Corps' first aces, eventually downing thirteen Japanese planes and receiving the Medal of Honor for "superb airmanship, outstanding skill, and personal bravery." Bored with Stateside duty—and advised by Washington officials that it was "too dangerous" to reassign him to another combat squadron—Galer worked his way back to the Pacific in the endeavor to improve the ragged state of close air support to landing operations. As an observer at Peleliu and Angaur, Galer saw firsthand both the promise and the problems of integrating air support to the landing forces with naval gunfire and artillery. Sensing the urgent need for better communications, he helped train three air control teams to use the new M-584 field radar and UHF radios. These teams evolved into the Landing Force Air Support Control Units that contributed so significantly to the storm landings of 1945. Galer then hit the road to supervise these teams in combat ashore at Iwo Jima, Luzon, and Okinawa. In the latter campaign, Galer's teams controlled as many as 375 aircraft on station simultaneously and directed night fighters to thirty-five confirmed kills. One of the few men to experience the tremendous growth of U.S. amphibious power from start to finish, his remark on the beach at Iwo Jima on D-Day is revealing: "Back at Guadalcanal it was 'can we hold?' Here it's 'when can we get it finished?'"

James Logan Jones, Amphibious Reconnaissance Marine. No unit better reflected the growth of amphibious virtuosity than the Fleet Marine Force, Pacific, Amphibious Reconnaissance Company, commanded throughout the war by James L. Jones. The Marines came close to losing Jones and his men in 1943 when friendly fire nearly sank the transport submarine *Nautilus* in the Gilberts. The sub and its troop contingent survived, going on to small-unit glory in the wholesale capture of Apamama Atoll. Thereafter, Jones and his men provided outstanding service in a series of pre-D-Day exploits in the Marshalls, Marianas, and Okinawa. Jones had chosen the Marine profession relatively late in life, at twenty-eight; for years he had sold farm tractors in west Africa. His international experience qualified him as an intelligence officer under Gen. Holland Smith's Amphibious Force, Atlantic Fleet. Smith had been intrigued with amphibious reconnaissance ("we're fighting blind without this") since sub-launched Marines first paddled ashore in fleet exercises in the 1930s. Jones formed his unique company, then followed Smith west to the Pacific. Over time, Jones's men became adept at launching rubber boats at night from subs or high-speed transports, paddling ashore, and securing vital intelligence. Prior to Tinian the unit executed a dangerous reconn of potential landing beaches under the very feet of Japanese sentries. At Okinawa Jones's well-conditioned scouts reconnoitered the 77th Division's beaches in the Kerama Retto, helped seize Keise Shima as a fire support base, and stormed Tsugen Jima. In each of these stealthy endeavors Jones enhanced the odds for amphibious success and built a solid operational foundation for the Force Reconn units of the succeeding fifty years.

Michael F. Keleher, Navy Surgeon, 4th Marine Division. "Irish Mike" Keleher was a newcomer to amphibious assault when he joined the 3d Battalion, 25th Marines, in 1943. Disembarking from a troop transport by cargo net into a boat alongside "required the timing of a flying-trapeze artist," he admitted, but he

Thomas J. Colley, intelligence officer, 2d Marine Division. *(Douglas J. Colley)*

Robert E. Galer, fighter ace, air control pioneer. *(U.S. Marine Corps)*

James L. Jones, amphibious reconnaissance pioneer. *(James L. Jones Jr.)*

Michael F. "Irish Mike" Keleher, battalion surgeon, 3d Battalion, 25th Marines. *(Barbara Keleher)*

soon put this practice to good use during Roi-Namur, Saipan, Tinian, and Iwo Jima. Keleher marveled that any human could survive the naval bombardment at Namur, "but we soon learned that the Japanese soldier is very tough." So was "Irish Mike." During a Japanese night attack on Saipan, Keleher worked desperately to save a Marine whose leg had been nearly severed in the fighting. Holding his flashlight in his teeth, the surgeon used scissors and a tourniquet on the battlefield to complete the amputation and staunch the bleeding. The Marine lived. The next day an artillery round knocked Keleher senseless, but he returned to duty in a few hours. By the Tinian landing, Keleher felt that "we were now well-trained, experienced, and blooded veterans." Then came Iwo. Keleher landed on D-Day amid absolute hell on earth and began treating casualties in a shell crater. On the third evening the battalion commander, Lt. Col. "Jumping Joe" Chambers, fell with a bullet in his chest. Keleher got to him quickly, applied a pressure bandage, dragged him out of the fire, administered plasma. He had to draw his pistol to convince a reluctant DUKW driver to take the critically wounded Chambers out to the hospital ship. Chambers would live to receive the Medal of Honor, but before being evacuated to the States he wrote "Irish Mike" a personal note: "I cannot leave without thanking you for my life. There's no question that you saved mine, in the same manner you have saved so many others."

Larry E. Klatt, Navy SeaBee. The Naval Construction Battalions and the Marines enjoyed a symbiotic relationship throughout the Pacific War. At one point each Marine division included a SeaBee battalion. For twenty-three-year-old Carpenter's Mate 1/c Larry Klatt, a former architectural draftsman from Denver, this meant the submergence of his 18th SeaBee Battalion into the 2d Marine Division for Tarawa. Klatt and his unit had tasted combat in the Solomons, but Tarawa would provide their defining moment. In that savage melee, the Marines learned that the most valuable vehicle on the beach was a SeaBee bulldozer, equally useful in burying low-lying Japanese bunkers, digging howitzer parapets, or clearing the runway. Klatt, ashore on D+3, received a personal welcome when a sniper's bullet zipped within an inch of his head. By Saipan, Klatt and crew considered themselves amphibious veterans, but the long hours spent in a bobbing LVT proved unsettling: "Some of those who trained the hardest lay greenest in the bottom of the boat." Ashore, Klatt survived sniper fire as a stretcher bearer, experienced profound fear when a Japanese 8-inch gunner methodically bracketed the beachhead with high explosive shells, felt compassion for a native Chamorro woman whose newborn baby died in the battle. Klatt's SeaBees then devised breaching ramps to help Marine LVTs assault Tinian's steep escarpments. But Klatt's greatest contribution to the storm landings of 1944–45 lay in his meticulous scale drawings of the Japanese fortifications on Betio at the demand of Chester Nimitz, appalled at the failure of naval shelling. Nimitz's engineers used Klatt's blueprints to build exact replicas on Kahoolawe in Hawaii. No gunship could thereafter go west to war without first assaulting "Klatt's pillboxes."

Lewis J. Michelony Jr., Marine First Sergeant, 2d Marine Division. Prewar Marine first sergeants tended to be grizzled veterans in their forties. "Micky" Michelony reflected the "New Corps," a young man so physically fit, forceful, and responsible that Maj. William K. Jones, commanding the 1st Battalion, 6th Marines, selected him as a top sergeant at the tender age of twenty-two. Michelony suffered no fools—he had been middleweight boxing champion of the Atlantic Fleet—and he took seriously his duties of training and discipline. He saw enough combat in Guadalcanal to fine-tune his reflexes. On D+3 at Tarawa, die-hard Japanese gunners ambushed Michelony's patrol. Desperate, Michelony dove headfirst into a nearby bunker, tumbling into what he thought was a pool of water. It was instead a foul residue of the bunker's Japanese defenders, some long dead, others still alive. Michelony spat, swore, scrambled to safety, reeking. He never regained his sense of smell. By Saipan, he figured he had used up his luck. The D-Day landing was "a mess—dead Marines all up and down the beach." That night his patrol encountered the major Japanese tank attack, caught between two fires as they raced back to their lines. Two weeks later Michelony tried to rescue a patrol that had been ambushed in a draw dominated by three Japanese cave positions. "I did the crazy thing. I hollered 'this is Micky, your Top Sergeant; if anyone's alive down there, sound off, otherwise I'm going to flame the whole draw.'" One Marine answered weakly. Michelony crawled down and rescued the survivor, then returned and destroyed each cave position. He had grown up in the Pennsylvania coal mines during the depression. "In a small town, everyone was family. So were my Marines. I loved them like brothers."

Minoru Ota, Imperial Japanese Navy rikusentai. The rikusentai were naval infantrymen, sailors with "advanced degrees" in infantry tactics and weapons. Initially organized to spearhead amphibious landings, these special naval landing forces fought prominently at Wake, Guam, the Bismarcks, and Solomons. When the tide turned, the rikusentai came to resemble defense battalions of the Fleet Marine Force, adapting heavy antiaircraft and coast-defense guns. These sailors became known for their discipline, esprit, and combat skills, but few survived the war. Their greatest commander, Adm. Keiji Shibasaki, died at Tarawa. Minoru Ota lived longer and fought the Americans at more places but met the same fate. Ota, fifty-four at the battle of Okinawa, was a native of Chiba Prefecture and a 1913 graduate of the Japanese Naval Academy. He was an exceptional naval gunner and served as executive officer of the battleship *Yamashiro,* but by mid-career he was commanding rikusentai units in China. As a captain in May 1942, Ota headed the 2d Combined Special Landing Force earmarked to seize Midway after Yamamoto's expected naval victory. Later, as a rear admiral, he commanded the 8th Combined Special Landing Forces in New Georgia. Here he fought against the 1st Raider Battalion in the jungles of Bairoko. At Okinawa, Ota commanded ten thousand men, but half were civilian laborers and the others were more gunners than naval infantry. Ota nonetheless galvanized them into a ferocious defense of the Oroku Peninsula against the attacking 6th Marine Division. In the end, he radioed Tokyo: "The troops under my command have fought gallantly, in the finest tradition of the Japanese Navy. Fierce bombing may deform Okinawa's mountains but cannot alter their spirit."

Eugene B. Sledge, Marine Rifleman, 1st Marine Division. Fittingly, the lowest-ranking man in this sample achieved the greatest postwar fame. Eugene Sledge attained renown by writing frankly of his wartime experiences. For all of amphibious warfare's great operational and doctrinal breakthroughs, the final executors were men like Sledge who had to storm ashore under fire. His book *With the Old Breed at Peleliu and Okinawa* became the classic rifleman's account of the Pacific War, favorably compared with World War I's *All Quiet on*

Larry E. Klatt, Carpenter's Mate 1/c, USN, 18th Naval Construction Battalion. *(Larry E. Klatt)*

Lewis J. Michelony Jr. 1st Sergeant, 1st Battalion, 6th Marines. *(Lewis J. Michelony Jr.)*

Eugene B. Sledge, rifleman, 3d Battalion, 5th Marines. *(Eugene B. Sledge)*

Donald M. Weller, naval gunfire support pioneer. *(U.S. Marine Corps)*

the *Western Front* and the Civil War's *Red Badge of Courage.* Of these, Sledge's work, manifestly nonfiction, is the most believable. Sledge was a twenty-year-old Alabaman, dutiful and observant, when he joined the 1st Marine Division (the Old Breed) in 1944 as a 60-mm mortarman in King Company, 3d Battalion, 5th Marines. Of his first combat landing at Peleliu, Sledge wrote, "Everything my life had been before and has been after pales in the light of that awesome moment when my amtrac started . . . toward that flaming, smoke-shrouded beach." Getting ashore was traumatic enough, then Sledge noted: "A number of amtracs and DUKWs were burning. Japanese machine-gun bursts made long splashes on the water as though flaying it with some giant whip. . . . I caught a fleeting glimpse of a group of Marines leaving a smoking amtrac on the reef. Some fell." Sledge's officers warned him Okinawa would be even rougher ("expect 85 percent casualties"). When no resistance materialized, Sledge's team sped ashore singing "Little Brown Jug." Then came Awacha Pocket, Half Moon Hill, Kunishi Ridge. Only a handful of the Peleliu vets in his company survived. When news of the A-bombs reached the men in the ranks, "we sat hollow-eyed and silent, trying to comprehend a world without war."

Donald M. Weller, Naval Gunfire Pioneer. Many prewar ground officers viewed naval gunfire as the fatal flaw of amphibious doctrine: the unnatural reliance on ships to suppress a defended beach until proper field artillery could land, register, and open fire. Fleet landing exercises in 1935–41 did little to dispel this bias. But naval gunfire support to amphibious war came of age in the Central Pacific. This feat had many fathers, none more farsighted than Marine artillery officer Don Weller. A Connecticut native, Weller graduated from the Naval Academy in 1930. He served on battleships and cruisers, attended the Army Field Artillery School, and in 1940 became Gen. Holland Smith's naval gunfire officer in what emerged as the Amphibious Corps, Atlantic Fleet. Smith chose Weller—as he had chosen Captain Jones of amphibious reconn—for his vision and work ethic. Like Jones, Weller followed Smith to the Pacific and helped him prepare for the Aleutians. Weller then took a "leave of absence" to command a 75-mm howitzer battalion in the 3d Marine Division during Bougainville and Guam. He rejoined Smith's staff to help plan Iwo Jima. "Iwo was the toughest nut to crack," said Weller. While he and Smith failed to sway the Navy to extend the preliminary bombardment, they did devise a unique "rolling barrage" by a destroyer squadron to precede the assault troops ashore and across the first terraces. Weller also convinced Admiral Blandy to focus all D-minus-1 fires against Suribachi and the Rock Quarry, dominating the beaches. But it was Tarawa, to Weller, that proved the watershed in this difficult art: "The Japanese shore battery could be attacked at short range with reasonable impunity; ships could 'fight forts,' at least Japanese forts." And smart naval gunfire could save American lives.

Textual Notes

The following abbreviations are used in the notes:

MCHC: Marine Corps Historical Center, Washington, D.C.

MCOHC: Marine Corps Oral History Collection, MCHC, Washington, D.C.

NHC: Naval Historical Center, Washington, D.C.

SS No.: *Senshi Sosho* No. (Japanese war history series)

USMC Operations 1–5: *History of U.S. Marine Corps Operations in World War II,* volumes 1–5

USNIP: U.S. Naval Institute *Proceedings*

USN Operations: Samuel E. Morison, *The History of U.S. Naval Operations during the Second World War*

Prologue

Epigraph cited in Dyer, *The Amphibians Came to Conquer,* 330. "Enemy troop strength is overwhelming" from USMC Operations, 1:264. Details on Baker Company's landing from Frank, *Guadalcanal,* 72, and USMC Operations, 1:263. Paramarines and others landing on Gavutu-Tanambogo from Frank, *Guadalcanal,* 74–79, and USMC Operations, 1:266–73. "The most far-reaching tactical innovation" by Gen. J.F.C. Fuller, quoted by Isely and Crowl, *The U.S. Marines and Amphibious War,* 6. "A soldier's battle" by Maj. Gen. Alexander A.Vande-grift, quoted in Frank, *Guadalcanal,* 79.

Chapter 1

Epigraph from Isely and Crowl, *Amphibious War,* 27. For Aboukir Bay, see Brendan P. Ryan, "Aboukir Bay, 1801," in Bartlett, *Assault from the Sea,* 69–73. For Caesar in Britain, see Brenda Ralph Lewis, "Caesar's Battle for Britannia," *Military History* 12 (February 1996), 46–53. Gallipoli summary from Isely and Crowl, *Amphibious War,* 17–23. Liddell Hart "one of the most difficult opera-tions of war" cited in Dyer, *Amphibians,* 318. (Kelly Turner had this quote in his sea cabin as he sailed for Guadalcanal.) General Eisenhower's "an amphibious landing is not a particularly difficult thing" is cited in full in Isely and Crowl, *Amphibious War,* 6. Gen. Eli Cole and Adm. Montgomery Taylor's reports of the 1924 landing exercises are cited in Isely and Crowl, *Amphibious War,* 30–31. Two works by Kenneth J. Clifford provide the background of amphibious doc-trinal development, *Progress and Purpose: A Developmental History of the U.S. Marine Corps* (1973) and *Amphibious Warfare Development in Britain and America from 1920–1940* (1983). "Pioneer work of the most daring and imagi-native sort" from Isely and Crowl, *Amphibious War,* 36. Japanese amphibious developments in the prewar years from Millett, "Assault from the Sea." See also chapter 2 of Alexander, *Utmost Savagery.* Nimitz's comment "only skill in keep-ing their plans disguised" from Frank, *Guadalcanal,* 597. Vandegrift comment "Landings should not be attempted in the face of organized resistance" from Dyer, *Amphibians,* 541.

Chapter 2

Epigraph from Gen. David M. Shoup Collection, Personal Journal, 2 July 1943, Hoover Institute Archives. Shoup served as observer to the 43d Infantry Division landing at Rendova, New Georgia. Experiences of first waves ashore at Tulagi from USMC Operations, 1:263–64. Maj. Gerald C. Thomas's Congressional tes-timony concerning defenses of Guam from Millett, *In Many a Strife,* 129–30, 138. Testing the reef-crossing abilities of Higgins boats from USMC Operations, 1:81. Details on development and employment of Higgins's LCVPs and LCMs from Strahan, *Andrew Jackson Higgins,* and Baker, *Allied Landing Craft.* Captain Ota's amphibious plans for Midway from Fuchida and Okumiya, *Midway: The Battle That Doomed Japan.* Details on the Makin and Dieppe raids and Opera-tion Torch from Lorelli, *To Foreign Shores,* 57–58, 58–60, and 70–84, respec-tively. Lt. Col. Jack Colley's intelligence plan for Tarawa from collection main-tained by his son, Cdr. Douglas J. Colley, USNR (Ret.), graciously shared with the author. Naval gunfire at Gavutu-Tanambogo from Dyer, *Amphibians,* 843–44.

"From daylight to noon this little island was bombarded" from Rear Adm. Herbert B. Knowles, USN (Ret.), letter 1 September 1962 to Headquarters, Marine Corps, p. 1, retained in "Comments on Vol. III" file, Archives Section, MCHC. Casualties from "friendly" aviation strikes on Gavutu from Frank, *Guadalcanal,* 76, 78. "Tinker toy level" from Wyckoff, "Let There Be Built Great Ships," 51–57. "Unloading French 75s" from del Valle, oral memoir, 1966,

MCOHC, 243. Sir Roger Keyes's "folly to storm a defended beach in daylight" cited in Dyer, *Amphibians,* 590. Russian Black Sea Fleet landings in 1943 from Paul Carell, *Scorched Earth,* 2:154–69. Details on amphibious transports and cargo ships from Silverstone, *U.S. Warships of World War II,* 260–61, 281, 335. Losses of troop transports from Silverstone, *U.S. Warships of World War II,* 266, 335, 404, and Morison, *The Two-Ocean War,* 233, 408. For the Japanese Ketsu-Go plan for attacking American troop transports with suicide forces, see chapter 9 this volume. Details on LSTs from Baker, *Allied Landing Craft.* The tattletale leaker from Barbey, *MacArthur's Amphibious Navy,* 39, 43. Turner's "You are the first to land!"—one of the all-time classic quotes of amphibious warfare—cited in Dyer, *Amphibians,* 545.

Chapter 3

Epigraph from Tadao Onuki, one of the eight rikusentai to survive Tarawa, in Ito, Tomiaka, and Inada, eds., *Jitsuroku Taiheyo sense* (Real accounts of the Pacific War), 3:31. Details on Admiral Shibasaki and the action on Betio Island, Tarawa Atoll, extracted from Alexander, *Utmost Savagery.* Details on the naval revolution in the Central Pacific engendered by the advent of the *Essex*-class carriers from Reynolds, *The Fast Carriers.*

Gen. Holland Smith's early recommendations for use of LVTs in amphibious assaults are found in CG, Amphibious Corps, Atlantic Fleet to CG, Army Ground Forces of 13 March 1942, p. 3, and CG, Amphibious Corps, Atlantic Fleet to Commander in Chief, United States Fleet of 31 March 1942, Annex G, p. 2, both copies provided courtesy Maj. Jon T. Hoffman, USMCR, in his research as the leading biographer of Merritt A. Edson. Lieutenant Colonel Krulak's 1943 "Crash Test" of LVTs is contained in his official report, "Tests of amphibian tractor under surf and coral conditions," 3 May 1943. Gen. Clayton B. Vogel forwarded the report to the commandant on 5 May. The assistant commandant (Maj. Gen. Keller E. Rockey) endorsed the report "for information" to the CG, Amphibious Corps, Pacific Fleet (Gen. H. Smith) on 9 June 43, five months before Tarawa. Document held in Archives Section, Marine Corps University, and provided the author courtesy of fellow historian Maj. James R. Davis, USMC (Ret.). Joint Planning Staff Report No. 205, "Operations against the Marshall Islands," 10 June 1943 is found in Record Group 165, ABC 384, National Archives.

Tank losses and problems at Tarawa from 2d Tank Battalion Special Action Report, 14 December 1943, Archives Section, MCHC. Development of the dock landing ship from Wyckoff, "Let There Be Built Great Ships," 56–57. The complaint about Spruance wanting "a sledgehammer to drive a tack" is attributed by Potter to Adm. John H. Towers in *Nimitz,* 255. Spruance's observation about the principal lesson learned at Tarawa came from Buell, *The Quiet Warrior,* 214–15. "Get the hell in and get the hell out" from Potter, *Nimitz,* 257. An excellent account of the Bougainville landing is contained in USMC Operations, 2:207–35. Details of close air support to the landing from Sherrod, *History of Marine Corps Aviation,* 131, 181, 190–92. Admiral Koga's belief that his aviators had so severely damaged Halsey's fleet that the Americans would be incapable of launching a new counteroffensive in the Central Pacific is reported in SS No. 62, 442.

Prof. Donald W. Olson identified the rare "apogean neap tide" in "Tide at Tarawa," 526–29. Admiral Shibasaki's death, now determined to have occurred the afternoon of D-Day vice D+3, is based on translations of survivors' accounts in SS Nos. 6 and 62, action reports of the two destroyers in Fire Support Area Four, and radio logs of the Shore Fire Control Party and the 2d Marine Division, as presented in Alexander, *Utmost Savagery,* 147–52. Turner "a goddamned painful lesson" cited in Dyer, *Amphibians,* 651. Shoup's dissatisfaction with support provided by VAC at Tarawa is scattered throughout his 1943–44 journals in the Shoup Collection, Hoover Institute Archives, and the "Volume 3 Comments" file in the Archives Section, MCHC. See also Merritt Edson to Gerald Thomas, 13 December 1943, Box 5, Edson Papers. The mystery of the missing two-thousand-pound daisy-cutters is discussed in Alexander, *Utmost Savagery,* 88, 108. See also Shoup's field notebook for Tarawa, Personal Papers Collection, MCHC.

"Not the nature of amphibious warfare to be bloodless" from Kelly, "The Achilles Heel," 41–45. "Carry a supply of wooden plugs" from VAC "SOP for Employment of Amphibian Tractors (LVTs)," 14, Navy Archives, Suitland. "SNAFU Leadership" from Lt. Col. Evans F. Carlson, USMCR, to CG, VAC, "Report of Observations on Galvanic Operation," 27 November 1943, p. 8, Archives Section, MCHC. "Landing teams should practice landings wherein all units are mixed up" from Lt. Col. Walter I. Jordan, USMC to CG, VAC, "Long-suit Operation, observation of," 27 November 1943, p. 5, Archives Section, MCHC. Japanese attempts to alert the Marshalls of tactical lessons learned from the loss of Tarawa are contained in radio intercepts reported in CINCPAC messages 212100 November 1943, ULTRA file, and 230127 November 1943, ULTRA file, both in SRMN-OI3, Part 3, Record Group 457, National Archives.

Chapter 4

Epigraph from CINCPAC Monthly Operations Report, July 1944, p. 37, cited in Dyer, *Amphibians,* 945. J. T. Rutherford account of D-Day landing from interview, April 1995. "On this day the enemy landed" from diary of Tarac Kawachi of the 43d Division Hospital Unit, found on Saipan 19 July 1944, copy provided author courtesy Raymond J. Hagberg, 2d Amphibian Tractor Battalion at Saipan. Composite U.S. casualties extracted from USMC Operations, 3:636. The concentration of so many significant naval and military landmarks in a mere six weeks vitiates their historical study: 6 June 44: D-Day at Normandy; 15 June: D-Day at Saipan; 18–19 June: Battle of the Philippine Sea; 21 July: W-Day at Guam; 24 July: J-Day at Tinian.

Nimitz's waffling on the Marianas vs. "the single axis," MacArthur's "Give me central direction of the war in the Pacific" letter to Secretary of War Stimson, and King's rebuke to Nimitz are contained in Potter, *Nimitz,* 279–83. The composition of Mitscher's Task Force 58 in the Marshalls from Miller, *War at Sea,* 435. Nimitz's plans for the amphibious invasion of Truk from Isely and Crowl, *Amphibious War,* 308. Quantities of LVTs available for the three landings in the Marianas from Croizat, *Across the Reef,* 243–44. Shortage of ships for the landing forces for Forager reflected in Turner to Wilkinson, 30 July 1944: "We simply didn't have enough troops here [Saipan], and the reason we didn't have enough troops was that we didn't have enough ships to bring them in," cited in Dyer, *Amphibians,* 917. West Loch disaster and shortage of qualified ammo ships from Dyer, *Amphibians,* 895. Incident of Nimitz endangered by venturing too close to exploding ammo ships at West Loch related to author by Loren F. "Sonny" Paulus, former bodyguard to Nimitz, during interview, February 1996.

The Japanese rigid adherence to defense at the water's edge in the Marianas is best summarized in Crowl, *Campaign in the Marianas,* 61–63, 67. See also Dyer, *Amphibians,* 873. Dyer (870–72) also substantiates the disruption of IGHQ efforts to reinforce the Marianas created by U.S. submarines. Major Yoshida interrogation from personal papers of Col. Thomas Jack Colley, USMC (Ret.), provided the author courtesy of his son, Cdr. Douglas J. Colley, USNR (Ret.). Holland Smith "We are through with flat atolls now" cited in Sherrod, *On to Westward,* 57–58. Incident of injury to Lieutenant Dodd on D-Day at Saipan in Sherrod, *On to Westward,* 77. Spruance's comments defending his decisions at the Battle of the Philippine Sea from Buell, *The Quiet Warrior,* 303. Nimitz's reaction to the civilian bodies at Saipan's Marpi Point on 17 July 1944 from Potter, *Nimitz,* 313–14, and Paulus interview, February 1996.

"I was particularly impressed to see Japanese soldiers still alive" attributed to Lt. Col. Calvin W. Kunz, USMC, 9th Marines, Guam, in USMC Operations, 3:458. Gaan Point action from same source, 3:461–62. General Shepherd's two D-Day quotes from same source, 3:474, 476. One-fifth of IIIAC committed to logistics functions from same source, 3:577–78. "The 77th Marine Division" from O'Brien, *Liberation,* 44. "Dick Conolly's and Roy Geiger's units were superbly schooled" from Morison, *New Guinea and the Marianas,* 383 (vol. 8 in USN Operations).

Tinian details summarized from Alexander, "Amphibious Blitzkrieg at Tinian," 10–17. The most concise and dispassionate summary of the "Smith vs. Smith Controversy" (more accurately: "Maj. Gen. Holland Smith, USMC, vs. Lt. Gen. Robert C. Richardson, USA") is contained in USMC Operations, 3:313–20. Excellent details of the J-Day night counterattack battle are found in same source, 3:388–92. "Each man fell in position" from interview, with Brig. Gen. Frederick J. Karch, USMC (Ret.), February 1994. Adm. Kishisaburo Nomura's "Everywhere you attacked before the defense was ready" appears in the USSBS Interrogation No. 429, 2:387.

Chapter 5
Epigraph from Vandegrift, "Amphibious Miracle of Our Time," *New York Times,* 6 August 1944, magazine sect., p. 38. Allan R. Millett's calculations concerning the number of amphibious assaults executed by Army and Marine divisions from Millet, *Semper Fidelis,* 439. Admiral Barbey's efforts with the Seventh Amphibious Force from Barbey, *MacArthur's Amphibious Navy,* 44–46, 66. Details on Operation Reckless (Hollandia) from Barbey, *MacArthur's Amphibious Navy,* 168–79, and Hoffman, "Legacy and Lessons of the New Guinea Campaign," 76. Regarding the differing tactical styles of the Army and Marines in beach assault, Admiral Spruance observed during the height of Okinawa's kamikaze attacks, "I doubt if the Army's slow, methodical method of fighting really saves any lives in the long run. It merely spreads the casualties over a longer

period. The longer period greatly increases the naval casualties when Jap air attacks on ships is a continuing factor" (Buell, *The Quiet Warrior,* 387). Vandegrift's "Out here too many commanders have been far too leery about risking their ships" cited in Potter, *Nimitz,* 193. Turner's "close the range or cease firing" cited in Dyer, *Amphibians,* 584. "Rock-throwing range" and Major Metzger's "beautiful seamanship" reported in USMC Operations, 3:463–65 and 3:461, respectively. Julian C. Smith's "crossing that beach with no more armored protection" (with the usually omitted profane adjective) appears in interview with Jeter A. Isely, 28–29 October 1948, contained in the "Princeton Papers," Personal Papers Section, MCHC.

Continuing problems with close air support to amphibious operations from USMC Operations, 3:573–74, 584. Growth of Marine Corps aviation units from Sherrod, *History of Marine Corps Aviation.* Details on DUKW performance from Baker, *Allied Landing Craft,* and comparing performance between LVTs and DUKWs from GHQ, Southwest Pacific Area, "Report of Landing Problem Using LSTs, DUKWs, Buffaloes, and Alligators, Carried out near Puni Puni on 16–17 November 1943," Navy Archives, Suitland.

Hill's "The reef marks the limit of Navy responsibility" cited in Dyer, *Amphibians,* 905. Details on LVT-As from Croizat, *Across the Reef,* and especially the series of letters from then Maj. Louis Metzger, USMC, who commanded the 1st Armored Amphibian Battalion in the Marshalls and Guam, as cited in USMC Operations, 3:441, 459, 543. Details on portable and mechanized flamethrower development from Meyer, "Tactical Use of Flame," 19–22; Unmacht, "Flame Throwing SeaBees," 425–26; Hunnicutt, *Sherman,* 402–7; and McKinney, *Mechanized Flame Thrower Operations,* 4–6, 83–90, 130, 151–55, 263–65, 288. Japanese antitank tactics from CINCPAC-CINCPOA Bulletin No. 144–45, "Japanese Antitank Warfare," 11 June 1945, Operational Archives, NHC. Japanese fear of white phosphorous munitions expressed in Yoshida Interrogation, Colley Papers.

Details of the F-Series Marine Division contained in USMC Operations, 3:618–19; 3:576 describes evolution of the Marine fire team. "Oh the BAR, now there was a weapon" from Shepherd, oral memoir, 1967, MCOHC, 232. Technical details of the Browning Automatic Rifle, as well as the Marines' preference for the older, lighter version, from Canfield, *U.S. Infantry Weapons,* 162–68. Losses of surgeons and corpsmen from USMC Operations, 3:636. "Only eleven divisions of troops" from Sherrod, *On to Westward,* 5–6. Details on Japanese antiboat mines from U.S. Department of War, *Handbook on Japanese Military Forces, Technical Manual TM-E30-480,* 373–74. Edson's "They've taken Indian warfare" cited in Hersey, *Into the Valley,* 11.

Chapter 6

Epigraph from Morison, *Leyte,* 4 (vol. 10 in USN Operations). Insights on Nimitz's way of dealing with stress from interviews with H. Arthur "Hal" Lamar, flag lieutenant, and Loren F. Paulus, bodyguard to CINCPAC, February 1996. Halsey's "I feared another Tarawa" and "the vulnerable underbelly of the Imperial Dragon" from Halsey and Bryan, *Admiral Halsey's Story,* 194–95 and

199, respectively. Geiger's initiative in going ashore at Peleliu on D-Day from Willock, *Unaccustomed to Fear,* 274–75. "Everything about Peleliu left a bad taste" from Silverthorn, oral memoir, 1969, MCOHC, 317. "Spigot of the Oil Barrel" from "Battlefronts," *Time,* 25 September 1944. "Breakwater of the Pacific" and "a picked Manchukuoan regiment" are the words of the commanding officer of the 15th Infantry Regiment, 14th Division, Imperial Japanese Army, cited in CINCPAC-CINCPOA, Item No. 9764, "Report on the 15th Infantry Regiment," 16 May 1944, Operational Archives, NHC. The role of Major General Murai and the Japanese account of the development of Peleliu's fortifications and defensive plans is well covered in SS No. 13, 102, 135, 142, 146–47, 151–53, 172, and 208–10. An outstanding summary of Japanese anti-amphibious research into lessons learned in the Gilberts, Marshalls, and Marianas, including the conversion from water's edge tactics to "endurance engagements" featuring Fukkaku honeycombed underground defenses, is contained in Kuzuhara, "Operations on Iwo Jima."

· Details on the battle for Biak from Smith, *Approach to the Philippines,* 282–300. "Momoji" from Funasaka, *Falling Blossoms,* 174. "Worn out more seabags" from McMillan, *The Old Breed,* 257. Personal insights regarding Major General Rupertus's family losses and operational injury from interview with Benis M. Frank, February 1995. Geiger's perception of 1st Marine Division shortcomings in preparations and lack of an assigned naval gunfire officer for Peleliu from Willock, *Unaccustomed to Fear,* 268–69 and 270–71, respectively. The division's lack of experience in conducting opposed amphibious assaults from USMC Operations, 4:78. Rupertus's reluctance to convert LVTs from logistics to tactical role cited in Isely and Crowl, *Amphibious War,* 188–89. Intelligence and shipping shortfalls from Isely and Crowl, *Amphibious War,* 395–96 and 398, respectively. Lt. Col. Kimber H. Boyer's armored amphibian battalion having to train with blueprints pending the last-minute arrival of their new vehicles from USMC Operations, 4:93. Lt. Col. Leonard F. Chapman Jr.'s "Pitiful expedient" from same source, 4:91–92. Ship collisions, other accidents from Isely and Crowl, *Amphibious War,* 398. Oldendorf's "run out of profitable targets" cited in Isely and Crowl, *Amphibious War,* 403.

Japanese mines reported in Underwater Demolition Team No. 6, "Anti-Invasion Mines on Peleliu," 1 October 1944, Archives Section, Marine Corps University, Quantico. Colonel Nakagawa's final defensive plans, including the possibility of "starting fires in fuel oil cans near reefs to make up fires on the seawater" from SS No. 13, 147. "Moments are getting tense now" from Kennard, *Combat Letters Home* (12 September 1944), 4. "Rough but fast" and "In again, out again Finnegan" from McMillan, *The Old Breed,* 269–70.

"The beach was a sheet of flame" from Sledge, "Peleliu 1944: Why Did We Go There?" 72–73. Tank action on D-Day from USMC Operations, 4:110. Saga of King Company, 3d Battalion, 1st Marines, at "the Point" from same source, 4:110–13, plus Hunt, *Coral Comes High,* and interview with Fred K. Fox of K/3/1, February 1996. "Can you observe?" from Platt, oral memoir, 1980, MCOHC, 72–73. Tom Lea quoted in McMillan, *The Old Breed,* 293. Smith accounts at Peleliu from Smith, oral memoir, 1969, MCOHC, 132–40. MacArthur's "They are waiting for me there" from "Battlefronts," *Time,* 25 September 1944. "As steep as the roof of a house" from Silverthorn, oral memoir, 1969, MCOHC, 318, 329. "I was always convinced that Lewie Puller would not have survived" from Davis, oral memoir, 1977, MCOHC, 132. Arrival of air units from Sherrod, *History of Marine Corps Aviation,* 256–59. Japanese officer captured on Ngesebus from Hough, *The Assault on Peleliu,* 125, and Walt, "The Closer the Better," 37.

Hirohito's nine separate decrees of praise from Funasaka, *Falling Blossoms,* 231. "It was a young man's war" from McLaughlin, oral memoir, 1978, MCOHC, 75. Swinging satchel charges into caves and smelling the Japanese cook-fires underground from McMillan, *The Old Breed,* 323. "Fifteen seconds over target" from Sherrod, *History of Marine Corps Aviation,* 257, and Hough, *The Assault on Peleliu,* 134. "The enemy plan seems to be to burn down the central hills" attributed to Col. Tokechi Tada, chief of staff, 14th Division, in Hough, *The Assault on Peleliu,* 139. *Time* mentioned the Peleliu campaign in its "Battlefronts" section during 18 and 25 September, 2 and 9 October, but only the latter carried any substance (an entire page, plus map). Delays in getting the B-24 bomber squadron operational from Smith, *Approach to the Philippines,* 573.

Colonel Nakagawa's final message from Funasaka, *Falling Blossoms,* 231. An average of 1,589 rounds of ammunition to kill each enemy soldier from McMillan, *The Old Breed,* 342–43. Sledge's "I shall always harbor a deep sense of bitterness" from Sledge, "Peleliu 1944: Why Did We Go There?" 74. "MacArthur's Marines" from interview with Fred K. Fox, February 1996. "Nimitz's greatest mistake of the war" from Miller, *The War at Sea,* 456.

Chapter 7

Epigraph from Task Force 56 Action Report, Iwo Jima, Archives Section, MCHC. Spruance's strategic views from Buell, *The Quiet Warrior,* 332–35. Nimitz "It is a cardinal principal of amphibious operations" from Isely and Crowl, *Amphibious War,* 449. General Schmidt's resentment of Holland Smith's postwar fame at Iwo Jima is revealed in an 11 December 1949 letter to Professor Isely: "I was the commander of all troops on Iwo Jima at all times. . . . Holland Smith . . . never had a command post ashore, never issued a single order ashore, never spent a single night ashore." Letter contained in the "Princeton Papers," Personal Papers Section, MCHC. Smith's "we welcome a counterattack" and other prelanding statements cited in Newcomb, *Iwo Jima,* 67. The intelligence report that could have answered many questions about Japanese defensive dispositions, soil trafficability, minefields, and the potential use of gasoline drums for a flame barrier along Iwo's beaches was CINCPAC-CINCPOA Bulletin No. 9-45, "Iwo Jima: First Supplement to Nanpo Shoto Information Bulletin No. 122-44," 10 January 1945, Operational Archives, NHC. Smith "toughest fight" from Newcomb, *Iwo Jima,* 240.

Biographical details concerning General Kuribayashi, his defensive assessment and preparations at Iwo Jima, and his meetings and correspondence with Major General Sanada are best presented in SS No. 13, 275–98. Kuribayashi's consideration of blowing the island in half is covered on p. 295. Corroborating details from Yoshitake Horie, "Explanation of Japanese Defense Plan and Battle of Iwo Jima," 25 January 1946, Reference Section, MCHC; Horie, "The Last Days of General Kuribayashi," 38–43; and Alexander, "The Americans Will Surely Come," 12–18. Smith re Kuribayashi: "Of all our adversaries in the Pacific," from Heinl, *Soldiers of the Sea,* 481. Technical details of 320-mm spigot mortars from Kenneth L. Smith-Christmas, "The Japanese 320-mm Spigot Mortar," in Alexander, *Closing In,* 29. The threat of Japanese fire drums along the beaches and the precautionary wearing of white greasepaint by the assault forces appear in VAC Intelligence Report, 16–17 March 1945, Archives Section, MCHC; Isely and Crowl, *Amphibious War,* 291; and Adm. Harry W. Hill memoirs in Hill, "The Landing at Iwo Jima," 291.

"Our units are taking advantage of the slackening of the bombardment" from Lofgren, "Diary of 1st Lt. Sugihara Kinryu," 122. Preparing in advance for Iwo's soft beaches: Dyer, *Amphibians,* 1027; Hill, "The Landing at Iwo Jima," 294, 298; Admiral Hill to Professor Isely, 13 January 1950, 2–3, the "Princeton Papers," Personal Papers Collection, MCHC. "I didn't like the idea of landing in a bight" from Cates, oral memoir, 1967, MCOHC, 192. Embarkation problems re tanks and LCMs and 105-mm howitzers and DUKWs from Bartley, *Iwo Jima: Amphibious Epic,* 33, and 4th Marine Division Special Action Report, Iwo Jima, Section 1, p. 4, Archives Section, MCHC. Details of UDT mission on D-2 enhanced by interview with participant E. F. "Andy" Andrews, August 1994. "The landing was a magnificent sight" from Williams, oral memoir, 1980, MCOHC, 180. "So the real landing has come at last" from Lofgren, "Diary of 1st Lt. Sugihara Kinryu," 124.

"Like an enormous tidal wave," from Lt. (jg) Satoru Omagari, Imperial Japanese Navy, 16, the John K. McLean Collection, Personal Papers Section, MCHC. "Enemy strength is approximately two thousand men" from Lofgren, "Diary of 1st Lt. Sugihara Kinryu," 124. "Crossing that second terrace" from Chambers, oral memoir, 1978, MCOHC 2, 638. Infantry regimental reports of the Japanese bombardment extracted from VAC C-3 Journal, D-Day, 19 February 1945, Archives Section, MCHC. Cates's "Look at that goddamned murderous fire" cited in Sherrod, *On to Westward,* 172. Sherrod's "Whether the dead were Japs or Americans" from Sherrod, *On to Westward,* 180. Lieutenant Colonel Youngdale's losses among his DUKW-loaded 105-mm howitzers from Newcomb, *Iwo Jima,* 147. Loss of eighty-eight LVTs at sea, principally because of refusal of LSTs to accommodate them at night reported in VAC LVT Officer Special Action Report, Iwo Jima, 30 April 1945, 9, Archives Section, MCHC, and Croizat, *Across the Reef,* 160. Newcomb, *Iwo Jima,* 152, relates the saga of LVT "Mama's Bathtub," which, out of gas and refused assistance by LSTs, drifted on the high seas for two days and nights.

David H. Susskind remarks from journal provided author courtesy Lt. Col. Joseph McNamara, USMCR, 1995. "Hot damn!" by former Lt. David Conroy, USNR, interview, July 1994. Role of Navy flight nurses in medevacs from Iwo Jima to Guam from Avery, *History of the Medical Department of the U.S. Navy,* 1:205–6, and interview with former flight nurse Norma M. Crotty, September

1994. Stanley Dabrowski "am I doing the right thing?" quoted by Herman, "Corpsman at Iwo," 11. Details on the eight flame tanks from Hunnicutt, *Sherman*, 406–7. Kuribayashi's "We need to reconsider the power of bombardment of ships" from Horie, "Explanation of Japanese Defense Plan," appendix A, p. 1, and Bartley, *Amphibious Epic*, 204. Japanese aerial resupply of bamboo spears related by Navy chief petty officer Kei Kanai, interrogation, 12, McLean Collection, Personal Papers Section, MCHC.

Kuribayashi's final pronouncements and the end of organized resistance on Iwo Jima are described in SS No. 13, 405–11; and Horie, "Japanese Defense Plan," 12–14. Horie, out of the line of fire on Chichi Jima, recorded in these pages the final message from the 145th Infantry Regiment ("Here we burnt our brilliant regimental flag completely. Good bye.") and General Kuribayashi's last words on 21 March ("We are going to fight bravely till the last"). Total landing force casualties of 24,053 compiled from USMC Operations, 4:797.

Chapter 8

Epigraph from Commander Task Force 54, "Okinawa Report, 5 May 1945," 29, cited in Dyer, *Amphibians*, 1094. Marine Division Table of Organization and equipment evolutions from appendixes I–J, USMC Operations, 5:843–51. Comments on M-7 105-mm self-propelled "siege gun" from USMC Operations, 5:725. Details on the Japanese 32d Army from Yahara, "The Defeat of the Japanese 32nd Army," and Huber, *Japan's Battle of Okinawa*. IGHQ decision to detach the 9th Division for service in the Philippines from USMC Operations, 5:41. Kamikaze details from Dull, *Battle History of the Imperial Japanese Navy*. Major Jones's VAC Force Reconn activities from USMC Operations, 5:104–6, and Alexander, "Okinawa's Other Beachheads," 14–17. "Through the din and smoke" from Isely and Crowl, *Amphibious War*, 15–16. L-Day landing and feint operations extracted from Nichols and Shaw, *Okinawa: Victory in the Pacific*, 63–69. "My amphibian tractor passed" from Kennard, *Combat Letters Home* (14 April 1945), 79. "But there are many thousands of Japs" from Buell, *The Quiet Warrior*, 379. TAF operations during April from USMC Operations, 5:176–87. Mount Yae Take insights from interview with Lt. Gen. Victor H. Krulak, USMC (Ret.), February 1995. Battle of Ie Shima from Belote and Belote, *Typhoon of Steel*, 172ff.

Kakazu Ridge tank battle losses and request for 1st Tank Battalion from Frank, *Okinawa: The Great Island Battle*, 86–87; del Valle, oral memoir, 1966, MCOHC, 190; Brig. Gen. Oliver P. Smith, USMC, "Personal Narrative: Tenth Army and Okinawa, 8 November 1944–23 June 1945," in Personal Papers Collection, MCHC, 88–89, 100. Navy losses to kamikazes from Dyer, *Amphibians*, 1104, and USMC Operations, 5:369. Details on Baku bomb and last sortie of the *Yamato* from Dull, *Battle History of the Imperial Japanese Navy*, 126–32, and 19–20, 140–45, respectively. "You take them" from Buell, *The Quiet Warrior*, 384. Giretsu commando raid on Yontan from USMC Operations, 5:228. "Witches on broomsticks" from Buell, *The Quiet Warrior*, 392. "Like a giant bat" from interview with Nick Floros (LSM 120), 22 November 1995. Logistic efforts from USMC Operations, 5:162. Impact of loss of ammunition ships from Nichols and Shaw, *Okinawa: Victory in the Pacific,* 85. "Losing a ship and a half a day" from Potter, *Nimitz,* 375.

"The amphibious card" debates from Shepherd, oral memoir, 1967, MCOHC, 73–79, 103; Vandegrift's position from USMC Operations, 5:196; Frank, *Okinawa: The Great Island Battle,* 88–89, 151–52; Potter, *Nimitz,* 375–76; "I get impatient for some of Holland Smith's drive" from Buell, *The Quiet Warrior,* 387; "The absence of a landing" from Yahara, "The Defeat of the Japanese 32nd Army," 3; and Taxis, oral memoir, 1981, MCOHC, 187. "Russian front" by Col. Frederick P. Henderson, USMC, cited in USMC Operations, 5:193. Target Information Centers and LFASCUs from USMC Operations, 5:382–83 and 5:181–93, respectively. "The front was too narrow" from Maj. Gen. Melvin H. Silverthorn, USMC, and Brig. Gen. Vernon E. Megee, USMC, letter, 21 November 1947, the "Princeton Papers," Personal Papers Collection, MCHC, 4–7. "Unsung heroes" by Colonel Henderson cited in USMC Operations, 5:377. "Quick retribution" from Yahara, "The Defeat of the Japanese 32nd Army," 11. "It was not uncommon" from USMC Operations, 5:278. "Like bones from the spine of a fish" from Snedeker, oral memoir, 1968, MCOHC, 7.

Oroku Peninsula fight from Shepherd, oral memoir, 1967, MCOHC, 106–8; Smith "Personal Narrative," 126–28; 6th Marine Division Special Action Report, Unit Journal, Phase III, 9–14 June 1945, Archives Section, MCHC. Admiral Ota's final message from USMC Operations, 5:321. Casualties provided by Reference Section, MCHC, and from USMC Operations, 5:369. For casualties to Okinawan natives, see Gudmundsson, "Okinawa," 73. "Bloody hellish prelude to the invasion of Japan," from Buell, *The Quiet Warrior,* 396.

Chapter 9
Epigraph from Twining, *No Bended Knee,* 195. "The Japanese are defeated" from an unspecified Fifth Fleet intelligence officer, 17 May 1945, in Dyer, *Amphibians,* 1108. On Japanese war aims in 1945, see Murray, "Armageddon Revisited," 6–11, and Maslowski, "Truman, the Bomb, and the Numbers Game," 103–7. Much of the information on casualty estimates, deception operations, Japanese order of battle and troop strength, shortages of mines, weapons, and cement, landing beaches, special weapons, and tactical atomic weapons from Skates, *The Invasion of Japan.* Details on Japanese deployments and net assessment from Drea, "Previews of Hell," 74–81; Drea, "Japanese Preparations for the Defense of the Homeland," (from whence "human breakwaters"); and Bauer and Coox, "Olympic versus Ketsu-Go," 32–44. Barlow's "The Question of Command for Operation Olympic" provides the most concise treatment of that sensitive issue. Figures on cumulative losses of the three Marine divisions and the entire Sixth Army provided by historian Richard B. Frank as a courtesy in advance of publication of his forthcoming book on the fall of the Japanese Empire. Details on Marine Corps aviation roles and missions from Sherrod, *History of Marine Corps Aviation,* 415–16, 420, and Gailey, *The War in the Pacific,* 474. JCS advisory to avoid bombing Japanese radio towers in COMINCH to

CINCPAC, 23 December 1944, copy provided courtesy Dr. Timothy K. Nenninger, National Archives. Military biographies of senior Japanese Army commanders and general order of battle on Kyūshū at war's end from Hayashi and Coox, *Kogun,* 157, 165–66, 223–40. Other assessments of Japanese intentions from Paschall, "Olympic Miscalculations," 62–63, and Sherrod, *History of Marine Corps Aviation,* 417–19. "Walls 3.5 meters thick" from "Japanese Deliberate Field Fortifications," Special Translation No. 72, CINCPAC-CINCPOA Bulletin No. 94-45 of 20 May 1945. "Hypothetical Defense of Kyūshū," Special Translation No. 72, CINCPAC-CINCPOA Bulletin No. 158-45 of 20 July 1945. New U.S. infantry weapons described in Appleman, *Okinawa,* 58. Losses in Ketcham's and Caldwell's rifle companies at Iwo Jima; comments on fear and combat fatigue by Cushman (MCOHC, 1:177) and Keleher based on research and interviews conducted by the author in preparation of Alexander, "Combat Leadership at Iwo Jima," 70–71. Combat fatigue cases in specified Pacific campaigns from Avery, *History of the Medical Department of the U.S. Navy,* 1:77–78. Turner "dead tired" from Dyer, *Amphibians,* 853. Poison gas option at Iwo from Newcomb, *Iwo Jima,* 207. "Would've been tough" from Taxis, oral memoir, 1981, MCOHC, 218–20. "Scared to death" from Brown, oral memoir, 1967, MCOHC, 220. Clement's combined landing force at Yokosuka from USMC Operations, 5:438, 476–87. "We cried" cited by syndicated columnist Joan Beck, "Vets Defend Atomic Bomb," *Asheville Citizen-Times,* 14 January 1995, p. 5B.

Epilogue

Epigraph: Admiral King, War Reports, 1947, cited in Frank and Shaw, USMC Operations, 5:653. Rubber boat landing for SecNav at Parris Island in 1941 from interview with Col. Robert J. Putnam, USMC (Ret.), 16 April 1996, the platoon commander for the occasion. 5th Marine Division landing craft summary from Sect. 4 (Ship-to-Shore Movement), CG, 5th Marine Division Action Report, Iwo Jima, 28 April 1945, Archives Section, MCHC. Tojo's failure to mention the American landings in the Solomons from Twining, *No Bended Knee,* 194. "We were unstoppable" from Shapley, oral memoir, 1971, MCOHC, 98. Joint Publication 3-02, Joint Doctrine for Amphibious Operations, was published 8 October 1992. "Chaos reigned" attributed to Brig. Gen. Eli Cole, USMC, in evaluating Fleet Problem Number Four, Culebra Island, 1 February 1924, cited in Isely and Crowl, *Amphibious War,* 30–31. "Amphibious warfare a l'outrance" from Heinl, "The United States Marine Corps," 1319. "Helpless victims" from Walt, "Landing Techniques—A Look to the Future," 20–27. Cumulative Marine Corps and organic Navy casualties for the landings cited extracted from vols. 3, 4, and 5, Marine Corps Operations. "What impels a young guy" from Robertson, oral memoir, 1976, MCOHC, 133. "American steel" from Sherrod, *On to Westward,* 14.

Appendix

Anderson. Biographic summary, Operational Archives, NHC. Unspecified Royal Navy liaison officer quoted in Morison, *Victory in the Pacific,* 50 (vol. 14 in USN Operations). Morison states that "Squeaky" came from Anderson's high-pitched voice, but others attribute the nickname to his use of booming bullhorns and amplifiers along the beaches. Hill, "The Landing at Iwo Jima," 294–300. Dyer, *Amphibians,* 745. "I yust pass it on" quoted by Robert Trumbull, *New York Times,* 25 February 1945, p. 28.

Colley. Interviews with son, Cdr. Douglas J. Colley, USNR (Ret.) 1995–96, and examination of the Colley papers held by his son. Among the more pertinent: "Estimate of Japanese Defenses of Betio," 25 October 1943; "Estimate of Japanese Situation at Saipan," 27 May 1944; "POW Interrogation Report c/o Major Kiyoshi Yoshida, Intelligence Officer, 43d Division, Imperial Japanese Army," 16 July 1944; field notebook for Tarawa, with entries concerning tides, moon, code names, combat correspondents; letters to parents about Tarawa dated 3 December and 25 December 1943; Colley, "The Aerial Photo in Amphibious Intelligence," 32–35. The collection contains the original "D-2 Situation Map" of Betio.

Galer. Biographic summary, Reference Section, MCHC. Interviews, October 1994, May 1996. Sherrod, *History of Marine Corps Aviation.* USMC Operations, vols. 4 and 5.

Jones. Biographic summary, Reference Section, MCHC. Interview with his son, Lt. Gen. James L. Jones Jr., USMC, 20 April 1996, which included an examination of his father's professional papers. Commanding Officer, Reconnaissance Company, VAC, "War Diary, Reconnaissance and Operations on Boxcloth Atoll [Apamama]," signed by James L. Jones, 12 December 1943. USMC Operations, vols. 3 and 5; Alexander, "Okinawa's Other Beachheads," 14–17; Alexander, *Utmost Savagery,* 55, 218–19, 221–23.

Keleher. Interviews February 1994, November 1995, May 1996. Keleher, *Dear Progeny,* chapter 13. Interview, Col. Robert J. Putnam, USMC (Ret.), February 1994. Chambers, oral memoir, 1978, MCOHC, 675–77. Silver Star citations, case of Lt. Michael F. Keleher, USNR.

Klatt. Interviews 1994, 1995, 1996. Klatt, "Letters," *Smithsonian,* January 1994, 11. *The Odyssey* (cruise book of the 18th Naval Construction Battalion, 1942–45). Commanding Officer, 3d Battalion, 18th Marines, "Combat Report, Tarawa," 19 December 1943, Archives Section, MCHC. Alexander, *Utmost Savagery,* 57, 90, 91, 204, 206. Klatt's distinctive logo appeared on many of the Betio fortifications drawings, including those later held in the files of the Office of Naval Intelligence. The logo also appears frequently in the attachments to Lt. Col. Vincent A. Wilson, USA, report to CG, VAC, "Helen [Betio], Study and Report of Conditions at," 23 December 1943, Archives Section, MCHC.

Michelony. Interviews 1993, 1994, 1995. Interviews, Lt. Gen. William K. Jones, USMC (Ret.), 1992, 1993. Jones, "Tarawa: That Stinking Little Island," 37. Alexander, *Utmost Savagery,* 64, 185, 201. Silver Star citation, case of First Sgt. Lewis J. Michelony Jr., USMC.

Ota. Hata, *Nihon Riku-Kaigun Sogo Jiten* (Japanese Army and Navy comprehensive dictionary), 175–76. USMC Operations, 2:47–48, 89–90, 5:46, 54–55, 205, 207, 292, 297, 310, 316, 321.

Sledge. Interviews 1994, 1995, 1996. Sledge, *With the Old Breed.* Alexander, introduction in Sledge, *With the Old Breed,* xi–xxv. Sledge, "Peleliu 1944," 72–74.

Weller. Biographic summary, Reference Section, MCHC. Weller, oral memoir, 1982, MCOHC, 90–105. USMC Operations, 5:672–74. Weller, "Firepower and the Amphibious Assault," 56. Weller, "Salvo—Splash," (August 1954): 839–49 and (September 1954): 1011–21 (both reprinted as "The Development of Naval Gunfire Support in World War II," in *Assault from the Sea,* ed. Bartlett, 261–81). Colonel Weller to Professor Isely, 26 January 1950, the "Princeton Papers," Personal Papers Section, MCHC.

Notes on Sources

I began with the original operations plans, action reports, "lessons learned," test reports, doctrinal debates, and battle analyses conducted by the survivors of the storm landings. These are contained principally in the National Archives, the Marine Corps Historical Center (MCHC), the Navy Historical Center, and the Marine Corps University at Quantico. I also researched private assortments, such as the David M. Shoup Collection at the Hoover Institute Archives, the McLean Collection at the MCHC, and those held by sons of the late James L. Jones and Thomas Jack Colley. I made extensive use of interviews with veterans, oral history collections, unit histories, and postwar battle studies, including the official fiftieth anniversary commemorative monographs published during 1992–96 by the Marine Corps. Of the principal postwar accounts, I referred most often to five reliable "veterans": the five-volume series *History of United States Marine Corps Operations in World War II*; Robert Sherrod's *History of Marine Corps Aviation in World War II*; George C. Dyer's two-volume *The Amphibians Came to Conquer*; Thomas B. Buell's biography on Raymond Spruance, *The Quiet Warrior*; and Jeter A. Isely and Philip A. Crowl's *U.S. Marines and Amphibious War*. Regarding the latter, the crown jewel of archival material on amphibious operations in the Central Pacific remains the assembly of letters between Dr. Isely and hundreds of key survivors immediately after the war, all beautifully preserved and indexed as "the Princeton Papers," maintained in the Personal Papers Section, Marine Corps Historical Center. Although Daniel E. Barbey's *MacArthur's Amphibious Navy* is not directly germane to storm landings, as defined here, I referred to the book often and profitably. Two recent (Fall 1996) books from the Naval Institute Press shed additional light on this general subject: Theodore L. Gatchel's *At the Water's Edge: Defending Against the Modern Amphibious Assault*, and Merrill A. Bartlett's biography, coauthored with Dirk A. Ballendorf, titled *Pete Ellis: An Amphibious Warfare Prophet, 1880–1923*.

Repeating the style of research performed for *Utmost Savagery*, I dedicated considerable effort to learning the Japanese side of the equation—how they reacted and adapted to the threat of American storm landings, how they passed the word, what changes we would have faced in the invasion of Kyūshū . Translations of the appropriate *Senshi Sosho* (Japanese war history series) volumes concerning Imperial Army and Navy units in the Central Pacific proved enlightening—and sometimes alarming. I balanced these accounts against U.S. intelligence translations issued during 1943–45, mainly from JICPOA bulletins and POW interrogations, as well as pertinent ULTRA radio intercepts. Edward J. Drea, a renowned authority on ULTRA in the Pacific, also shared several contemporary research papers by officers of the Japanese Self-Defense Force. Other military historians are using the combined Allied-Japanese research approach very effectively. The best of these to date in my view is Thomas M. Huber, *Japan's Battle of Okinawa, April–June 1945*.

Finally, I had the good fortune during the past three years to participate in the production of military history television documentaries that commemorated all seven of these storm landings for the Arts and Entertainment Network and the History Channel. This provided a golden opportunity for one-on-one interviews with such luminaries as Robert Sherrod, Hal Lamar, Gen. Ray Davis, USMC, Lt. Gen. Victor H. Krulak, USMC, and Dr. Eugene Sledge, among many others.

Bibliography

This is a simplified bibliography. I have not included the special or private collections, nor the original source documents cited in the notes and held in the service historical centers. What follows is principally a list of books, essays, oral histories, and interviews.

Abbreviations used:
  HQMC: Headquarters Marine Corps
  MCG: *Marine Corps Gazette*
  MCOHC: Marine Corps Oral History Collection
  USNIP: U.S. Naval Institute *Proceedings*

Alexander, Joseph H. *Across the Reef: The Marine Seizure of Tarawa*. Washington, D.C.: HQMC, 1993.
———. "The Americans Will Surely Come." *Naval History* 9 (January–February 1995): 12–18.
———. "Amphibious Blitzkrieg at Tinian." *Leatherneck* 77 (August 1994): 10–17.
———. "Approaching Showdown: The Planned Assault on Japan." *Leatherneck* 78 (September 1995): 16–23.
———. "Bloody Tarawa." *Naval History* 7 (November–December 1993): 10–16.
———. "Capture of Apamama." *Leatherneck* 76 (November 1993): 50–51.

———. *Closing In: Marines in the Seizure of Iwo Jima.* Washington, D.C.: HQMC, 1994.

———. "Combat Leadership at Iwo Jima." MCG 79 (February 1995): 66–71.

———. "David Shoup: The Rock of Tarawa." *Naval History* 9 (November–December 1995): 19–24.

———. *Final Campaign: Marines in the Victory on Okinawa.* Washington, D.C.: HQMC, 1996.

———. "Iwo Jima: Amphibious Pinnacle." USNIP 121 (February 1995): 28–33.

———. "Okinawa: The Final Beachhead." USNIP 121 (April 1995): 78–81.

———. "Okinawa's Other Beachheads." *Leatherneck* 78 (June 1995): 14–17.

———. "Peleliu, 1944: King Company's Battle for 'The Point.'" *Leatherneck* 79 (November 1996): 18–25.

———. "Red Sky in the Morning." USNIP 119 (November 1993): 39–45.

———. "Saipan's Bloody Legacy." *Leatherneck* 77 (June 1994): 12–19.

———. "Tarawa: The Ultimate Opposed Landing." MCG 77 (November 1993): 52–61.

———. "The Turning Points of Tarawa." *MHQ* 8 (summer 1996): 42–51.

———. *Utmost Savagery: The Three Days of Tarawa.* Annapolis: Naval Institute Press, 1995.

———. "Volcanic Fortress: The Battle of Iwo Jima." *Officer Review* 35 (January–February 1995): 1–3.

Andrews, E. F. (Navy UDT). Interview by author. 1994.

Appleman, Roy E., et al. *Okinawa, The Last Battle: The U.S. Army in World War II.* Washington, D.C.: Department of the Army, 1948.

Avery, Bennett F., ed. *The History of the Medical Department of the U.S. Navy in World War II.* Vols. 1 and 2. Washington, D.C.: GPO, 1953.

Baker, A. D. *Allied Landing Craft of World War II.* Reprint, Annapolis: Naval Institute Press, 1985.

Barbey, Daniel E. *MacArthur's Amphibious Navy.* Annapolis: Naval Institute Press, 1969.

Barlow, Jeffrey G. "The Question of Command for Operation Olympic." Paper presented at the 12th Naval History Symposium, U.S. Naval Academy, Annapolis, Md., 26–27 October 1995. Copy provided author by Dr. Barlow.

Bartlett, Merrill L. *Assault from the Sea.* 1983. Reprint, Annapolis: Naval Institute Press, 1985.

Bartley, Whitman S. *Iwo Jima: Amphibious Epic.* Washington, D.C.: HQMC, 1954.

Bauer, K. Jack, and Alan C. Coox. "Olympic versus Ketsu-Go." MCG 49 (August 1965): 32–44.

Belote, James H., and William M. Belote. *Typhoon of Steel: The Battle of Okinawa.* New York: Harper and Row, 1970.

Boyd, Carl, and Akihiko Yoshida. *The Japanese Submarine Force and World War II.* Annapolis: Naval Institute Press, 1995.

Brown, Wilbert S. Oral Memoir, 1967, MCOHC.

Buell, Thomas B. *The Quiet Warrior: A Biography of Adm. Raymond A. Spruance.* Boston: Little, Brown, 1974.

Caldwell, Frank C. (26th Marines). Interviews by author. 1994, 1995.

Canfield, Bruce N. *U.S. Infantry Weapons of World War II.* Lincoln, Neb.: Andrew Mowbray, 1994.

Cates, Clifford B. Oral Memoir, 1967, MCOHC.

Carrell, Paul. *Scorched Earth: Hitler's War on Russia.* London: George Harrap, 1970. Translated from the German by Ewald Osers.

Chambers, Justice M. Oral Memoir, 1978, MCOHC.

Clifford, Kenneth J. *Amphibious Warfare Development in Britain and America from 1920–1940.* Laurens, N.Y.: Edgewood, 1983.

———. *Progress and Purpose: A Developmental History of the U.S. Marine Corps.* Washington, D.C.: HQMC, 1973.

Colley, Douglas J. Interviews by author. 1995, 1996.

Colley, Thomas J. "The Aerial Photo in Amphibious Intelligence." MCG 29 (October 1945): 32, 34–35.

Conroy, David. (USN, TBM Pilot, VC 84). Interview by author. 1994.

Cooper, Norman V. "The Military Career of Gen. Holland M. Smith, USMC." Ph.D. diss., University of Alabama, 1974.

Croizat, Victor J. *Across the Reef: The Amphibious Tracked Vehicle at War.* Quantico: Marine Corps Association, 1992.

Crotts, Hubert D. (2d Tank Battalion, Tarawa, Saipan). Interview by author. 1997.

Crotty, Norma M. (USN Flight Nurse). Interview by author. 1994.

Crowl, Philip A. *Campaign in the Marianas: The War in the Pacific.* Washington, D.C.: Department of the Army, 1960.

Cushman, Robert E., Jr. "Battalion Landing Teams in Amphibious Operations." MCG 29 (January 1945): 11–20.

———. Oral Memoir, 1977, MCOHC.

Cutler, Thomas J. *The Battle of Leyte Gulf.* New York: Harper Collins, 1994.

Davis, Raymond G. Interview by author. 1995.

———. Oral Memoir, 1977, MCOHC.

Day, James L. Interview by author. 1996.

———. Oral Memoir, 1988, MCOHC.

del Valle, Pedro A. Oral Memoir, 1966, MCOHC.

———. "Ship to Shore in Amphibious Operations." MCG 16 (February 1932): 11–16.

Drea, Edward J. "Japanese Preparations for the Defense of the Homeland." Paper presented at the Admiral Nimitz Seminar, San Antonio, Tex., 18–19 March 1995. Copy provided author by Dr. Drea.

———. *MacArthur's Ultra: Codebreaking and the War Against Japan, 1942–45.* Lawrence, Ks.: The University Press of Kansas, 1992.

———. "Previews of Hell." *MHQ* 7 (spring 1995): 74–81.

Dull, Paul S. *A Battle History of the Imperial Japanese Navy, 1941–1945.* Annapolis: Naval Institute Press, 1978.

Dyer, George C. *The Amphibians Came to Conquer: The Story of Adm. Richmond Kelly Turner.* Washington, D.C.: GPO, 1969.

Floros, Nick (USN, *LSM 120*). Interview by author. 1995.

Fox, Fred K. (K/3/1 Peleliu). Interview by author. 1996.

Frank, Benis M. Interview by author. 1995.

———. "Lt. Gen. Holland M. Smith, USMC." In *Men of War,* ed. Stephen Howarth. New York: St. Martin's Press, 1992.

———. *Okinawa: The Great Island Battle.* New York: Dutton, 1978.

Frank, Benis M., and Henry I. Shaw. *Victory and Occupation: History of U.S. Marine Corps Operations in World War II.* Vol. 5. Washington, D.C.: HQMC, 1968.

Frank, Richard B. *Guadalcanal.* New York: Random House, 1990.

Fuchida, Mitsuo, and Masatake Okumiya. *Midway: The Battle That Doomed Japan.* Annapolis: Naval Institute Press, 1953.

Funasaka, Hiroshi. *Falling Blossoms.* Singapore: Times Books, 1986.

Gailey, Harry A. *The War in the Pacific: From Pearl Harbor to Tokyo Bay.* Novato, Calif.: Presidio Press, 1995.

Garand, George W., and Truman R. Strobridge. *Western Pacific Operations: History of U.S. Marine Corps Operations in World War II.* Vol. 4. Washington, D.C.: HQMC, 1971.

Gatchel, Theodore M. *At the Water's Edge: Defense against the Modern Amphibious Assault.* Annapolis: Naval Institute Press, 1996.

Gudmundsson, Bruce I. "Okinawa." *MHQ* 7 (spring 1995): 64–73.

Halsey, William F., and Joseph Bryan. *Admiral Halsey's Story.* New York: Whittlesey House, 1947.

Hata, Ikuhiko. *Nihon Riku-Kaigun Sogo Jiten* (Japanese Army and Navy comprehensive dictionary). Tokyo: Tokyo Daigaku Shuppankai, 1991.

Hayashi, Saburo, and Alvin D. Coox. *Kogun: The Japanese Army in the Pacific War.* Quantico: Marine Corps Association, 1959.

Hayes, Grace P. *The History of the Joint Chiefs of Staff: The War against Japan.* Annapolis: Naval Institute Press, 1982.

Heinl, Robert D. *Soldiers of the Sea: The U.S. Marine Corps, 1775–1962.* Annapolis: Naval Institute Press, 1962.

———. "The United States Marine Corps: Author of Modern Amphibious War." USNIP 73 (November 1947): 1317–21.

Henderson, Frederick P. Interview by author. 1995.

———. Oral Memoir, 1974–76, MCOHC.

Herman, Jan K. "Corpsman at Iwo." *Navy Medicine* 86 (January–February 1995): 6–11.

Hersey, John. *Into the Valley: A Skirmish of the Marines.* New York: Alfred A. Knopf, 1943.

Hill, Harry W. "The Landing at Iwo Jima." In *The Pacific War Remembered: An Oral History Collection,* ed. John T. Mason Jr. Annapolis: Naval Institute Press, 1986.

———. Oral Memoir, 1969, MCOHC.

History of U.S. Marine Corps Operations in World War II. Frank O. Hough, Verle E. Ludwig, and Henry I. Shaw Jr. *Pearl Harbor to Guadalcanal.* Vol. 1. Washington, D.C.: HQMC, 1961.

———. Henry I. Shaw Jr. and Douglas T. Kane, *Isolation of Rabaul.* Vol. 2. Washington, D.C.: HQMC, 1963.

————. Henry I. Shaw Jr., Bernard C. Nalty, and Edwin T. Turnbladh. *Central Pacific Drive.* Vol. 3. Washington, D.C.: HQMC, 1966.

————. George W. Garand and Truman R. Strobridge. *Western Pacific Operations.* Vol. 4. Washington, D.C.: HQMC, 1971.

————. Benis M. Frank and Henry I. Shaw. *Victory and Occupation.* Vol. 5. Washington, D.C.: HQMC, 1968.

Hittle, James D. (3d Marine Division). Interview by author. 1994.

Hoffman, Carl W. *Saipan: The Beginning of the End.* Washington, D.C.: HQMC, 1950.

Hoffman, Jon T. "The Legacy and Lessons of New Guinea." MCG 77 (September 1993): 74–77.

————. "The Lessons and Legacy of Okinawa." MCG 79 (April 1995): 64–71.

————. *Once a Legend: "Red Mike" Edson of the Raiders.* Novato, Calif.: Presidio Press, 1994.

Hofmann, George F. "Technology, Ideas, and Reality: The U.S. Marine Corps and the First Assault Amphibian Tank." In *Perspectives on Warfighting No. 3: Selected Papers from the 1992 Meeting of the Society for Military History,* ed. Donald F. Bittner, 151–73. Quantico: Marine Corps University, 1994.

Horie, Yoshitake. "The Last Days of General Kuribayashi." MCG 39 (February 1955): 12–18.

Hough, Frank O. *The Assault on Peleliu.* Washington, D.C.: HQMC, 1950.

Hough, Frank O., Verle E. Ludwig, and Henry I. Shaw Jr. *Pearl Harbor to Guadalcanal: History of U.S. Marine Corps Operations in World War II.* Vol. 1. Washington, D.C.: HQMC, 1961.

Huber, Thomas M. *Japan's Battle of Okinawa: April–June 1945.* Fort Leavenworth: Combat Studies Institute, 1990.

Hunnicutt, Richard P. *Sherman: A History of the American Medium Tank.* Belmont, Calif.: Taurus Enterprises, 1978.

Hunt, George P. *Coral Comes High.* New York: Harper, 1946.

————. "Point Secured." MCG 29 (January 1945): 39–42.

Ito, Masanori, Sadatoshi Tomiaka, and Masazumi Inada, eds. *Jitsuroku Taiheyo sense* (3) (Real accounts of the Pacific War, vol. 3). Tokyo: Chuo Koron Sha, 1970.

Isely, Jeter A., and Philip A. Crowl. *The U.S. Marines and Amphibious War.* Princeton: Princeton University Press, 1951.

Joint Chiefs of Staff. Joint Publication 3-02: *Joint Doctrine for Amphibious Operations,* 8 October 1992.

Joint Planning Staff No. 205, "Operations against the Marshall Islands," 10 June 1943.

Jones, James L., Jr. Interview by author. 1996.

Jones, William K. Interviews by author. 1992, 1993.

————. "Tarawa: That Stinking Little Island." MCG 71 (November 1987): 30–41.

Karch, Frederick J. (14th Marines). Interview by author. 1994.

————. Oral Memoir, 1971, MCOHC.

Keleher, Michael F. *Dear Progeny.* Amherst: Values Quest Group, 1992.

————. Interviews by author. 1994, 1995.

Kelly, John P. "The Achilles Heel." USNIP 111 (November 1985): 41–45.

Kennard, Richard C. *Combat Letters Home.* Bryn Mawr: Dorrance, 1985.

Ketcham, William T., Jr. (24th Marines). Interviews by author. 1994, 1996.

Klatt, Larry E. (18th NCB). Interviews by author. 1994, 1995, 1996.

Krulak, Victor H. *First to Fight.* Annapolis: Naval Institute Press, 1984.

———. Interviews by author. 1994, 1995.

Kuzuhara, Kazumi. "Operations on Iwo Jima: Utility of Combat Lessons." Paper presented at the Japan-U.S. Military History Exchange Conference in Fort Leavenworth, Kans., September 1990. Copy provided the author courtesy of Dr. Edward J. Drea, chief, Research and Analysis Division, U.S. Army Center of Military History.

Lamar, H. Arthur (Flag Lieutenant to CINCPAC). Interview by author. 1996.

Lewis, Brenda Ralph. "Caesar's Battle for Britannia." *Military History* 12 (February 1996): 46–53.

Lofgren, Stephen J., ed. "Diary of 1st Lt. Sugihara Kinryu." *Journal of Military History* 59 (January 1995): 97–133.

Lorelli, John A. *To Foreign Shores: U.S. Amphibious Operations in World War II.* Annapolis: Naval Institute Press, 1995.

Maslowski, Peter. "Truman, the Bomb, and the Numbers Game." *MHQ* 7 (spring 1995): 103–7.

McCutcheon, Keith B. "Close Air Support on Luzon." MCG 29 (September 1945): 38–39.

McKinney, Leonard L. *Mechanized Flame Thrower Operations in World War II.* Washington, D.C.: U.S. Army Chemical Corps, 1951.

McLaughlin, John E. Oral Memoir, 1978, MCOHC.

McMillan, George. *The Old Breed: A History of the 1st Marine Division in World War II.* Washington, D.C.: Infantry Journal Press, 1949.

Megee, Vernon Edgar. Oral Memoir, 1967, MCOHC.

Metzger, Louis. "Okinawa." MCG 79 (April 1995): 81–87.

Meyer, Lewis. "Tactical Use of Flame." MCG 29 (November 1945): 19–22.

Michelony, Lewis J., Jr. (6th Marines). Interviews by author. 1993, 1994, 1995.

Miller, Edward S. *War Plan Orange.* Annapolis: Naval Institute Press, 1991.

Miller, Nathan. Interview by author. 1996.

———. *The War at Sea: A Naval History of World War II.* New York: Scribner, 1995.

Millett, Allan R. "Assault from the Sea: The Development of Amphibious Warfare between the World Wars." Typescript prepared for the director of Net Assessment, OSD, 1993. Copy provided author by Dr. Millett.

———. *In Many a Strife: General Gerald C. Thomas and the U.S. Marine Corps, 1917–1956.* Annapolis: Naval Institute Press, 1993.

———. *Semper Fidelis: The History of the U.S. Marine Corps.* Rev. ed. New York: Free Press, 1991.

Morison, Samuel E. *The History of U.S. Naval Operations during the Second World War.* 15 vols. Boston: Little, Brown, 1947–62. (Especially, vol. 8, *New Guinea and the Marianas;* vol. 10, *Leyte;* vol. 14, *Victory in the Pacific.*)

———. *The Two-Ocean War.* Boston: Little, Brown, 1963.

Moskin, J. Robert. *The U.S. Marine Corps Story.* 3d rev. ed. Boston: Little, Brown, 1992.

Murray, Williamson. "Armageddon Revisited." *MHQ* 7 (spring 1995): 6–11.

Newcomb, Richard F. *Iwo Jima.* New York: Holt, Rinehart and Winston, 1965.

Nichols, Charles S., and Henry I. Shaw Jr. *Okinawa: Victory in the Pacific.* Washington, D.C.: HQMC, 1955.

O'Brien, Cyril J. *Liberation: Marines in the Recapture of Guam.* Washington, D.C.: HQMC, 1994.

Olson, Donald W. "The Tide at Tarawa." *Sky and Telescope,* November 1987, 526–29.

Paschall, Rod. "Olympic Miscalculations." *MHQ* 7 (spring 1995): 62–63.

Paulus, Loren F. (CINCPAC Staff). Interview by author. 1996.

Platt, Jonas M. Oral Memoir, 1980, MCOHC.

Potter, E. B. *Nimitz.* Annapolis: Naval Institute Press, 1976.

Putnam, Robert J. (1st Marines). Interviews by author. 1992, 1994, 1996.

Reynolds, Clark G. *The Fast Carriers: The Forging of an Air Navy.* New York: McGraw-Hill, 1968.

Robertson, Donn J. Interview by author. 1994.

———. Oral Memoir, 1973–76, MCOHC.

Rutherford, J. T. (2d AmtracBn). Interviews by author. 1993, 1994, 1995.

Ryan, Brendan P. "Amphibious Warfare, 1801 Style." MCG 63 (July 1979): 47–51.

Senshi Sosho (Japanese war history series). No. 6, *Chuba Taiheyo homen rikugen sakusen* (1) (Army operations in the Central Pacific, vol. 1). Tokyo: Asagumo Shimbunsha, date unknown.

———. No. 13, *Chuba Taiheyo homen rikugen sakusen* (2) (Army operations in the Central Pacific, vol. 2). Tokyo: Asagumo Shimbunsha, 1968.

———. No. 62, *Chuba Taiheyo homen Kaigun sakusen* (2) (Navy operations in the Central Pacific, vol. 2). Tokyo: Asagumo Shimbunsha, 1973.

Shapley, Alan. Oral Memoir, 1971, MCOHC.

Shaw, Henry I., Jr., and Douglas T. Kane, *Isolation of Rabaul: History of U.S. Marine Corps Operations in World War II.* Vol. 2. Washington, D.C.: HQMC, 1963.

Shaw, Henry I., Jr., Bernard C. Nalty, and Edwin T. Turnbladh. *Central Pacific Drive: History of U.S. Marine Corps Operations in World War II.* Vol. 3. Washington, D.C.: HQMC, 1966.

Shepherd, Lemuel C. Oral Memoir, 1967, MCOHC.

Sherrod, Robert. *History of Marine Corps Aviation in World War II.* Washington, D.C.: Association of the U.S. Army, 1952.

———. Interview by author. 1993.

———. *On to Westward: The Battles of Saipan and Iwo Jima.* New York: Duell, Sloan, and Pierce, 1945.

Silverstone, Paul H. *U.S. Warships of World War II.* New York: Doubleday, 1968.

Silverthorn, Merwin H. Oral Memoir, 1969, MCOHC.

Skates, John Ray. *The Invasion of Japan: Alternative to the Bomb.* Columbia: University of South Carolina Press, 1994.

Sledge, Eugene B. Interviews by author. 1994, 1995, 1996.

———. "Peleliu 1944: Why Did We Have to Go There?" USNIP 120 (November 1994): 72–74.

———. *With the Old Breed at Peleliu and Okinawa.* Classics of Naval Literature Edition. Annapolis: Naval Institute Press, 1996.

Smith, Oliver P. Oral Memoir, 1969, MCOHC.

———. "Personal Narrative: Tenth Army and Okinawa, 8 November 1944–23 June 1945." Typescript in Personal Papers Collection, MCOHC.

Smith, Robert R. *The Approach to the Philippines: The War in the Pacific.* Washington, D.C.: Department of the Army, 1963.

Snedeker, Edward W. Oral Memoir, 1968, MCOHC.

Spector, Ronald H. *Eagle against the Sun.* New York: Free Press, 1985.

Stebbins, Owen T. Interview by author. 1995.

———. "A Maneuver That Might Have Been . . . ?" MCG 79 (June 1995): 69–72.

Strahan, Jerry E. *Andrew Jackson Higgins and the Boats That Won World War II.* Baton Rouge: Louisiana State University Press, 1994.

Taxis, Samuel G. Oral Memoir, 1981, MCOHC.

Toland, John. *The Rising Sun.* New York: Random House, 1970.

Twining, Merrill B. *No Bended Knee: The Battle for Guadalcanal.* Novato, Calif.: Presidio Press, 1996.

Unmacht, George F. "Flame Throwing SeaBees." USNIP 74 (April 1948): 425–26.

U.S. Department of War. *Handbook on Japanese Military Forces: Technical Manual TM-E30-480,* 1944.

U.S. Navy. Fleet Training Publication No. 167, *Landing Operations Doctrine,* 1938, with Change Three, 1 August 1943.

Walt, Lewis W. "The Closer the Better." MCG 30 (September 1946): 37–38.

———. "Landing Techniques—A Look to the Future." MCG 35 (February 1951): 20–27.

Weller, Donald M. "Firepower and the Amphibious Assault." MCG 36 (March 1952): 56–57.

———. Oral Memoir, 1982, MCOHC.

———. "Salvo—Splash." USNIP 80 (August 1954): 839–49, and (September 1954): 1011–21.

Wheeler, Richard. *A Special Valor.* New York: Harper and Row, 1983.

Williams, Robert H. Oral Memoir, 1980, MCOHC.

Willock, Roger. *Unaccustomed to Fear: A Biography of the Late General Roy S. Geiger.* Reprint, Quantico: Marine Corps Association, 1983.

Willoughby, Malcolm F. *The U.S. Coast Guard in World War II.* Annapolis: Naval Institute Press, 1957.

Wyckoff, Don P. "Let There Be Built Great Ships." USNIP 118 (November 1992): 51–57.

Yahara, Hiromichi. "The Defeat of the Japanese 32nd Army on Okinawa in 1945." Recounted from POW interrogation. Privately published by USMC 8th Defense and AA Battalion Reunion Association, 1977.

Index

About the Author

Col. Joseph H. Alexander served for twenty-nine years as an assault amphibian officer in the Marine Corps. He commanded a company in Vietnam and a battalion in Okinawa and served five years at sea on board amphibious ships. As a colonel, he served as chief of staff, 3d Marine Division, director of the Marine Corps Development Center, and military secretary to the Commandant of the Marine Corps.

Colonel Alexander is an independent military historian now living in Asheville, North Carolina. A 1960 graduate of the University of North Carolina, he holds master's degrees from Georgetown and Jacksonville Universities and is a distinguished graduate of the Naval War College. He is a member of the U.S. Naval Institute, the Marine Corps Historical Foundation, and the Society for Military History.

He is the author of *Utmost Savagery: The Three Days of Tarawa* (Naval Institute Press, 1995), a main selection of the Military Book Club and winner of the 1995 Wallace M. Greene Award, 1995 Roosevelt Naval History Prize, and 1996 Alfred Thayer Mahan Award. He also coauthored, with Merrill L. Bartlett, *Sea Soldiers in the Cold War* (Naval Institute Press, 1994) and three World War II fiftieth-anniversary monographs (Tarawa, Iwo Jima, and Okinawa). His recent essays on the Pacific War have been published in the U.S. Naval Institute *Proceedings, Naval History, MHQ: The Quarterly Journal of Military History, Leatherneck,* and the *Marine Corps Gazette.* From 1993 to 1996 he participated as scriptwriter and principal on-screen authority for eleven historical documentaries with Lou Reda Productions for the Arts and Entertainment Network and the History Channel.